IM

THE
CASE
AGAINST
LEE
HARVEY
OSWALD
(VOLUME ONE)

BARRY KRUSCH

Manufactured in the United States of America

ISBN: 978-0-9620981-4-7

First Edition

Author contact: bkrusch@yahoo.com

Table Of Contents

This is an extensive work, over 1000 pages spread out over three volumes. Due to the scope of this project, the author feels it would be helpful to explain some key details before proceeding with the book itself.

What This Book Is About

Over the last three years, if people asked me what I was doing, I would say I was writing a book on "Lee Harvey Oswald." And sometimes people would ask me in response, *"Who's* Lee Harvey Oswald?"

So, if you are one of those people, here is some essential background: on November 22, 1963, a President of the United States, President John Fitzgerald Kennedy, was assassinated in Dallas, Texas. The man accused of the assassination was named Lee Harvey Oswald. Oswald was arrested, but never had a trial: two days later, he was killed by another assassin, a man named Jack Ruby. The Vice President of the United States at the time, Lyndon Johnson, became President, and appointed a body known as the Warren Commission to investigate the assassination. The Warren Commission concluded that Lee Harvey Oswald fired the shot that killed President John F. Kennedy. A subsequent investigation by the House Select Committee on Assassinations concluded the same thing.

The claim of this book is that *that conclusion would be impossible to support in a court of law.* This claim has at least 3 important implications:

1. The actual murderers of a President of the United States were never brought to justice.
2. Because there is no statute of limitations for murder, Kennedy's assassination would therefore very much be an open case . . . even *today*, decades later. Consequently, we are not talking about "history", we are talking about something that is important real-time, right now . . . right this very *second*.
3. People who insist that the case is "closed" when it is not are doing the American people a great disservice, aborting an inquiry into what *really* occurred, and all the consequences that would naturally flow after that inquiry was conducted.

For many years, the claim that Oswald was the lone assassin was disputed, and it was generally acknowledged that the case was, at best, extremely shaky. However, as the 50th anniversary of the assassination of the President approaches ever closer, there has been a new push to validate the conclusions of the Commission. Books by Vincent Bugliosi, John McAdams, Stephen King, and an upcoming book by Bill O'Reilly, all ride the lone assassin bandwagon. Even many people who do not accept the conclusions of the Commission believe, based on the latter books I have discussed, that there is some sort of genuine controversy.

I am writing this book to put an end to this nonsense once and for all. This book is going to challenge these authors to justify their point of view, in a very interesting way which we will get to shortly.

Frankly, I doubt that they will accept my challenge. If I am right, you will learn something, and if I am wrong, you will learn something.

About the Author

The vast majority of the books written on the Kennedy assassination up to this time have been written by people who knew where they were when Kennedy was shot. One day there will come a time when these books will be written by authors without direct personal experience.

I am not one of those authors. I remember very well where I was when Kennedy was shot. I was in school, kindergarten, and the one vivid memory I have is of teachers running through the halls crying. That was the dominant image of the day, lots and lots of people crying, wherever you went. A big steel-gray cloud had rolled over America, and was not to leave for many weeks.

Yes, I knew this was a very big deal, not just because so many people were crying, but because they also canceled Saturday morning cartoons. That was when I knew that this thing was really huge, when the cloud hit really close to home.

Of course there was a funeral procession after that, and all I can remember about that was the truly awful silence, the only sound being drumbeats. Spooky. My wife recalled it as a "black parade," her only experience with processionals like that being the Thanksgiving Macy's Day Parade. I also remember watching the processional (or a re-broadcast of the processional), only to have it interrupted by a commercial, for Salvo detergent tablets as I recall:

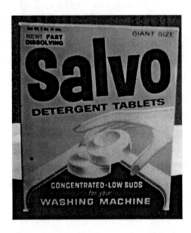

I remember even at that early age being shocked that something as somber as that procession would be interrupted by a commercial for detergent.

To help give you some context, here is what I looked like when I was young, with my mom and sister:

I am not sure when that picture was taken, but I'm sure that at the time of the Kennedy assassination I was older, because I was 5 years and 9 months when Kennedy was assassinated, and I look like I am about 4 or 5 in that picture.

I think in the next picture I am older than 5 years, 9 months, probably 6. It is me holding a book called *Turtles*, which I think was one of the first books I ever owned (it probably is the first, otherwise, why else take a picture of me holding a book about turtles?):

Innocent times. A boy and his book on turtles. How things have changed . . .

I am showing these photographs because I want to contrast them with a famous photograph I'm sure that you have seen, the one where John Kennedy's son saluted his father at the funeral procession, his mother and his uncle behind him, a photo which marks a clear historical turning point:

This is a heartbreaking image even today, but you can imagine the effect this image had on me when I was only 5 years 9 months old. When I saw the picture, I remember thinking "how sad that little boy must be." Even though I was 5 years 9 months, I remember thinking of him as a "little boy" because he was only 3, not a "big boy" like me.

(Today I think of him not only as saying goodbye to his father, but metaphorically saying goodbye to a bygone era.)

Well, in light of the image above, and dozens and hundreds of similar images broadcast daily on television and seen in newspapers, you can just imagine how people felt about Lee Harvey Oswald. Oswald was truly the Osama bin Laden of his day, and I doubt that even bin Laden achieved the level of revulsion and hatred that Oswald stirred up him in the hearts of the American people. Consequently, when Oswald was killed by Ruby,

there were cheers and excitement all across America, with most people ecstatic that "justice was done." I do remember, though, that my parents did not seem enthusiastic like other people did. I wondered why. After all, wasn't John Kennedy a *good* man? And wasn't Lee Harvey Oswald, because he killed John Kennedy, a *bad* man? And didn't that make Jack Ruby, who killed Lee Harvey Oswald, a *good* man?

My schema was *good man shoots bad man who killed good man*, and I remember thinking at the time that what Jack Ruby did was perfectly logical, and in fact I even expected it. I was really surprised when my parents did not feel the same way.

Well, after Ruby shot Oswald, a flurry of historical events followed. By the time I was seven, I began to notice that the nightly news was, night after night after night after night, sending the same images, from a place called Vietnam:

We were in a war. I did not understand that war. All I knew was, when the news came on, we were going to see pictures from that war. And invariably, these pictures would have shots of helicopters. Lots and lots of helicopters. Thousands of them. If you were in the helicopter business then, you would have made a *killing*. But there were other pictures without helicopters, pictures of women and children. And what terrible pictures they were. I'm sparing you the gory details.

Little did I know, after the Kennedy assassination, we were leaving the world of a boy and his turtles and entering a time when the images we did not want to see came firing at us like rounds from a Gatling gun with an ammunition pool the size of Lake Michigan.

The images revolved around historical events, events which at the time we thought were disconnected, such as the assassination of Martin Luther King . . .

The assassination of Robert Kennedy. . . .

Watergate and the resignation of a President (VP at the time: Gerald Ford) . . .

Two assassination attempts on Ford (VP at the time: Nelson Rockefeller) . . . .

An assassination attempt on Reagan (VP at the time: George Bush Sr.). . . .

the Persian Gulf War . . .

9/11 . . .

And the Iraq/Afghanistan wars . . .

. . . which takes us to the present day.

But were *all* these historical events *really* disconnected? And if they *were* connected, either in whole or part, were they somehow, someway, connected to the Kennedy assassination, and if so, how?

Well, if Lee Harvey Oswald was truly the assassin of President Kennedy, then people can make a case that those historical events were not connected to the assassination. But if he was not the assassin, the case they want to make is going to be more difficult. So the stakes are high.

Well, I have seen the evidence, and I have seen the light. So here I am, over forty years later, the kid with the book on the turtles now all grown up, writing a book defending a man who I once hated with a passion. But now I realize that my hatred was based on solely on the images I saw broadcast on the television, not on evidence that actually connected Oswald to the assassination.

Since reading that book on "Turtles", I have read thousands of books, and over 100 of them on the Kennedy assassination. I'm older now. I know a lot more now. I question more now.

You might be interested in my qualifications to write a book on the Kennedy assassination, and there are at least five of them.

First, I do have direct personal experience with the assassination, and authors of books that are written in the future are going to lack this connection. So it is important to have a record written now by "one who was there," in the sense that it affected his or her personal life.

Second, I went to law school for a year at the University of Georgia, worked as an investigator for Atlanta Legal Aid for four years, and was a paralegal for four years. Consequently, I have a deeper background in law than many authors who have written books on the Kennedy assassination, though not as nearly as deep as others, most notably attorney Mark Lane, a man to whom the American people owe a great debt for the work he did in bringing this issue to people's attention. I saw Mr. Lane speak at Emory University in 1977, and that was the first time I knew that there was another side to this story. Mr. Lane almost single-handedly kept the issue alive for many years when most people wanted to forget it.

Third, I have written several books, two on constitutional law. One of them, *The 21st Century Constitution*, was called by Richard Bernstein in his book *Amending America* "the most thoughtful and thorough reframing of the Constitution yet attempted," and I appeared on C-SPAN and the Tom Snyder radio show discussing the book. The book even landed me an entry into the *Encyclopedia of Constitutional Amendments, Proposed Amendments, and Amending Issues, 1789-2002*.

Fourth, I have been an instructional designer for twenty years specializing in instructional technology (first CD-ROM, now web-based training), and have a Masters degree in Education. I have written courses on a wide variety of topics for a wide variety of clients, including *American Express, Bank of America,* and *Hartford Life*. As far as I know, I'm the first instructional designer to write a book on the Kennedy assassination. My experience in writing courses, which involves evaluating and analyzing hundreds, sometimes thousands of pages of complex material that has to be converted into a course that could last anywhere from 2 to 4 hours, has proven to be very useful in helping me to understand and explain the complexities of what is in all likelihood the most complex murder case ever.

Fifth, and finally, I have extensive experience in the analysis of film, which began at Emory University with my friends Scott Greene and Bill Blagg. At least one, usually two times a week, we would go to a theater called *The Silver Screen* in Atlanta, Georgia, and watch foreign film double features. Many times we would go to the film more than one time. Scott was an art history major, and had an amazing ability to find nuances in films that I was simply unable to find. But, discussing these films with Scott for years built up my skills in this type of analysis as well. Eventually, I wrote a document called *The Kubrick FAQ*, which analyzed the films of Stanley Kubrick. I must have watched the films of Kubrick dozens of times, and on each go-round discovered something that I hadn't seen before.

You might not think that experience very relevant, but I think of all the experience that I've had that I've listed, this has been the experience that has proven most valuable in finding the holes in The Case Against Oswald.

How This Book Is Different
Because there are hundreds of books on the Kennedy assassination, a fair question is "why another one?" Thus, I believe that every author who jumps into this field is obliged to provide an answer.

In my view, this book is different for at least three reasons:

1. How it was written.
2. What it seeks to achieve.
3. How it achieves what it seeks to achieve.

Details follow.

How This Book Was Written

I am not sure how other people have written books on the Kennedy assassination, but I am pretty confident that I am one of the few that use the method I ultimately deployed, because the method I ultimately deployed was not even available when hundreds of these books were written.

My first strategy in writing this book was a fairly standard one, to read a book, and as I read it, index it along the way. So, I would read book after book, and classify each point of evidence by topic. Then, I compiled those smaller indexes into one large master index which allowed me to find evidence using those topics.

This worked pretty well, but I found it was taking too long, so I came up with another strategy.

Whenever I bought a book on the Kennedy assassination, I would scan it into the computer, and then use optical character recognition to create searchable text. Then, I would index the book. Finally, I would create a master index of all the books.

By having this electronic master index, I was able to search the contents of over 100 books simultaneously by keyword. This made it extremely easy to locate the sources of information for any particular topic, which in a case like this, would be impossible to do if you did not have this method, since we are talking about searching literally tens of thousands of pages.

I not only did this with the books, I also did it with the most important relevant documents in the case, including the records of the Warren Commission and the House Select Committee on Assassinations.

Because I was able to locate information quickly, this book has dozens of compare and contrast scenarios that would have been extraordinarily difficult, you might even say practically impossible, to discover any other way.

Because of this method, and because I was also able to build on the hard work of all the fantastic researchers and writers who came before me, this book only took three years to write, when it should have taken over a hundred years to write. In an acknowledgments section coming up, I will be thanking many of these authors.

Now let's go to the second reason this book is different.

What This Book Seeks to Achieve

It is amazing how many excellent books have been written about this topic. And yet, even though the authors of those books presented to me compelling evidence that there was no Case Against Oswald, we are still, to this day, debating the topic. It is almost as if people thought that whether or not the Holocaust existed was a legitimate topic for debate. That would be crazy, right? Well, that's the way it is with the Kennedy assassination.

If everyone read those books, there would be no need for this book. But everyone has not read those books, and many of them are now out of print. So it looks like we are going to need at least one more book.

Yes, brilliant as these books were and are, due to a variety of circumstances including the out-of-print status of some of these books as well as the relatively high cost of some of the others, the books as a group only been able to get the ball to the one-yard line (through no fault of their own), with some very determined, very well-financed people trying to move that ball back to the five, ten, or even twenty yard line.

Because the ball has never crossed the goal, there is always this back-and-forth motion, and there always will be, until someone proves the point *definitively*, that there is no case at all.

But how do you write a book that conclusively proves that there is no case against Oswald? How could such a thing be done?

Well, in thinking about this, I decided to structure the book logically, categorizing all the evidence by topic, the topics related to key facts in the assassination which had to be true if Oswald was indeed the culprit. With the evidence categorized by factual topic, people could then make up their mind as to whether or not the evidence supported that particular fact.

So, with this method, it would be very easy for people to determine the strength or weakness of the case.

If this book is successful, it is going to break a decades-old logjam, and allow the intellectual efforts of people to be focused in what I view as the right direction, creating a short-list of suspects in the murders, and then deciding what would be the appropriate action to take.

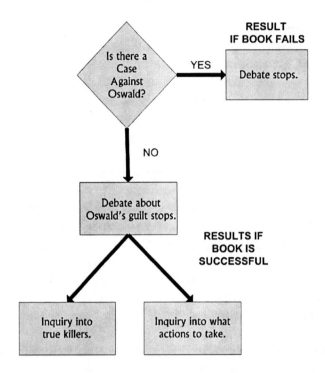

Now the question is, how *do* I prove it? That takes us to the third reason this book is different, how it achieves what it seeks to achieve, and to that point, there is one primary method, *The JFK Challenge*.

The *JFK Challenge*

Here is how the *Challenge* works: I make certain claims in the book. As a result of these claims, people will conclude that there is no case against Oswald. Others will challenge me, saying that I have either distorted or omitted information. To those people I say, "Fine. If you have purchased my book, you have the right to take me before an arbitrator and demonstrate before him or her the strength of what you're saying. Prepare a rebuttal to my book, and I will prepare a counter-rebuttal, and we each have a second right of reply, and we will take all this material before an arbitrator. We will let them decide which one of us has distorted or omitted information."

This is a strong concept! Suppose a person claims that I have distorted or omitted information. Yet, curiously enough, *that person refuses to take me before an arbitrator to prove his or her case.* What does that tell you? I know what it tells me. It tells me they can talk the talk, but they can't walk the walk. It tells me who is real, and who was just posing. *The JFK Challenge* allows me to smoke out the phonies.

By the way, you should know that at the very beginning of this book, even before this book was written, I knew I was going to have a *JFK Challenge*. The amount I used in my mind was $5000 at risk. At each stage in the writing of the book, when I put a fact down, I asked myself "is there any evidence out there that *should be* included that someone is going to claim should be included for this point?" I did this over and over and over, multiple times a day.

That is why, when you read this book, you're going to find every fact footnoted, and all the evidence in the case before your eyes in the form of screen captures. You will be able to check everything that I've said against the public record. This is how you are going to know that I did not distort information. Someone defending Oswald must have absolute integrity, and this is the check I placed against myself to ensure the integrity of the information I presented.

So, if you wanted to know why this book is different, you just read three very good reasons.

Other Ways This Book Is Different
Apart from these three points, there are other reasons this book is different:

- Because it is going to be used as evidence before an arbitrator, there are far more illustrations in this book than most of the books on the Kennedy assassination. I can only think of a handful that have more.
- I am going to allow future Kennedy researchers to use the images which I've created especially for this book without having to ask me permission first, and obviously at no charge. See the copyright notice.

Why "Who Killed JFK?" Is Not The Right Question
We are now about to enter the book itself. Before we move to the first part of the book, the *Foreword*, I want to discuss another issue which comes up.

I already told you one question that people ask me when I mentioned that I was working on a book on Lee Harvey Oswald. Only a few people ask me that question. Everyone else asks me this one: "Okay, if Oswald didn't kill Kennedy, who did?" That is a fair question, and believe me, I would like to answer that question, but before answering, I have a question for them: "What is your standard of proof? If I have evidence, am I supposed to prove it beyond a reasonable doubt?"

If the answer to that question is "yes," then I would say we're going to be waiting a long long time for evidence that is going to enable anyone to achieve that standard. Much evidence has been destroyed, the vast majority of witnesses are already dead, or very soon will be, so with no truly reliable evidentiary base, I think that proving the actual identities of the killers beyond a reasonable doubt is going to also be impossible.

Does that mean that we can never know who killed the President with reference to *any* standard of proof? No, not at all; I think if we shift the standard of proof, we can definitely make out a short list of suspects, the ones most likely to have shot the President. And that will be good enough to take action.

Eventually we are going to realize in addition to asking who is on the short list of suspects, that there are even more, even better questions to ask, as follows:

- Is it more important to know who *fired* the shots, or who *called* the shots?
- Should the question be "*Who* killed JFK?" or "*What* killed JFK?"
- Was it an *individual* who planned the assassination, or a *group*?
- If it was a group, is that group *still in existence* today, even as we speak?
- Is the government structured in such a way that a group like that could hijack the government without us knowing?
- If that group is still in existence today, is that group so important and tied-in to the government that it can make sure that it will never be investigated by the government?
- Has the government cooperated with this group over the years to cover up the true identity of the murderers?
- If Oswald didn't kill JFK, why does the first layer of evidence say that he did? And if a second layer of evidence proves that he didn't, why doesn't the government acknowledge the existence of the second layer, and why do they only discuss the first?
- If this group was powerful enough to assassinate the President and create the illusion that Oswald was responsible, and that group is still in existence today, do they have any other treasonous plans up their sleeves and/or on the drawing boards?

There is one absolutely critical thing to note about the questions above. If there was such a group, and that group is still active, *would it matter the names of the people in the group at the time*? I think you can see, it would not! So, we don't need to spend a lot of time wasting time arguing about who was in the group and who was not, all we need to establish is that in fact there *was* such a group. That's what counts!

And one final question:

- If we are convinced that there is no case against Oswald, what are the next steps?

What Are the Next Steps
Back in the old days, before I learned what I've learned in the process of writing this book, I probably would have, like numerous other people, called for a new official investigation by the government, and called for all previously unreleased documents to be released.

I now realize that either of these approaches would be a mistake.

In the first place, we don't need any new government investigations. Government investigations can't be trusted, and if you don't believe that now, you will after reading this book. As far as a call for more documents goes, we don't need any additional documents to show that the case against Oswald is dead, and I think it is extraordinarily unlikely that any existing documents possessed by the government are going to be pointing to the real perpetrators of the assassination. Also, given the illegitimacy of many of the documents that we already have, I don't believe all the documents that will be released can be trusted, and validating the documents would be a time-consuming, time-wasting, and ultimately hopeless task.

The bottom line is that people will waste a lot of time asking the wrong questions and looking for information that will be impossible to get (because the evidence is destroyed), and therefore we can't conclude anything beyond a reasonable doubt, and no one is going to agree on an alternate standard of proof anyway.

To me, if you want to discover what the next steps should be, you should be asking yourself the following question:

"If I was 100% convinced that the same group that was behind the assassination of President Kennedy was still in power today, and had control of the government, what action would I take?"

That's really the question, isn't it? Notice how now the responsibility has shifted away from the *government* to *you*.

If you were 100% convinced of that, what action would *you* take?

Surprisingly, and shockingly, I think the answer of many people would be "no action." They would say something like "you can't fight City Hall," "the system is too big to take on," "I just don't have time for that," and then they would go back to whatever they were doing.

I think you can see that that one would be pretty much a nonstarter. The government loves people who don't take action when action is called for. That's how government — or, more precisely, the people who have hijacked the government — gets away with murder.

So, what action *do* you take? Well, I have listed a number of possibilities in my book *Peak Oil And What To Do About It*, a book which could also be called *The National Debt And What To Do About It*, or could also be called *The Kennedy Assassination And What To Do About It*.

If you don't have time to read that book, and the ideas within it, take these as a brief takeaway:

- Cancel your cable. Get a *Roku* and *Netflix* and *Hulu* accounts. Congratulations, you just saved around $50 a month, and now have an 5-7 additional hours free a week which are not spent watching commercials. You're going to need that time.
- Now that you can't watch *CNN* and *Fox News* anymore (lucky you!), you can get your information from *Netflix* documentaries and by reading books: much higher quality sources of information because they were not produced on ridiculously short deadlines. Here are some *Netflix* documentaries I highly recommend:

  > *Flow*
  > *The Corporation*
  > *Inside Job*
  > *Enron: The Smartest Guys in the Room*
  > *The Best Government Money Can Buy*
  > *Unprecedented*
  > *Uncounted*
  > *Outfoxed*

And here are some excellent books:

Dissolving Dollars
Web of Debt
The Creature From Jekyll Island
The Long Emergency
Into the Buzzsaw

Of course, these are just a few ideas for you, I am sure that you will have no problem in discovering your own topics of interest. The main thing is this: the issues that *you* think about as important should be driven by what *you* actually think important, and not by what the box is telling you to think.

If you follow this strategy, and all your neighbors do the same thing, eventually you and your neighbors are going to stop thinking about the items that are on the agenda of the day as defined by *The Associated Press* and *The New York Times*. You won't be thinking about whether or not "Obamacare" is a good or bad thing, or whether the best candidate is Palin or Romney or Trump or Gingrich, and you are going to start thinking about questions that the media does not talk about very much, questions that actually require answering, like "how come the national debt always seems to be going up and up and there is never any solution?" and "if the Democrats and Republicans are *opposed*, why do they always seem to agree to raise the debt and to fight wars that people don't want?" and "why are we being held hostage to high oil prices when we should have had an energy policy developed over forty years ago that would have gotten us off of the need to use oil, using alternative energy sources such as solar thermal, solar photoelectric, wind, geothermal, etc.?" and "why is the city trying to privatize my water supply, which will ultimately raise my rates?" Lots and lots and lots of other questions you should be thinking about, and having conversations with your neighbors about. It's where your brain time should be if you want to get the answers to those questions.

- Here is one answer to all those questions: never, ever, ever, ever again vote for a Democrat or Republican! Now, when I say never, I mean *never*. **You must absolutely sever the umbilical cord that connects the master planners in**

Washington with the politicians of the district you live in. You want the politicians that you vote for to represent *you*, not put into place the agendas created by someone in Washington, DC, New York, or wherever these people live. Instead, you're much better off voting for a third-party, if there is one, but a far better strategy is simply to write in the name of a candidate. This is not necessarily a plug-and-play strategy, there are nuances involved, just read the *Write-In America FAQ* document included inside *Peak Oil And What To Do About It*. **If you sever that umbilical cord, you will simultaneously be severing the vacuum cleaner hose that is sucking bills out of your wallet**, which takes us to the next point.

Do you want more reasons to not vote for a Democrat or Republican? How about this: both parties have given us a $15,620,637,197,295 national debt!

U.S. NATIONAL DEBT CLOCK

The Outstanding Public Debt as of 04 Apr 2012 at 08:41:54 PM GMT is:

$15,620,637,197,295.65

And that figure became obsolete even before I was able to paste the screen capture. It's higher now. Go to http://www.brillig.com/debt_clock/ for the latest figures.

There, I just gave you over 15,000,000,000,000 reasons not to vote for a Democrat or a Republican. Now, if that is not enough reasons for you, I will give you one more. Let's follow a chain of logic related to the Kennedy assassination.

Let's say that hypothetically there was some group that was responsible for planning the assassination of the President. I think it is pretty obvious that the members of this group were not patriots!

Now, if that was the case, after the election of President Johnson, the members of this group, who were not patriots, got control of the government. Having gotten control of the government, they were in a position to consolidate their power. Because the television stations in the United States are licensed by the government, the government had control over the people who own those licenses, and if they happened to broadcast the "wrong" information, the government could take those extremely valuable licenses away. Consequently, the broadcasters would broadcast officially approved material defining the agendas of the day, and before you know it everyone would be dancing to the beat of that drummer.

A group like this, who we know are not patriots, could basically be using the government for whatever purpose they wanted, like siphoning off dollars from the public treasury and delivering them into their own pockets. Where do those dollars come from? Ultimately, from you, either visibly through higher taxes, or invisibly through higher inflation (cutting of services is also a type of inflation. For example, notice how your medical deductibles have been going up over the years, and your co-pays have increased, while the percentage insurance pays for procedures has decreased? Ever notice how the amount of coffee in that coffee can went from 16 oz. down to 11 oz. without you even knowing it?).

Now, if we assume that a group like this could get power over the *government*, then it could certainly get control over the Republican and Democratic parties, right? Nothing a few campaign contributions can't solve! We know they had the money for those contributions, because the firehose of government spending was pointed directly at their swimming pools.

And, if a group like this got control of *both* the Republican and Democratic parties, then any candidate who you voted for that was a member of those parties would have to follow the party line so that they would receive contributions that would enable them to be elected to office, which means that they too would have to dance to the beat of the drummaster in Washington.

And you are going to elect these people to office? Are you crazy?

Now, I'll make you a deal . . . if you read this book, and you conclude that Lee Harvey Oswald was actually the assassin of the President, forget the advice I just gave. But, if you read this book and conclude that there is *no way* that anyone could say that they were convinced that there was a Case Against Oswald beyond a reasonable doubt, then take my advice!

Deal?

What You Can Do To Spread The Word

When you finish this book, you will no longer have the illusion that there is a case against Lee Harvey Oswald. But you will be surrounded by the people who do. That won't change until you let them know. To let them know, you need to take some action. Post something about this on your *Facebook* page, your blog, send out in an e-mail. Even better, review this book on *Amazon* or *BN.com,* or review other books related to the Kennedy assassination, and link to this book. Tell them Volume One is free on the 22nd of every month.

Are you getting the idea that I want people to read this book?

Acknowledgments

The book you have in your hands you would never have had in your hands were it not for the work of hundreds of Kennedy researchers who did the basic legwork and discovered numerous key documents that had been buried in all kinds of places. The bulk of the work for me was simply discovering the pieces of the puzzle they were able to uncover, and then putting those pieces together to form the big picture related to the case (although I definitely was able to make quite a few discoveries of my own, as you will see).

We all owe these individuals a big "thank-you," for the research and insights that they provided. The researchers and authors I most relied on are listed below:

Harold Weisberg	Sylvia Meagher	Mary Ferrell
Mark Lane	Josiah Thompson	George Evica
Jim Fetzer	Jim Douglass	Jim Garrison
Vincent Salandria	David Lifton	Stewart Galanor
Gary Shaw	Wim Dankbaar	John Armstrong
Robert Groden	Harrison Livingstone	Gary Aguilar
David Mantik	Douglas Horne	Jim DiEugenio
Bruce Adamson	Peter Dale Scott	Donald Gibson
William Davy	Howard Roffman	Walt Brown
Jerry Rose	Michael Wiseberg	Joachim Joesten

I also want to thank the people at the website *The Education Forum* who provided so many observations that found their way into this book, and some other individuals as well:

William Kelly	Gil Jesus	Martin Hay
John Simkin	Vince Palamara	Larry Hancock
Pat Speer	Rex Bradford	Tom Scully

Thanks for reading. Now to the book.

". . . if you knew the facts you would be amazed."
                        – Jack Ruby, March 16, 1965.[1]

Foreword

Prepare to be amazed.

You might think that this is a book about the Kennedy assassination. And, at one level, it is. But more importantly, it is really a book about the *perception of reality* — or, more accurately, what people *claim* to be the perception of reality. What people *claim* to be true isn't always the case, and in this case, that is everything!

Yes, what people *claim* to perceive as reality can *indeed be changed*; scary thought, huh? Consider the following experiment by Solomon Asch, reported in 1951: [2]

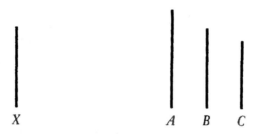

In Asch's experiment, subjects were asked to make a very simple determination: decide which line on the right was the closest in length to line X on the left.

Not too difficult — the answer is simple — line B.

But now imagine that you are in a room and you are the fourth person to be asked the question. And, to your amazement, when asked the question, each person in front of you instead says that the answer is "line A." What will you do, stick to your guns, or go along with the crowd?

When Solomon Asch performed this experiment in 1950, he found that a significant percentage of people conformed (or pretended to conform) with the majority opinion as listed in the table below: [3]

---

[1] Quoted in *Accessories After the Fact*, p. 453; see also *Evidence Of Revision* DVD # 1, at 1:24.

[2] *Effects of group pressure upon the modification and distortion of judgment*, found in H. Guetzkow (Ed), *Groups, Leadership, and Men*, pp. 177-190.

[3] http://en.wikipedia.org/wiki/Solomon_Asch (retrieved March 23, 2011). See also *The Social Animal*, Third Edition, p. 19. Data in the table is from "Opinions And Social Pressure," *Scientific American*, Volume 193, Number Five (1955).

Never conformed	Conformed *at least once*	Conformed the *majority* of the time	*Always* conformed
25%	75%	37%	5%

What Asch learned is that people will *claim* to conform their judgments based not on what they *themselves* perceive as reality, but on what *others* claim to perceive as reality.

It is important to be clear here: the confederates in front of the subjects *did not actually believe* what they were saying. However, the subject had no way of knowing that. The problem with the subjects who conformed with the false view of reality is that they not only doubted their own judgment — evidence right in front of their eyes — but they also had a misplaced faith in the judgments of others well-undeserving of trust.

The Asch experiment is the key to understanding Kennedy assassination analysis as it has developed over the years. Consider the following multiple-choice question related to the Kennedy assassination, and think of the answers as choices in an Asch–like experiment:

Based on the evidence developed so far, which statement is the *most likely* to be true?

A) **There was *no* conspiracy to kill President Kennedy.**
B) **There *was* a conspiracy to kill President Kennedy.**
C) **We can *never know* whether or not there was a conspiracy to kill President Kennedy.**

Now, only *one* of these answers can be correct. The contention of this book is that the *only* answer consonant with the evidence is B, and yet this answer fails to conform with the judgment of the establishment media. School textbooks, newspapers, television programs, historians, all will tell you that the answer is A, and if they are pressed with much contradictory evidence, may be moved to C, but they will rarely admit B.

Notice how much trickier is this situation versus the Asch situation. In the example of the 3 lines, it is perfectly obvious what the correct answer is, and so it is very easy to tell fact from fiction. However, with the Kennedy assassination, things are not nearly as clear-cut on the surface, and even if they are clear-cut once you examine the evidence, your evidence-based perception will come under fire from a media-driven world whose members, Asch-*protégés* all, are constantly telling you otherwise.

To prove that studying the Kennedy assassination will test your ability to distinguish reality from illusion, we will explore a few examples.

Let's start with the arrangement of boxes where Oswald was supposedly situated. According to the Warren Commission (the first major government investigation of the Kennedy affair in 1964, followed by the second, the *House Select Committee On Assassinations* in 1979), only *one* of the photographs below represents the original position of the boxes at the "sniper's nest," the position they were in after the assassin (if indeed the assassin was located at that position) left the scene.

But which one?

COMMISSION EXHIBIT 733   COMMISSION EXHIBIT 509

These photographs are evidence in The Case Against Oswald, Warren Commission Exhibit 733 on the left, and 509, on the right. *(Note: Exhibit 733 can be found in Volume 17 of the Warren Commission Hearings, at page 509, which will be cited as **17 H 509**. Exhibit 509 is found at **17 H 220**. These exhibits can be viewed at http://www.history-matters.com/jfkmurder.htm and http://www.maryferrell.org.)*

Now, you can immediately see that we've got ourselves a real problem here!

A compare and contrast between the photographs, which any third-grader familiar with similar exercises found in *Highlights* should easily be able to do, results in a series of questions.

To prove any third-grader can do it, we can divide these questions into roughly 2 types named in honor of the two main rivals for Darla's affection in the old *Our Gang* series, rivals who now have decided to stop squabbling and join forces. From this corner emerges Alfalfa, the straight-up earnest cow-licked boy lifted straight out of a Norman Rockwell painting . . .

. . . and from this corner, Butch, the snarling pugilist:

"Alfalfa" questions, just like their namesake, are polite and proper like questions should be, but "Butch" questions, by contrast, are rude and in-your-face in the best Gordon Ramsay style.

These archetypes firmly in mind, *Alfalfa* comes out swinging with his queries about the incompatible box *feng shui*:

- Why are these boxes in different positions?
- Did anyone at the Warren Commission notice?
- If they did notice, did the Warren Commission not think that *we* would notice that these boxes were in different positions — and then start wondering why?

Not to be outdone, Butch chimes in with his point of view:

Are you kidding me?

Alfalfa adds some fast jabs:

- Which of these two photographs, if either, represents the *original* position of the boxes at the so-called "sniper's nest?"
- If we are told that the position of the boxes in Exhibit 733 is the one which represents the way the boxes were originally positioned, how come there is an *alternate* photo?
- Boxes don't move themselves — someone obviously moved them. *Who* moved them? *When* did they move them? *Why* did they move them?

And even more *Alfalfa* flurries:

- If I am told that the position of the boxes in Exhibit 733 represents the *original* position, how do I know that I'm being told the truth?
- How can anyone *prove* that this is the original position? If it is not, doesn't this affect any analysis related to trajectories and the ability of the assassin to make his shot?
- In any event, doesn't the movement of boxes violate everything we have been told about maintaining the integrity of the crime scene?

But of course, as always, we can rely on Butch to go straight to the point:

Hey, what *is* this, a *con job*?

That Butch . . . you gotta love him!

And there are many other questions, which you could easily formulate given the time.

But before you can get to those questions, defenders of the Warren Commission will always come back at you with answers, exposing you to the *First Law Of Kennedy Assassination Motion*:

**For every bizarre contradiction
there is an equal and opposite "innocent explanation."**

And what is the innocent explanation in this case?

"Tut, tut, my man, 'tis no problem at all. The Warren Commission never tried to pass off CE 509 (also known as Studebaker Exhibit D) as a photo depicting the Sniper's Nest boxes as they were first found by the police. Nor did they attempt to pass off CE 733 as a photograph of the boxes in their original position.

Quite the contrary, in fact. The Commission has testimony that CE 509 was a picture that was taken after boxes were moved for fingerprints before photographs were taken, and that CE 733 was a 'reconstruction' of the original position, and neither photo represented the configuration of the boxes in their exact position when they were first discovered by police. It's all very innocent, you see."

And yet, like the mythological Hydra, the "innocent explanations" you get just lead to even more *Alfalfa* queries:

- You mean, in the murder of the century, we do not have an original photographic record of the crime scene!!??
- You say this innocent explanation is true, but how are we to know that?
- Why did the Dallas Police Department feel it was necessary to photograph the boxes in different positions after they had been dusted and moved around?
- How does this comport with crime scene protocol at the time?
- Why wasn't the photograph taken *before* the fingerprinting was done?
- Is there another, more sinister explanation that the innocent explanation hides?

And if you happen to get more innocent explanations in reply, if you're lucky enough to get a reply, you are just going to have to go back to the well again to dredge up more questions.

Instantly you can see that this is no ordinary case!

But this is only the beginning, trust me. There will be seemingly no end to the eye-popping question-inspiring multiple descriptions of reality in the historical record we will have to choose from, as we will continually be confronted with gaps between the representations of reality and the reality represented (that's a fancy way of saying *we are being lied to*).

But *who* is doing the lying? It's that old *Invasion Of The Body Snatchers* conundrum: is your best friend a *person* or a *pod*? There's no choice in the matter, we have to decide.

Consider these competing versions of the so-called single-bullet path (the image on the left is from Jim Marrs' *Crossfire*. The image on the right is from page 189 of the second volume of the *House Select Committee On Assassinations Appendix*, which will be cited as 2 HSCA 189, JFK Exhibit F-145):

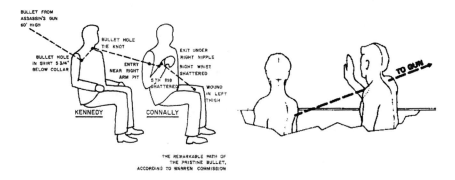

Zig-zag vs. straight-line. Both of these views can't be correct, of course.

Now, your first inclination, when you see these two drawings, is to attempt to determine their respective legitimacy by asking yourself which of the two (purporting to describe reality) conforms to your prior knowledge. Of course, we all are familiar with the laws of physics, at least intuitively. We know that bullets that travel in a straight line on a downward path don't immediately shoot upward, and then, a fraction of a fraction of a fraction of a second later, immediately reverse course. From the laws of physics perspective, you can completely rule out the drawing on the left, which illustrates not the *laws*, but the *loss* of physics. That leaves you with the drawing on the right, which, of these two, is the *only* possible one which could be true.

But the question now is, *which of these drawings best describes the state of the evidence gathered by the Warren Commission?* If the answer is the drawing on the left, then you can instantly see that the *evidence* the Warren Commission claims to be legitimate cannot possibly be true, or the *conclusion* derived from that evidence cannot possibly be true — or both.

As it turns out (and as you will find out), the evidence gathered supports *neither* of these images, which leads us right back to square one: if we were going to draw a picture of the reality (if indeed it was reality) of the single-bullet path based on the best evidence, what would it look like?

This question has very deep ramifications, and leads to other questions: What is the data we need to draw this picture? Do we need *more* data? Or should we simply analyze the data we have and draw the conclusions which most naturally flow? And if we should just analyze the data we have, whose *version* of the data is dispositive?

As you might expect, there are multiple versions of what "the data" is. According to prosecutor Vincent Bugliosi (writing in the book *Reclaiming History*), the data partially consists of five reasons that one should have more faith in the image on the right we previously saw (and that therefore one should ignore the obvious evidence in the Zapruder film which on its face indicates that that image is flawed in what may be more ways than one). Bugliosi's dataset is as follows (*Reclaiming History* pp. 458-64 [hereinafter to be cited as RH 458-64]):

- The alignment of Kennedy and Connally's bodies to each other at the time the shot was fired is consistent with the single-bullet theory.
- No physical evidence supports a second gunman.
- The entrance wound in Governor Connally's back was not circular, but oval.
- The bullet alleged to have traversed the bodies of both Kennedy and Connally, Warren Commission Exhibit 399, was fired from Oswald's rifle.
- No separate bullet was available to hit Connally.

The validity of the foregoing statements, obviously, will be discussed extensively later on in this book. However, one might argue provisionally that this is molehill data on which to base such a mountainous conclusion, particularly since the conclusions inherent in the statements are not necessarily consistent with the evidence. Yet note the Mount Everest conclusion Bugliosi tells us emerges from this molehill data (RH 464-65; emphasis supplied):

Each of the above five reasons, alone and by themselves, proves the single-bullet theory independent of the Zapruder film. (I would defy any conspiracy theorist to *come up with even one — much less five — logical arguments that are independent of the Zapruder film and support the proposition that Kennedy and*

Connally were hit by separate bullets.) All five of these reasons, when taken together, prove the proposition that Connally was hit by the same bullet that hit Kennedy not just beyond all reasonable doubt, but **beyond all possible doubt**. Therefore, the film itself cannot, by definition, show something else. As I said earlier, any interpretation of the film that contravenes the single-bullet theory either must be a misinterpretation by the person analyzing the film, or *is explainable in some other way.*

Quite a compelling proclamation, even from a prosecutor who gives numerous indications in this paragraph that he never met a hyperbole he didn't like. Unfortunately for Bugliosi's overly-optimistic summary, there actually is another way to describe the single-bullet theory which on its face trumps Bugliosi's five reasons, a description which encompasses far more of the physical evidence unearthed (as will be seen, Bugliosi's summary suffers from an invisible *factectomy*). George Evica takes on Bugliosi's challenge to come up with more than one logical argument to support the proposition that Kennedy and Connally were hit by separate bullets, in his brilliant *reductio ad absurdum* of the Single-Bullet Theory (*And We Are All Mortal*, p. ix):

Though such a theory was not necessary to the Commission's case (except that in its absence conspiracy was certain), the *Report* argued it *could* have happened. A single-bullet could have caused Kennedy's back of the neck wound (somehow moved up six inches from its observed location), continued through his neck (at a rather acute angle to the horizontal plane of the limousine despite the fact the round was allegedly fired from a sixth-floor window at an original angle of about 45 degrees) and, striking no bones, exited from the front of the neck through what *had* been an entry wound, turned down, leaving particles of lead throughout Kennedy's neck, but keeping its copper alloy jacket intact, and, losing no weight, either paused for 1.3 seconds before striking Connally or so lightly and swiftly struck him that he did not respond for 1.3 seconds, then plunged through the thorax of the Governor, shattering a rib, yet losing no weight and, with its copper alloy jacket still intact, its diabolical velocity still undiminished and possessing an uncanny direction-changing ability, exited through a gaping wound in the Governor's chest, turned right, smashing through the Governor's right wrist and breaking one of the hardest bones in the human body, leaving lead particles behind, yet losing no weight, its copper alloy jacket still intact, exited the wrist, turned down and left, and imbedded itself in the femur bone of the Governor's left thigh, where, exhausted, it would drop *up* and out, its copper alloy jacket still intact *and* without weight loss, leaving lead fragments in the Governor's thigh, but with *one last great effort*, tucking itself under the mattress of a stretcher used in the emergency *red blanket* treatment of a small black boy at Parkland Memorial Hospital, from which, helpfully, it would heave itself out when it was needed as evidence.

Uh . . . . what? Something is very wrong here . . . Vincent Bugliosi is a well-respected prosecutor. How can his conclusion that the single-bullet theory has been proven "beyond all possible doubt" (based on his five reasons) *possibly* be reconciled with the previous paragraph?!

At this point, as the Immortal Bard could have told us, you may be sensing something rotten in the state of the Union. Psychiatrist Dr. Martin Schotz, in a speech entitled "The Waters of Knowledge versus The Waters of Uncertainty," delivered on November 20, 1998 to the *National Conference of the Coalition on Political Assassinations* (COPA), smelled a rat, and began to follow the thread:

Over and over again we hear people asking for more and more information from the government. I suggest to you that the problem is not that we have insufficient data. The problem is that we dare not analyze the data we have had all along. In fact we need very little data. Honestly, as far as I'm concerned you can throw almost the whole 26 volumes of the Warren Commission in the trash can. All you need to do is look at this . . .

And then Schotz contrasted two images related to the aforementioned single-bullet theory, the first an illustration produced under the supervision of autopsy doctors for the Warren Commission, and the second a photograph of President Kennedy's jacket produced by the FBI, both said to show the entry point of a bullet shot from the *rear* of the President:

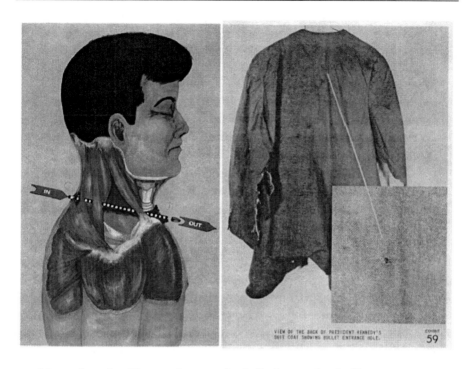

Note that the *illustration* on the left shows the bullet entry wound at or *above* the collar; the *photograph* on the right reveals that the bullet entry wound actually entered over 5 inches *below* the collar, and that the neck "exit wound" in the left illustration therefore had to have been not only a *separate* wound, but *also* a wound of *entry*, indicating a separate shot from the *front* . . . where Oswald was *not*. So much for the single-bullet theory, and so much for the idea of Oswald as the "lone assassin," two hypotheses elegantly destroyed with a mere two images.

But there is more to the tale than that. Schotz tells us where the thread is heading: [1]

> On the left is the Warren Commission drawing of the path of the "magic" bullet. To the right is a photograph of the hole in the President's jacket. Now what does this tell us? It tells us without a shadow of a doubt that the President's throat wound was an entry wound, and that there was a conspiracy without

---

[1] The Schotz speech is contained in Vincent Salandria's book *False Mystery*, quotes from pp. 180-1 (emphasis supplied). The image on the left is CE385, found at 17H977 (that is *Commission Exhibit* 385, which can be found in volume 17 of the *Warren Commission Hearings And Exhibits*, page 977). The image on the right is from the *FBI Supplemental Report to the Warren Commission* dated January 13, 1964, CD105, p. 69 (*Commission Document* 105, page 69).

any question. But it tells us much more. It tells us that the Warren Commission knew that the conspiracy was obvious and that the Commission was engaged in a criminal conspiracy after the fact to obstruct justice. The Chief Justice of the United States was a criminal accessory to the murder of the President. Senator Arlen Specter is a criminal accessory to murder. **The Warren Report was not a mistake; it was and is an obvious act of criminal fraud.**

Think of this for a moment. The Warren Report is an obvious criminal act of fraud and no history department in any college or university is willing to say so. What does such silence mean?

Didn't see that one coming, did you? I told you to prepare to be amazed!

Dr. Schotz's extraordinarily provocative point takes us back to where we began. Studying the Kennedy assassination brings us out of the realm of mere history, and into the world of what has academically and euphemistically been termed the "social construction of reality": just what is history anyway? Is it what *actually* occurred, or is it the version that we *are told* occurred? How do we decide which is the correct version of history? What version of history best conforms to the evidence? And if there is a version of history which best conforms to the evidence, why would anyone report a *different* version of history?

And, if a different version of history *is* reported, and *all* the evidence goes *against* that version, how do we explain the fact that so many people have been, and continue to be, perpetually fooled?
If so, *the real story* of the Kennedy assassination would be that *we don't know the real story* of the Kennedy assassination!

Think *The Matrix.*
Think *The Truman Show.*
Think *The Prisoner.*
This is what we are talking about, people!

If Schotz is right, then the citizens of America have a real problem on their hands . . . the information they have been given in this case, and, by extension, possibly dozens or hundreds of other cases related to historical events, could possibly be describing a parallel (but opposing) world of *fiction* masquerading as a world of *fact*.

And since no evidence has been provided that there are parallel worlds, the apparent ability to convince us that what is true is *false*, and that what is false is *true*, has the most disturbing implications, to wit:

> *The authorities promulgating the Lone Assassin Scenario, if it is indeed false, would be functioning like the confederates in the Asch experiment, telling you that lines A or C are the correct answer when it's really line B. And if the true facts of the matter are unavailable to you, your only option is to go along . . .*

Think about it: what is the ultimate hat trick of political power? To convince you that a shot from a low-velocity weapon came from a high velocity weapon . . . or that a shot from the front came from the back . . . or that a shot over 5 inches below the collar "really" entered at the base of the neck!

With power like that — the power to convince you that what is demonstrably *false* is *true* — what *couldn't* the mythmakers do?

The power to modify our view of reality is a power that we have granted to our authorities when we ignore the fine print and put away the fine-tooth comb. When our authorities have talked, we, good citizens all, have listened. But that's a power we only want to grant to authorities who have *themselves* correctly viewed reality. If they have not, the risk of being fooled — and all the consequences which naturally flow — are great. If the mind can be changed, can the soul be far behind?

In this book, we are going to focus predominantly on the *physical* evidence that has been proposed to buttress The Case Against Oswald. Because of this exclusive focus, you won't find extensive information here about many familiar names in Kennedy assassination literature, such as Guy Bannister, Allen Dulles, John McCloy, Henry Luce, David and Nelson Rockefeller, Joseph Ball, Edward Lansdale, David Ferrie, David Atlee Phillips, James Files, Chauncey Holt, "Tosh" Plumlee, Phillip Twombly, Johnny Roselli, Charles Nicoletti, Santo Trafficante, Carlos Marcello, Gerry Hemming, Charles Harrelson, George Bush Sr., E. Howard Hunt, William Harvey, Sam Giancana, Clay Shaw, Lloyd Cobb, Alton Ochsner, Walter Dornberger, Earle Cabell, William Gaudet, Donald Kendall, Richard Nixon, Cord Meyer, Frank Sturgis, Ed Butler, D.H. Byrd, Clint Murchison, Curtis LeMay, William Reily,

Judith Vary Baker, Mary Sherman, and a host of other personalities who may or may not be related in one way or another to the events of November 22, 1963. Understanding who these people are, and the role they played or possibly played, is important, but until you are absolutely convinced that The Case Against Oswald is completely impossible, their relationship to the case, if any, will be perpetually mysterious.

With that in mind, let us continue. You are about to enter a world where black is white, but so is red. Where a fact may be true one day, but false the next. Where the innocent are guilty, while the guilty frame our perception.

Welcome to the world of Kennedy assassination research!

Once again, prepare to be amazed, and brace yourself for a brush with the impossible.

Introduction

You want a difficult, what some would call an *impossible* task? Try defending Lee Harvey Oswald. If the government and the mass media are to be believed, even *thinking* that he was not the sole assassin of John Fitzgerald Kennedy on November 22, 1963 certifies you as a bona-fide la-la-lander, proud possessor of a lifetime complimentary membership with the Flat Earth Society. (And yes, there really is one; visit *http://theflatearthsociety.org* if you feel so inclined.)

Do you think that characterization unfair? If so, you probably weren't reading the *Dallas Observer* on July 6, 2000, and if you were, you certainly weren't reading this article by Robert Wilonsky: [1]

> **The Nut lives just outside a small town called Paradise**, a few miles northwest of Fort Worth. With his wife of more than 30 years, The Nut inhabits 25 acres of land deserving of its proximity to a town called Paradise, because even the still, damp air of summer feels light and sweet here. . . .
>
> **The Nut — with his short pants and denim shirt and hiking boots and straw hat and walking cane — and his four dogs walk up here when it's time to think, to clear the brain and focus on shadow governments and assassinated Presidents and spacemen who live among us.**
>
> **"This," says The Nut, pointing toward the spectacular horizon, "is where I come to be alone."**
>
> It is hard to reconcile such a placid, idyllic setting with the man who has lived on it since 1979. For a decade, The Nut — who has a name, Jim Marrs, a most appropriate moniker for a man who not long ago wrote a book titled *Alien Agenda: Investigating the Extraterrestrial Presence Among Us* — has been among the most high-profile of conspiracy theorists . . .

Now, if you were a rigorous fact-checker, you would want to make sure that Mr. Wilonsky wasn't telling a tall one. He wasn't:

---

[1] "The truth is way out there; Jim Marrs believes that Kennedy was murdered as part of a vast conspiracy, that aliens visit us regularly, and that the Trilateral Commission controls our government. So, what if he's right?" by Robert Wilonsky, *Dallas Observer* (Texas), July 6, 2000.

Ouch!

Well, you might think that the unfortunately-named Marrs is just a blip, and maybe he is, but he is not the only blip. To hammer home the point that "conspiracy theorist" = nut job, we have this fine work by Kenn Thomas which first graced our shores on May 31, 2011:

It is hard for me to imagine how the Kennedy researchers in the forums I perused in the course of writing this book missed this scholarly effort: on the other hand, maybe they believe, like me, that if there is one time it's okay to judge a book by its cover, this is it.

While it is safe to say that *JFK & UFO* is probably a long shot to be included in any Kennedy assassination bibliographies going forward, we can see that the Thomas book one-ups Marrs: while *Alien Agenda* happens to be written by the same author of *Crossfire* (a book on the Kennedy assassination cited in the previous chapter), the content of those two books is separate; this book, on the other hand, explicitly identifies JFK "conspiracy theorists" with people who believe in UFOs.

Yes, it is true that at least two of the millions of people who claim to believe that the evidence supports a conspiracy to kill President Kennedy also claim to believe in . . . dare I utter the word . . . *aliens.* Ouch again!

So now we know that at least two of the defenders of the thesis of this book are potentially off their rockers.

Hardly an auspicious beginning!

Armed with book covers like these, the defenders of the lone assassin thesis feel emboldened to stipulate that what they have to say is the gospel truth, as we learned in this article in the *Digital Journal* on September 11, 2011: [2]

> **[A]ny individual who claims Oswald did not shoot the President** or that the 9/11 attacks were not carried out by fanatics with hijacked commercial aircraft **is prima facie unworthy of belief with regard to any discussion of world affairs,** because the failure to accept the absolutely overwhelming evidence adduced in support of these two propositions is indicative of a totally denialist mentality.

The Wilonsky article pairs JFK assassination researchers with people who believe in aliens, and this uncredited *Digital Journal* article pairs the hypothesis that Kennedy was assassinated as a result of a conspiracy with the unsubstantiated belief (held by some) that the twin towers were not felled by hijacked commercial airliners. In both cases, these articles leverage the inertia of a discredited known A (aliens/no aircraft) to pair with an unknown B (conspiracy), and through the pairing attempt to identify B with A, and thereby drag B through A's mud.

You have to admit, it's a pretty successful technique. Who wants Marrs and Thomas on their side? If you don't — and you can be forgiven for that — your tendency is to want to go to the other side, where all the well-thought-of authorities await your companionship.

Faced with this, we have to ask, why not join the "responsible" crowd, Asch theory be damned?

Yes, for the most part, that "responsible" mass media crowd is in agreement. Say you were going to watch the miniseries *The Kennedys*

---

[2] *Digital Journal,* "9/11 Truth - Governors, veterans, and loonies." (September 11, 2011).

(which was originally lined up to air on *The History Channel*, and later *Showtime*, but was not shown on either of those networks), available at the time of this writing on *Netflix*. If you hover your mouse over a description of *Episode Seven*, the callout gives you that miniseries' version of reality — "Lee Harvey Oswald finalizes his assassination plan":

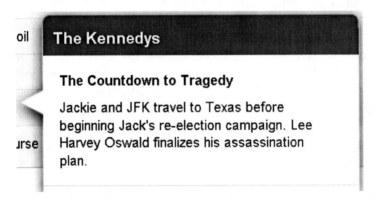

oil **The Kennedys**

The Countdown to Tragedy

Jackie and JFK travel to Texas before beginning Jack's re-election campaign. Lee Harvey Oswald finalizes his assassination plan.

And, if you decided to watch that episode, over 2/3 of the way through, you would be treated to this image of Oswald loading up:

Not a television watcher? Readers of mass-market books received the same information. At the top of the bestseller lists in 2012 was Stephen King's book *11/22/63*, whose primary thesis was that Oswald was the lone assassin:

A TV series. A book. But just the iceberg's tip. Over the years, the following respectable entities have, at one time or another come out in favor of Lee Harvey Oswald as the lone assassin of President Kennedy: high school textbooks, college textbooks, at least one Nobel prize winner (Luis Alvarez), a chief judge of the Supreme Court (Earl Warren), the PBS series *Nova* ("Who Shot President Kennedy?"), the PBS series *Frontline* ("Who Was Lee Harvey Oswald?"), CBS ("A CBS News Inquiry: The Warren Report"), ABC ("The Kennedy Assassination: Beyond Conspiracy"), the *Discovery Channel* ("JFK: Inside the Target Car"), *Showtime* ("On Trial: Lee Harvey Oswald"), *Life* magazine (multiple articles in the 60's identifying Oswald as the assassin), the *Journal Of The American Medical Association* (which published a series of articles in 1992 attacking the credibility of Dr. Charles Crenshaw and Gary Shaw (who co-authored a book called *Conspiracy Of Silence*), resulting in a defamation lawsuit settled favorably in Crenshaw and Shaw's behalf after the JAMA agreed to pay $213,000 [see *Journal of the American Medical Association*, May 24/31 1995, v. 273, No. 20, p. 1632, and *Assassination Science*, p. 19]), *Wikipedia* (article on Lee Harvey Oswald, etc.), and *The New York Times* (articles too numerous to mention, with several examples in this book).

Yes, there are exceptions, such as the Oliver Stone film *JFK*, and a series which appeared on *The History Channel* called *The Men Who Killed Kennedy*, and several others which have appeared over the years, including documentaries by Jesse Ventura, but these have to be seen as mere ripples in a much larger pond, especially when you consider that the most potent evidence of conspiracy was contained in the last three episodes of *The Men Who Killed Kennedy*, episodes which were subsequently banned from distribution (go to *Amazon* to buy the DVDs: you can buy six, but there were originally nine).

But for the fiftieth anniversary of the assassination of President Kennedy, additional high-profile Lee-Harvey-Oswald-dunnit works are planned, including a book by Bill O'Reilly, and a movie slated to be made from *Reclaiming History* (the extremely well-documented Bible of the lone assassin position), with Tom Hanks handling the role of executive producer. From an appeal-to-authority standpoint, it looks like those not kowtowing to the party line should, like Marrs, run for the hills.

Now, all of this really looks bad for those who want to challenge the lone assassin position, but if you are an independent thinker, you're going to be brushing all of this off. Sure, anyone can focus on a lone nut or two who happen to believe in aliens, and ignore the thousands of responsible people — forensic pathologists and investigators and attorneys and radiation oncologists and philosophy professors and physicists and educators — who believe that the evidence does not support the official version of what transpired in Dealey Plaza on November 22, 1963. Those individuals look at the *evidence*, and ignore the two dozen+ media outlets who have reported the alternative view as true; as history shows, two dozen media outlets, and even twenty dozen, can be wrong wrong wrong, as we saw with respect to the "weapons of mass destruction" rationale for the Iraq war. Just because people are marching together in lockstep . . .

. . . doesn't mean that what they have to say is *legitimate*.

Remember the Asch effect! We learned a powerful lesson from that experiment: make your decision exclusively by looking at the *facts*, and *ignore what the crowd says*. This can take some guts, and can on occasion be hazardous to your health:

So, inspired by the latter of the photographs above, we decide to take a chance and look at the facts related to The Case Against Oswald. Unfortunately, we have a problem there too, and at first glance, it is a big one.

When we examine the data on a cursory basis, it appears that this time the mass media may have got one right; the evidence against Oswald does *indeed* initially appear overwhelming. There is not just one piece of evidence which goes against him, not even two, nor three, or four, but *dozens upon dozens* of isolated facts which, when added up together, apparently point out — seemingly irrefutably — to his guilt.

Let's start from where the shots were fired. According to the Warren Commission and the *House Select Committee On Assassinations* (HSCA), all the shots that were fired in Dealey Plaza on November 22 originated from the sixth floor of the Texas School Book Depository, where Oswald was employed. Whose gun was found on the sixth floor? Oswald's! A bullet was said to have been found on John Connally's stretcher, and from whose gun was it fired? Oswald's! Three shells that were ejected from Oswald's rifle were claimed to have been found on the sixth floor, and since the majority of witnesses reported that only three shots were fired (according to the Warren Commission), the most likely perpetrator had to be — of course — Oswald.

And further . . . Oswald's palm print was found on the rifle; his fingerprints were found on some of the boxes; Oswald was observed to be in the building at the time of the assassination; a bag was found on the sixth floor, and Oswald had told a co-worker the extremely suspicious story that the contents of a paper bag he was going to carry into the building contained curtain rods; however, this bag could have also held a disassembled rifle, and considering what happened, a far more likely alternative.

And if you needed any more evidence than the hard data items listed above, just consider the fact that Oswald was a "loner," a Marxist, a person who defected from the United States, a person accused of earlier firing a shot at another public figure, General Edwin Walker (the natural inference: if true, his alleged attack on the President would not have been an isolated incident), and to top it all off, a person suspected of killing a police officer in an "escape from the scene of the crime."

Let's see . . . killed a cop? Check! Fled from the scene? Check! Caught red-handed in a photograph holding a rifle and two militant newspapers? Triple-check!

"It's not Oswald"???? . . . who else *could* it be?

Do you really need any more facts? Let's face it, just based on the above, you have to conclude that this guy was a sure candidate for the electric chair. Jack Ruby did us all a favor, and saved us the cost of what could have been an extremely expensive trial. And did the Warren Commission really have to write over 24,000 pages of documentation proving Oswald's guilt, supplemented by several thousand more by the HSCA? Why did Vincent Bugliosi have to write *Reclaiming History*? His 2800+ page extensive analysis *proves*, in Bugliosi's schema, that Oswald was guilty far beyond a reasonable doubt.

Forget Stephen King and *The Kennedys*. That's just fiction anyway. If you want the facts, Bugliosi is your man. The eminent district attorney and author told us just how difficult defending Oswald is, and how naïve Warren Commission critics and "conspiracy theorists" are, and given the evidence, who could blame him? (RH 952)

> [T]here is a simple fact of life that Warren Commission critics and conspiracy theorists either don't realize or fail to take into consideration, something I learned from my experience as a prosecutor; namely, that in the real world — you know, the world in which when I talk you can hear me, there will be a dawn tomorrow, et cetera — you cannot be innocent and yet still have a prodigious amount of highly incriminating evidence against you. That's just not what happens in life.

Bugliosi then went on to quote his opening argument to the jury in the 1986 mock trial of Oswald broadcast on *Showtime*, with Bugliosi successfully squaring off against famed defense attorney Gerry Spence (RH 952; emphasis supplied):

I articulated this fact in my opening argument to the jury in London: "Ladies and gentlemen of the jury, when a man is innocent of a crime, chances are there isn't going to be anything at all pointing towards his guilt. Nothing at all pointing towards his guilt. But now and then, because of the very nature of life, and the unaccountability of certain things, there may be one thing that points towards his guilt, even though he is innocent. In an unusual situation, maybe even two things point to his guilt, even though he is innocent. And in a very rare and strange situation, maybe even three things point to his guilt, even though he is completely innocent. But **with Lee Harvey Oswald, everything, everything points towards his guilt. In fact, the evidence against Oswald is so great that you could throw 80 percent of it out the window and there would still be more than enough to prove his guilt beyond all reasonable doubt.**"

And then, in case his level of doubt was in doubt, Bugliosi removed all doubt (RH 952; footnote omitted, emphasis supplied):

Indeed, **the evidence against Oswald proves his guilt not just beyond a reasonable doubt, but beyond all doubt**, or, as they say in the movies, beyond a shadow of a doubt. In other words, not just one or two or three pieces of evidence point toward Oswald's guilt, but more than fifty pieces point irresistibly to his guilt. And not only does all of the physical, scientific evidence point solely and exclusively to Oswald's guilt, but virtually everything he said and did points unerringly to his guilt. Under these circumstances, **it is not humanly possible for him to be innocent, at least, as I said, not in the real world in which we live. Only in a fantasy world could Oswald be innocent and still have all this evidence against him. I think we can put it this way:** *If Oswald didn't kill Kennedy, then Kennedy wasn't killed on November 22, 1963.*

Powerful words. Persuasive words. Unambiguous words. And Bugliosi was no wet-behind-the-ears kid fresh out of law school. As a Los Angeles Deputy District Attorney, he won 105 out of 106 felony cases. [3] Who could possibly want to begin to try to refute the remarks of an extremely competent prosecutor with seemingly every fact of the Kennedy assassination at his fingertips?

Your answer: yours truly!

Incredible though it may seem, I am convinced that Bugliosi is wrong, and for that matter, Stephen King, Tom Hanks, Bill O'Reilly, and anyone else who happens to agree with him, whether CBS, ABC, PBS, Peter Jennings, Walter Cronkite, Dan Rather, Bill Clinton, the history textbook you read in high school or college, etc. etc. etc.

How sure am I? So sure that I'm willing to put anywhere from $1,000 to $25,000 on the line, and possibly higher, to prove I'm right.

Yes, as Rodgers and Hammerstein once told us in the classic musical *Cinderella*, "impossible things are happening every day," and to show that's no fairy-tale, I want to prove the impossible, that *there is <u>absolutely no case</u> against Lee Harvey Oswald*!

Nada. None whatsoever. Zip. Zero. Zilch.

But, if you can prove me wrong to the satisfaction of a unanimous virtual jury of 12 arbitrators, the money is yours . . .

Are you salivating yet? Got that cruise planned already? (I recommend *The Jazz Cruise*, or maybe a poker cruise, where you can parlay those thousands into multiples of thousands).

The rules for this engagement, which I will refer to using the umbrella term *The JFK Challenge*, are contained later in this book (partly) and more specifically and more completely the third volume of this book, as of this writing. Information related to *The JFK Challenge* (whether in fact anyone accepts the challenge or not, the amounts to be awarded, and the results, if any) will be contained at the following link:

http://www.krusch.com/jfk
(then click the "JFK Challenge" link)

Why create *The JFK Challenge*? Because I am convinced of one other thing that you simply won't believe. Here it is:

Not only do *I* believe there is no Case Against Oswald whatsoever, I don't believe that there is *even one person* in the United States, and possibly the *world*, that will *accept* the challenge, proving that *no one else* believes it either!

[3] http://www.thenation.com/node/22710 (Retrieved March 17, 2011).

Now, wouldn't *that* be something? Just think: millions upon millions upon millions of media impressions that "Oswald did it, Oswald did it, Oswald did it", creating what we can call *The Oswald Wall*, Oswald's guilt assumed in history courses throughout the land and DVDs formerly littering the shelves of *Blockbuster* (now streaming video from *Netflix* and *Amazon*), and millions of people exposed to these impressions who supposedly buy into this blarney, and yet no one — not *one* — who is confident enough to take on the challenge.

I mean, what would that mean? The thought is staggering. Here's one implication:

A chief judge of the United States Supreme Court was *wrong*, and a guy meandering in the woods pondering alien agendas was *right*!

(let us all pause to let this sink in . . .)
Of course, whether this turns out to be the case, only time will tell.

While we wait for the results (tick, tick, tick . . .), let's proceed and take a look at the method by which I seek to prove that The Case Against Oswald is impossible — *actually* impossible, not one of the "impossible" things that can and do happen every day.

I will start here with the low-hanging fruit, and zero out the really bad arguments, like this one:

Communists are bad.
Assassins are bad.
<u>Oswald was a Communist.</u>
Therefore, Oswald killed Kennedy.

Now, I don't know if anyone actually believes anything like this, but if they did, they really must have some wires crossed in their mind. To have any hope whatsoever of turning this into something logically sound, we would have to articulate the implicit, unstated premises here, which is that "all Communists are assassins" and "all assassins are Communists." These unarticulated premises can be destroyed simply by observing that if the lone assassin theory was true, and there were 10,000 Communists in the United States in 1963, we would know for a fact that *9999 of them could not have killed Kennedy*. In addition, if there were 1000 assassins in 1963, we would also know that 999 did not kill Kennedy either. Even this wouldn't do it. To save this syllogism, we would have to manufacture yet another (obviously false) premise "All assassins killed Kennedy," and what would be the point of that? So this logic is clearly incorrect, and anyone who believes it is . . . dare I say it . . . *crazy.*

Just as bad is this one:

People who believe in aliens are crazy.
Jim Marrs believes in aliens, and a conspiracy to kill Kennedy.
People who believe in a conspiracy to kill Kennedy are crazy.

Hits a lot closer to home, doesn't it? This unstated syllogism is what lies behind articles like we saw in the *Dallas Observer*, and this chapter title in *Reclaiming History* (RH 872):

The Zanies (and Others)
Have Their Say

Or this marvelous writing by Bugliosi (RH 872):

Comedy feeds on tragedy. And whenever there's a major catastrophe or tragedy, as sure as death and taxes a chorus of cuckoo birds will voice their bizarre observations. It's automatic, as automatic as the bird whistles in the stands when there's a controversial call in an athletic event. But unfortunately for the conspiracy theorists in this case, although an enormous number of crackpots have surfaced to tell their silly stories about every single aspect of the Kennedy assassination, not nearly as many cuckoo birds as the conspiracy

"A chorus of cuckoo birds will voice their bizarre observations." Pure poetry from our legal Longfellow (love that meter!). But underlying this poetics is logic, Bugliosi-style, and that's where the beauty ends.

Again, returning to the syllogism, to disprove this "logic," all we have to do is take a look at *all* the beliefs that Jim Marrs has. If this logic were true, *every single thing* that Jim Marrs believed would have to be *false*. Yet we know this could not possibly be the case, as shown in the following counter-syllogism:

People who believe in aliens are crazy.
Jim Marrs believes in aliens and that $2 + 2 = 4$.
People who believe that $2 + 2 = 4$ are crazy.

Now *that* is crazy!

With two of the most poorly-conceived syllogisms disposed of, let's also eliminate the disreputable tests some people may have silently used in their minds to convict Oswald, most of these related to the Asch effect:

- *The Bestseller Test* (if a bestseller says it, it must be true);
- *The Friend Test* (if all my friends say it, it must be true);
- *The Television Test* (if the television reports it, it must be true);
- *The Personal Feeling Test* (if I hate Communists, Oswald did it);
- *The Textbook Test* (if my textbook tells me so, it must be so);
- *The Timing Test* (if I have been exposed to ten hours of information that Oswald did it, and one hour of information that he did not do it, then he did it);
- *The Stack Of Books Test* (if John reads a stack of books 1 foot high on the subject, and Ted reads a stack of books 2 feet high on the subject, and they are opposed, Ted is right, and John is wrong, particularly if Ted thinks Oswald did it);
- *The Majority Rules Test* (if the majority thinks that Oswald was involved, he is guilty);
- *The Lots Of Letters Test* (people with lots of letters after their name should always be trusted over people with no letters after their name. NOTE: having a Nobel Prize = 20 letters after your name, and testifying for the Warren Commission gives you double points);
- *The Famous Person Test* (if a famous person says something, and a person we don't know says something else, believe the famous person);
- *The Hall Of Mirrors Test* (the more media outlets that report something, the more likely it is to be true).

But these likewise fail: I think we can take it on faith that truth is not determined by the number of bestsellers which report something as true, or the number of friends we have, or whether or not a television show reports *x*, or any of the above, and if faith doesn't do the job, numerous counter-examples in the real world would. Now, if anyone can come up with any compelling reasons why I am wrong, please let me know.

So much for the easy ones. But while easy to show invalid, they are not the most common reasons why Oswald gets virtually burned at the stake in our 21st century version of the Salem witch trials (at least in the 17th century version, the "witches", unlike Oswald, *had* a trial). The most common reason is a meme that lies silently in people's minds, unarticulated. If you want to know why PBS, CBS, ABC, Tom Hanks, and a whole host of others are wrong, you have to understand this meme, and that is this:

They are applying the wrong standard of proof!

And, because they are applying the wrong standard of proof, they can convict in their minds someone who is actually *unconvictable*.

It took me a long time to figure out how so many people could be off the mark, until I finally realized that many of these people have their belief because they are not applying the correct standard — that of *reasonable doubt* — but a different and illegitimate standard, the standard of *unreasonable chance*.

Yes, the *unreasonable chance* standard is alive and well in America, and for my money (up to $25,000 or possibly higher, remember?), if you want an explanation of how so many people can be so wrong, this is it.

To prove that this standard does its dirty work silently in people's minds, an elegant proof is provided by none other than Stephen King, in the afterword to his book. Extra points if you spot the doublethink before I highlight it for you (*11/22/63*, p. 845):

> Early in the novel, Jake Epping's friend Al puts the probability that Oswald was the lone gunman at ninety-five percent. After reading a stack of books and articles on the subject almost as tall as I am, I'd put the probability at ninety-eight percent, maybe even ninety-nine. Because all of the accounts, including those written by conspiracy theorists, tell the same simple American story: here was a dangerous little fame-junkie who found himself in just the right place to get lucky. Were the odds of it happening just the way it did long? Yes. So are the odds on winning the lottery, but someone wins one every day.

(While you are scoping out the doublethink, I have to point out something about the "fame-junkie" crack: if Oswald was such a fame-junkie, why did he *deny* killing Kennedy? Isn't that something a fame-junkie would be *proud of*?)

Okay, I'll forget about the crack, and move to the issue at hand, focusing on two opposing key statements in the King paragraph:

1. "I'd put the probability at ninety-eight percent, maybe even ninety-nine."
2. "Were the odds of it happening just the way it did long? Yes. So are the odds on winning the lottery, but someone wins one every day."

Now there's a contradiction for you. A *glaring* one. We can see why when we realize that *winning a lottery is not an easy thing to do*; for example, in the *Mega Millions* lottery in America, 5 numbers are drawn from a group of 56, 1 number is drawn from a group of 46, and you must match all 6 balls to win the jackpot. Good luck: the chance of winning is a whopping *1 in 175,711,536!* [4]

To simplify matters, let's say the lottery King is talking about is a much easier lottery to win, where the chances of winning are a much less intimidating one in a million. Now, let's restate what King said using common terminology in both statements, and the contradiction will really pop out at you:

1. "I'd put the probability at **980,000 chances in a 1,000,000**, maybe even 990,000 chances in a 1,000,000."
2. "Were the odds of it happening just the way it did **1 chance in a 1,000,000**? Yes. So are the odds on winning the lottery, but someone wins one every day."

Now, how ridiculous is that? *The confidence level that one should have for an event to occur should be <u>directly related</u> to its probability!!* So, for example, if you flip a coin one time, you should be **50%** confident that heads will come up, not **100%**. If you flip a coin three times, you should be **12.5%** confident that heads will come up three times in a row, not **50%**.

Yet what King is saying is that even though the *odds* of Oswald being guilty were around <u>1 in 1,000,000</u>, he puts the *probability* of Oswald being guilty at <u>980,000 chances in 1,000,000</u>!!!

[4] http://en.wikipedia.org/wiki/Lottery (Retrieved March 15, 2012).

Folks, that just does not compute! 980,00 ≠ 1!!

Oswald gets inappropriately burned at the virtual stake because King rides down a slippery slope from the *reasonable doubt* height and some way, somehow, ends up mired in the *unreasonable chance* quicksand: in other words, if there is *any* chance that you are guilty, then you *are* guilty, even if the chance is one in 1000 or one in 1,000,000 or one in 1,000,000,000! Therefore, you are damned if you did, and damned if you didn't.

Object to King's reasoning? Well, shame on you, because someone *does* win the lottery . . . don't they? Well, eventually. But that's not really the point, is it? If you put people in jail based on the results of a *coin flip*, that approach would be light-years more fair than this standard!

Can you imagine how full our prisons would be if we convicted people using the *unreasonable chance* standard of 1 in a 1,000,000??? If you can't, consider the insight which emerges when we come at the ratio from another angle:

**If the chance you are *innocent* is 999,999 out of 1,000,000,
get ready to do some hard time in the slammer!**

That's right, under the Stephen King lottery-odds-are-the-benchmark version of the *unreasonable chance* standard, we'd *all* be calling Sing Sing home! And if that were true, would King be singing a different tune?

I don't know, probably not: if that person knocking at your door with a warrant for your arrest turns out to be Stephen King, I'd suggest you git while the gittin' is good.

Uh oh, too late . . . heeeeeeeeeere's Stephen!

Ahhhh, you say, now the light bulb is turning on!

Yes, unfortunately for the premise of King's novel, it turns out that we do not live in North Korea, nor China, nor any imaginary dystopia which would employ a standard so bizarre . . . and so *unjust*.

Instead, we live in the United States of America, where the standard of proof is much higher, and thank G-d for that (if you're an atheist, thank the Constitution). Equally important, that standard of proof has to be determined by not just *one* person, but *twelve* people, *all* in agreement, gathered together in a group we call a "jury", who listen to testimony from a jury box. Count the seats:

So, whatever the standard happens to be, we know that it is much, much higher than the unreasonable chance standard, and because of it, the chance of convicting Oswald would be much, much lower, perhaps even approaching . . . *zero!*

"But Barry, how can you say that?", you say, "didn't Bugliosi win before a jury on *Showtime* in 1986?"

Yes, indeed; in 1986. But new evidence has come out since then, and the defense is a lot more refined than that presented by Gerry Spence. And who knows how *that* "trial" was controlled, anyway? And how the jurors were selected? And what nondisclosure agreements did they sign? Was it on *Showtime* for a reason?

Indeed, another (later) mock trial did not have the same result ("Jury Deadlocks in Oswald Mock Trial," *ABA Journal*, October, 1992, p. 35):

> ## A mock jury, selected to represent a cross section of the population of northern California, reached a deadlock after about 2½ hours of deliberations. Seven of the jurors voted to convict Oswald; the other five favored acquittal.

Note what this article concludes, as I mentioned above: there have to be *twelve* people on the jury, and they *all* must agree. If they don't *all* agree, that is a *deadlocked* jury, what is sometimes known as a *hung jury*. If the jury can't reach a decision, then there has to be a new trial, with a new jury, and the cycle will start all over again, if necessary.

And that is the way the justice game is played in the U.S. of A. Love it or leave it. For my part (for what it's worth), I love it. I hope you do too.

Now that the cobwebs have begun to clear away from our mind, it is time to get serious. We had a lot of fun with aliens and UFOs earlier on, but when the evidence doesn't fit the conclusion, that hard dose of reality is going to wipe the smile off our faces. And the reality is that the standard of proof required to convict Oswald is a very difficult one to meet.

Let's learn more about it.

Chapter 1: An Introduction to Reasonable Doubt

While typically thought to be a quintessentially American concept, it turns out that the concern for protecting the rights of the innocent by applying an extremely high standard of proof has an ancient, very rich history, a history by no means confined to the United States.

Maimonides, writing in the 12th century, codified 613 commandments in the Jewish Bible, and wrote the following about Commandment 290 (emphasis supplied): [1]

> **The 290th commandment is the prohibition to carry out punishment on a high probability, even close to certainty . . . .** Do not think this law unjust. The Almighty shut this door and commanded that **no punishment be carried out except where there are witnesses who testify that the matter is established in certainty beyond any doubt . . . it is better and more desirable to free a thousand sinners, than ever to kill one innocent.**

Nor was this view by any means confined to Judaism. It is part of what might be considered "natural law."

According to Professor Sandy Zabell, Professor of Statistics at the University of Chicago, the earliest reference in non-religious legal literature was authored by Justinian: [2]

> The Divine Trajan stated in a Rescript to Assiduus (sic) Severus: "It is better to permit the crime of a guilty person to go unpunished than to condemn one who is innocent."

But, though the concept was an ancient one, America did provide a vehicle for formal recognition of this value in the Constitution of the United States of America, specifically, the Fifth and Fourteenth Amendments, which provide (respectively) in pertinent part as follows:

> No person shall be . . . deprived of life, liberty, or property, without **due process** of law . . . [1]

---

[1] Maimonides, Saeer HaMitzvot, Negative Commandment 290, quoted in N. L. Rabinovich, *Probability and Statistical Inference in Ancient and Medieval Jewish Literature,* 111 (1973)

[2] Justinian, Digest, 48.19.5 (collected in 9 S. P. Scott, *The Civil Law* 110 (1932). Trajan ruled A.D. 98-117.

No State shall make or enforce any law which shall abridge the privileges or immunities of citizens of the United States; nor shall any State deprive any person of life, liberty, or property, without **due process** of law . . . [2]

According to these Amendments, due process is the framework within which the mechanisms of criminal law operate. But what processes are "due?" There is an entire suite of these, and it is in the *definition* of these processes that we find the stipulation of the *means* by which the *innocent shall be protected,* and that means is through the creation of *a high standard of proof.*

Here is the standard:

In criminal law, *innocence is presumed* until guilt has been proven to the factfinder — a jury — *beyond a reasonable doubt.*

Note that the standard specifically refers to *being found guilty* of a crime. In other areas of criminal law, and also throughout civil law (lawsuits between two parties involving negligence, defamation of character, etc.), there are other, lower, standards of proof. Two of these standards are "preponderance of the evidence" and "clear and convincing evidence," as noted by Dorothy Kagehiro (Kagehiro, 1990, pp. 194-5; paragraph on separate pages combined by author):

The standard of proof refers to the degree to which the trier of fact must be satisfied that the necessary facts have been established. This degree of satisfaction varies from case to case and has three basic levels: (a) preponderance of the evidence; (b) clear and convincing evidence; and (c) beyond a reasonable doubt. The lowest or least stringent standard of proof, preponderance of the evidence, is used in most civil cases and concerns whether or not the existence of a fact is more probable than its nonexistence. Thus, the standard requires a plaintiff to

But these lower standards are also applied not only in civil law, but also in a different area of criminal law, pretrial detentions, as reported

---

[1] http://en.wikipedia.org/wiki/Fifth_Amendment_to_the_United_States_Constitution (retrieved June 17, 2011).

[2] http://en.wikipedia.org/wiki/14th_Amendment_to_the_United_States_Constitution (retrieved June 17, 2011).

in 2010 in *The Georgetown Law Journal Annual Review Of Criminal Procedure* (footnotes omitted; emphasis supplied): [1]

> The *Bail Reform Act* allows courts to detain an arrestee pending trial if the government demonstrates by ***clear and convincing evidence*** after an adversarial hearing that no release conditions will reasonably ensure the safety of the community. In *United States V. Salerno*, the Supreme Court held that pretrial detention of a defendant based solely on the risk of danger to the community does not violate due process. Nor does pretrial detention on the ground of dangerousness constitute "excessive bail" under the Eighth Amendment; the prohibition against excessive bail applies only to cases where it is appropriate to grant bail.
>
> A judicial officer may also detain a defendant if the government proves by a ***preponderance of the evidence*** that the defendant poses a risk of flight such that no condition or combination of conditions will reasonably assure the defendant's presence at trial. In assessing risk of flight, courts consider a variety of factors, including the defendant's ties to the community, past criminal history, and availability of assets. To detain a defendant, a judicial officer must find the defendant to be either a risk of flight or a danger to the community; proof of both is not necessary.

As noted above, these lower standards can be utilized in arrest *before* trial. But to find a person *guilty* of a crime after they have been arrested and *after* a trial, the *reasonable doubt* standard rules. The purpose of the standard from the American perspective was described by Barbara Underwood, Associate Professor of Law at Yale University, writing in the *Yale Law Journal* (emphasis supplied): [2]

> **The first function of the reasonable doubt rule is to reduce the chance of conviction in an individual case, by putting a thumb on the defendant's side of the scales of justice.** . . . One reason for putting a thumb on the defendant's side is to compensate for a systematic flaw in the scales. That

---

[1] 39 Geo. L.J. Ann. Rev. Crim. Proc. 1 (2010).

[2] "The Thumb on the Scales of Justice: Burdens of Persuasion in Criminal Cases", Barbara Underwood, 86 *Yale Law Journal* 1299 (1977).

is, factfinders may favor the prosecution rather than weigh the evidence objectively. . . . In reducing the likelihood of an erroneous conviction, the reasonable doubt rule does not, however, simply restore an accurate balance; **it is also understood to introduce a deliberate imbalance, tilting the scales in favor of the defendant**. It represents "a fundamental value determination of our society that it is far worse to convict an innocent man than to let a guilty man go free."

Professor Underwood noted that the status of this right was explicitly recognized by the Supreme Court in 1970: [1]

The requirement of proof beyond a reasonable doubt in criminal cases was given constitutional status by the Supreme Court in 1970, in the case of *In re Winship* . . .

The Court itself noted in that case that their decision was merely the logical outcome of a line of previous cases (*In Re Winship*, 397 US 358, 361-2; March 31, 1970; emphasis supplied):

The requirement that guilt of a criminal charge be established by proof beyond a reasonable doubt dates at least from our early years as a Nation. . . . Expressions in many opinions of this Court indicate that **it has long been assumed that proof of a criminal charge beyond a reasonable doubt is constitutionally required.** See, for example, *Miles v. United States*, 103 U.S. 304, 312 (1881); *Davis v. United States*, 160 U.S. 469, 488 (1895); *Holt v. United States*, 218 U.S. 245, 253 (1910) . . .

In *Winship*, the Supreme Court quoted noted judge Felix Frankfurter, who reminded us that the burden of proof is not on the *accused*, but on the *government* (*Winship* at 361-2; emphasis supplied):

[i]t is **the duty of the Government** to establish . . . guilt beyond a reasonable doubt. This notion — basic in our law and rightly one of the boasts of a free society — is **a requirement**

[1] "The Thumb on the Scales of Justice: Burdens of Persuasion in Criminal Cases", Barbara Underwood, 86 *Yale Law Journal* 1299 (1977).

and a safeguard of due process of law in the historic, procedural content of "due process."

The Supreme Court linked the *reasonable doubt* standard with the related concept of the *presumption of innocence*, which they referred to as "axiomatic and elementary" (*Winship* at 363 (quoting *Coffin v. United States*)):

> The reasonable doubt standard plays a vital role in the American scheme of criminal procedure. It is **a prime instrument for reducing the risk of convictions resting on factual error.** The standard provides **concrete substance for the presumption of innocence** — that bedrock "**axiomatic and elementary**" principle whose "enforcement lies at the foundation of the administration of our criminal law."

The Supreme Court contrasted the standard of proof for criminal cases to civil litigation. In the litigation of civil cases, the risk to one of the parties is relatively minimal. However, in criminal cases, the risk to the accused is always his *liberty*, and in cases where the death penalty is involved, sometimes his *life* — consequently, a higher standard is called for (*Winship* at 364; quoting *Speiser v. Randall*):

> There is always, in litigation, a margin of error, representing error in factfinding, which both parties must take into account. Where one party has at stake an interest of transcending value — as a criminal defendant his liberty — this margin of error is reduced as to him by the process of placing on the other party the burden of . . . persuading the factfinder at the conclusion of the trial of his guilt beyond a reasonable doubt.

The Supreme Court went on in the *Winship* opinion to describe the notion of "moral force," and the importance of the reasonable doubt standard in maintaining the confidence of society by only securing convictions in which there was "utmost certainty" (*Winship* at 364; emphasis supplied):

> Moreover, use of the reasonable doubt standard is indispensable to command the respect and confidence of the community in applications of the criminal law. **It is critical that the moral force of the criminal law not be diluted by**

a standard of proof that leaves people in doubt whether innocent men are being condemned. It is also important in our free society that every individual going about his ordinary affairs have confidence that his government cannot adjudge him guilty of a criminal offense without convincing a proper factfinder of his guilt with *utmost certainty.*

"Utmost certainty": sound like a high standard to you? It does to me!

The Supreme Court finally concluded with this ringing and completely unambiguous proclamation (*Winship* at 364; emphasis supplied):

Lest there remain any doubt about the constitutional stature of the reasonable doubt standard, we explicitly hold that the Due Process Clause protects the accused against conviction except upon *proof beyond a reasonable doubt of every fact necessary* to constitute the crime with which he is charged.

With the reasonable doubt standard established as axiomatic in American jurisprudence — that convictions cannot be secured without the *utmost certainty* — we can therefore use it to create a deductive argument that demonstrates why the presumed innocence of Lee Harvey Oswald must always so remain.

Chapter 2: Reasonable Doubt: The Deductive Case

Because the Constitution as interpreted by the Supreme Court has given us the inviolable standard of *reasonable doubt* which can — and indeed, *must* — be used for the purpose of legal analysis, we can see instantly that the possibility or impossibility of the conclusion of a legal case can be determined *deductively*. Consider the following syllogism derived from that standard:

> **PREMISE 1:** **If there is reasonable doubt in this case, there can be no conviction.**
> **PREMISE 2:** **There is reasonable doubt in this case.**
> **CONCLUSION:** **There can be no conviction (and, accordingly, the presumption of innocence for the defendant remains).**

The beauty of deductive logic is that it is *absolutely certain*: it removes all doubt (from the legal perspective) regarding the presumption of innocence of the accused. This argument, because it is deductively structured, proves that it is *impossible* for there to be a conviction in any case brought forth by the prosecution where the above two premises are true!

Now, we have seen that *the truth of Premise 1 is conclusively established simply by virtue of our residing under the Constitution of the United States* as interpreted by the Supreme Court in *In re Winship*. This premise is *stipulated* as true simply by virtue of its legal status.

Accordingly, **all we need to do in the Kennedy/Oswald case to demonstrate that conviction for Oswald is impossible is establish the truth of Premise 2**: that, regarding the case against Lee Harvey Oswald, there is reasonable doubt. If we establish that truth, then we have deductively demonstrated the truth of the conclusion, that there can be no conviction in this case, and, accordingly, the presumption of innocence for the defendant will remain.

To further proceed logically, we must first define a "case," which we will do as follows:

A "case" consists of a set of premises (to be referred to hereinafter as *propositions*), *which, if true, would deductively prove a conclusion, each proposition comprised of a series of necessary subpropositions (to be referred to as* *elements*), *those elements to be justified beyond a reasonable doubt (or not) by an analysis of all the evidence supporting (or contradicting) them.*

So, if we had a case whose charge was first-degree murder, a proposition of the case might be "**John Defendant fired a gun proximate to the temporal and spatial location of Jane Victim.**" Then, this proposition could be *further* subdivided into subsidiary facts supporting the proposition. In this regard, it is critically important to distinguish between the subsidiary facts *necessary* to establish guilt — the subpropositions which going forward we will refer to as *elements* — and facts which *may or may not* indicate guilt.

Let's use our murder case as an example: if the contention is that **the victim was murdered in the city of Dallas**, then the prosecutor must provide *comprehensive, credible, sufficient,* and *consistent* evidence that the person accused of the murder was actually in the city of *Dallas* at the time. If the defense can present evidence that the person accused was located in *Los Angeles* at the time of the murder (i.e., evidence *inconsistent* with the conclusion), then obviously reasonable doubt is thrown on that proposition, by virtue of outright refutation.

So, a *necessary* subsidiary fact (i.e. subproposition or *element*) for this murder case would be **John Defendant was located in the city of Dallas at the time of the murder**. (Of course, this could be refined further, that is to say, in the real world we would make sure that the murderer was located close enough and in the right position to commit the murder, and determine the precision of the necessary elements as needed.)

We could also formulate subsidiary facts that are *not* necessary, for example, that **John Defendant had a prior criminal conviction**. This statement is *not* necessary because if the person accused of the crime had no prior criminal conviction, he or she still could have committed the murder. In this case, the subsidiary fact might indicate a *tendency* to commit the crime, but it is not *required* to establish guilt.

Once we know that a case can be divided into *propositions*, which can then be further subdivided into *necessary* subsidiary facts known as "elements", we can sum up the foregoing analysis into the following statements:

A. The case for conviction regarding a particular charge rests on propositions that, taken together, can deductively establish the truth of the charge (i.e., the conclusion).

B. The validity of each proposition rests on necessary factual elements E1 through En.

C. Because *each* of these elements is *necessary* to establish the truth of the proposition, the proposition can be considered functionally disproven when there is reasonable doubt for *even one* of these elements.

D. For each element, there is a set of *evidentiary data*, which taken as a whole may create no reasonable doubt (or varying degrees of reasonable doubt) regarding the veracity of that element.

E. Reasonable doubt can be created for one of the necessary elements if the evidentiary data for that element (taken as a whole) is either not *comprehensive*, not *credible*, not *sufficient*, not *consistent*, or any combination thereof, *to the extent necessary* to create reasonable doubt.

F. Consequently, if the evidentiary data for an element (taken together) falls into one or more of the foregoing categories in Paragraph E, reasonable doubt will be created for that element, and the proposition will be functionally disproven.

So, here, in a nutshell, we have the framework for establishing the guilt or maintaining the presumption of innocence of Lee Harvey Oswald:

1. First, we must determine the *propositions*.

2. Then, for each proposition we must determine the factual *elements* underlying that proposition.

3. Next, for each element, we must establish the total set of evidentiary *data*.

4. Next, we need to *evaluate* the total set of evidentiary data, and analyze the extent to which the data, taken as a whole, tends to confirm or disconfirm each element, thereby decreasing or increasing reasonable doubt regarding that element.

5. Because these are *necessary* elements, if our determination shows that there is reasonable doubt for *even one* of these elements, then the proposition to be supported by that element is functionally disproven and, the case shown not proven beyond a reasonable doubt, the presumption of innocence shall remain.

The above statements, because they are derived from the law of the United States, and the laws of logic, are the basic foundation underlying all that follows.

However, as ironclad as these statements might seem, there is actually some "wiggle room" from the deductive perspective: what doubt is *reasonable*? Normally, what constitutes reasonable doubt is determined by a juror subject to *instructions* from a judge on how to define the term. Unfortunately, these instructions generally lack that all-important helpful quality we seek to uncover in a well-formed judicial directive. Consider the following example from a prominent federal pattern jury instruction treatise: [1]

A reasonable doubt is a doubt based upon reason and common sense — the kind of doubt that would make a reasonable person hesitate to act. Proof beyond a reasonable doubt must, therefore, be proof of such a convincing character that a reasonable person would not hesitate to rely and act upon it in the most important of his or her own affairs.

Does that settle it for you? Probably not, since this "instruction" is of the prototypical clear-as-mud variety. But it is all too typical of the typical "reasonable doubt" instruction. As Erik Lillquist, Associate Professor of Law at Seton Hall University School of Law noted, [2]

These instructions appear to do little to educate the jurors in what is meant by proof beyond a reasonable doubt. They certainly do not quantify how much proof is needed to convict a defendant. But what is most remarkable is how vague and opaque they are. These instructions used in the federal system

---

[1] 1A Kevin O'Malley et al., *Federal Jury Practice & Instructions: Criminal* 12.10, at 168 (2000).

[2] Erik Lillquist, "Recasting Reasonable Doubt: Decision Theory and the Virtues of Variability," 6 U.C. Davis L. Rev. 85, 126-7 (2002).

talk about hesitating to act in an important matter. What does that mean? State instructions are no better. They talk about proof beyond a reasonable doubt as "an abiding certainty" or what occurs after a "careful and honest review" of the evidence. What is a juror supposed to draw from these statements?

That's a good question. When faced with this problem, what is a good juror supposed to do?

From our perspective, as either potential jurors ourselves or as potential future defendants in front of these jurors, we must realize that because these instructions are vague, they are basically empty vessels into which any thought, whether nonsensical or well-formed, can be poured.

And, in the legal world, this is not a good thing. In fact, elsewhere in the legal world, laws in general can be struck down for being too ambiguous, per the *void for vagueness doctrine*, as Mary Vales told us in the *Seventh Circuit Review* (Vales, p. 251):

SEVENTH CIRCUIT REVIEW	Volume 6, Issue 2	Spring 2011

V.   WHAT EXACTLY IS THE VOID FOR VAGUENESS DOCTRINE?

A statute that is void for vagueness is unconstitutional because it violates due process of law.[149] Due process requires fairness in the legal system and that notice and the opportunity for a fair trial are provided to all.[150] Historically, a statute that is void for vagueness is one which fails to provide notice: it is one "which either forbids or requires the doing of an act in terms so vague that [persons] of common intelligence must necessarily guess at its meaning and differ as to its application."[151]

From this we learn the following global lesson: specificity, good — vagueness, bad.

How are we to know a statute or a reasonable doubt instruction are vague? With a standard we can call the "guess" standard: if you have to *guess* what it means, it's *vague*. So, if a reasonable doubt instruction is vague, you will be guessing. When you are guessing, you have no true guidance. And the impact of a reasonable doubt instruction that provides no true guidance should be clear: in a country which tells its children to expect "liberty and justice for all," and whose most primary document talks of "inalienable rights," how can the right to a *fair* trial be subject to a term that even a professor of law does not understand!?

With essentially no content, a vague reasonable doubt standard functions as a ruler that can be inappropriately (and silently) expanded or contracted from case to case, and how can a standard that can be inappropriately *rigorous* in one case and inappropriately *lenient* in another provide any standard at all, and without any standard at all, how could there be any protection from an incompetent and/or immoral government absent the standard that could provide that protection, and if there was no protection from an incompetent and/or immoral government, how could there be any *preservation* of the rights we formerly saw as "inalienable"?

Ponder this: if a *professor of law* is confused, how confused would be the *average citizen*, with absolutely no background in the meaning of the term, or in any other areas of legal practice that would enable meaning to be determined?

If you are guessing that empirical studies would show confusion across the United States in this regard on the part of jurors, you're right. As Dorothy Kagehiro wrote in 1990, [1]

> It is therefore disturbing in its implications for the quality of justice in verdict decision making that a good deal of empirical research indicates low comprehension levels by jurors of pattern (or model or standard) instructions. Comprehension levels of 50% or less have been found for mock jurors and representative samples of jurors from jurisdictions such as Arizona, California, Florida, Michigan, Nevada, and Washington (Bucha-

The instructions did little, if anything, to increase juror comprehension (Kagehiro, p. 194):

> Buchanan, 1976). Only half of the instructed jurors in a Florida sample understood that a criminal defendant did not have to present any evidence of innocence (Strawn & Buchanan, 1976). Severance and Loftus (1982) found that the comprehension levels of jurors concerning legal concepts explained in pattern instructions were not significantly different from the comprehension levels of jurors who had received no instructions.
>
> Moreover, low comprehension levels for pattern instructions were found despite jurors' assurances to the contrary. Eighty-

---

[1] "Defining the Standard of Proof in Jury Instructions," Dorothy Kagehiro, *Psychological Science*, Vol. 1, No. 3, May 1990, p. 194.

To see just how confused jurors can be, and the effect that vague terms have on determinations of innocence or guilt by jurors, the following table related to juror verdicts tells you all you need to know.

The table below has different standards of proof subdivided into three columns, *preponderance* (for "preponderance of evidence"), *clear and convincing* (for "clear and convincing evidence"), and *reasonable doubt* (for "beyond a reasonable doubt").

The layout of the standards, left-to-right, is no accident: the easiest standard to meet is the *preponderance of evidence* standard, the next easiest standard is the *clear and convincing* standard, and the hardest standard is *beyond a reasonable doubt*.

So, going from left to right across the rows in the table, the numbers ought to *decrease*: if a plaintiff could win **50%** of their cases using a *preponderance* standard on body of evidence x, then you might expect they could only win, say, **25%** of cases using a *reasonable doubt* standard on the same evidence. You certainly wouldn't expect the opposite.

To test the effect of methods of instruction on juror perception of the standards, and to see if the instructions produced the predicted result, Kagehiro decided to use several methods of definition, one using the verbal instructions used in a courtroom (in the screen capture below, the California pattern from the Committee on Standard Jury Instructions along with the Texas Supreme Court's instruction in *State v. Addington* (1979)), and one of the others a quantified (numeric) standard based on probability terms.

In one of the more alarming developments in the literature, Kagehiro found that *the prototypical judicial approach using vague language produced a result opposite from what ought to have been expected!* (Kagehiro, p. 197):

Table 1. *Summary table for the laboratory studies: proportion of verdicts for plaintiffs by type of definition and standard of proof (percentage)*

Definition	Standard of Proof		
	Preponderance	Clear and Convincing	Reasonable Doubt
Legal (California/*Addington***)**	31 WRONG!	38	43
Quantified	66[a]	52[a]	31[b]

There it is, in black-and-white, that the wrong method of providing instructions can result in jurors seeing black as white.

Kagehiro discovered essentially the same problem with other types of instructions, and concluded that "[a]cross the studies, only the quantified definitions consistently had their intended effect" (Kagehiro, p. 196). Kagehiro summarized the problem with unquantified definitions:

Thus, verbally expressed, unquantified definitions have the twin disadvantages of being less capable of communicating precisely and concisely an intended certainty level than quantified definitions and of involving complex syntax (Charrow & Charrow, 1979; Severance & Loftus, 1982). The latter may be a serious disadvantage since concern has been expressed in some quarters about deficiencies in language skills among segments of the general population (Kozol, 1979; Kreitlow, 1977; Labov, 1973; Northcutt, 1975; Park, 1981; St. John Hunter & Harman, 1979).

Well, I've learned my lesson, and I think you have too. So what does this mean to us? Just this: because Oswald was deprived of his right to a jury trial — as well as a judge who could provide a *definition* of the reasonable doubt standard that we are compelled to apply — *we* need to discover what constitutes reasonable doubt; to make sure that we do the job right, we are going to learn from what the Kagehiro study has taught us.

To achieve ironclad deductive certainty — *and* to satisfy the requirements of due process as a not insignificant side benefit — we must define "reasonable doubt" *objectively,* in *quantified* terms.

Let's put some meat on these bones.

Chapter 3: Reasonable Doubt: An Objective Standard

So, how is one to define "reasonable" objectively? At first glance, this would seem to be extremely difficult, if not impossible. For most of us, "reasonable" seems to embody the quintessential essence of wishy-washiness. And yet, once we more closely analyze the concept, it becomes evident that we can translate the term into a number, and, once this is done, we can then set a lower and upper numerical range for "reasonable" within which that number must fall, based on well-established societal norms.

The ease of doing this can be more readily seen when we talk about reasonable doubt from the standpoint of a concept easier to understand, *confidence level.*

We can make this transition because doubt and confidence stand at the opposite ends of the spectrum, and that any statement expressed in terms of *doubt* can simultaneously be expressed in terms of *confidence*, both of which can be expressed *numerically*.

The following continuum will illustrate this point:

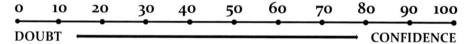

| 0 | 10 | 20 | 30 | 40 | 50 | 60 | 70 | 80 | 90 | 100 |

DOUBT   CONFIDENCE

The numbers at the top of the line indicate percentages. If you are 100% confident that an event will occur, then you are absolutely sure it *will* occur; to state it another way, we say you have "no doubt" it will occur. On the other hand, if you are 0% confident that an event will occur, then you are absolutely sure it *will not* occur, the most extreme doubt possible.

The concept of confidence level is typically used in weather forecasts. When the weather forecast for tomorrow says that there is "an 80% chance of rain," this means that the meteorologist is 80% confident that it will rain tomorrow. But, to the point just mentioned, this could be expressed another way, that it is 20% doubtful that it will rain.

Notice here that doubt and confidence are *inversely related*: to say that one is 70% *confident* of a proposition is to simultaneously say that one is 30% *doubtful* of a proposition.

Why do meteorologists express their propositions in terms of confidence versus doubt? Because, as you have undoubtedly seen, it is easier to conceive of a proposition in terms of confidence level rather than that of doubt (e.g. "80% confident that it will rain" is easier to conceptualize than "20% doubtful that it will rain", even though the two statements are essentially the same, just expressed in opposite ways).

So, going forward, for the purposes of clarity, we will attempt to translate the concept of reasonable doubt into a percentage expressed as a confidence level, and we will do that by asking this question: *when someone uses the phrase "beyond a reasonable doubt," to what specific percentage level of confidence does this translate?*

If we are able to nail down the concept of reasonable doubt to a specific confidence level, we will have a useful analytical tool that will enable us to precisely measure the effect evidence will have on reasonable doubt.

To find our number, let's start by working our way from both ends. Suppose you are **100%** confident that a defendant is guilty. Then, obviously, you have **0%** doubt (absolutely no doubt) that the defendant is guilty, which is obviously *well past* the reasonable doubt standard. This is the confidence level that the prosecutor, ideally, wants you to have for his charge. You *are* confident beyond a reasonable doubt.

On the other hand, suppose you are **0%** confident that a defendant is guilty. Then, you have **100%** doubt that the defendant is guilty, which needless to say, falls *well short* of the reasonable doubt standard. In other words, to dramatically understate the matter, "you are *not* confident beyond a reasonable doubt."

So, since we know that **100%** confidence easily *surpasses* the reasonable doubt standard, and **0%** confidence obviously *does not*, what is the number that should be used to demarcate the division between reasonable and unreasonable doubt? 50%? 75%? Some higher number?

To find the answer to this question, let's start with a rather mundane example which will lead us to a very useful conclusion:

You are a very well-paid office manager, and have been asked by the President of the firm to plan the office picnic. The President is a rather obsessive fellow, and he *loves* picnics in the sunshine. In fact, if you make a mistake, and choose a day where the picnic is aborted by rain, the President will *fire you*. Period. *Gulp*! Accordingly, it is your task to pick a day in the summer where you are confident it will be sunny *beyond a reasonable doubt*.

Now, ask yourself, what confidence level will you require before you pick a day for the picnic? Remember, your very well-paid job is at stake!

Suppose you assign this important task to your assistant, who comes to you and says that he has found the day. You check the meteorological records, and you find out that, on average, rain has fallen on that date 50% of the time. In other words, if you choose that date, you are 50% positive that it will *not* rain (which means that you are 50% positive that it *will* rain).

Now, would you chance your very well-paid job on a coin flip? Obviously not! So you tell your assistant to go back to the drawing board. And he comes back to you and says he has found a much better day. You check the meteorological records, you find out that rain has fallen on that date 25% of that time — a 75% chance of a sunny day. That is better, but is it good enough? You know that there is a one out of four chance it is going to rain. Would you risk your job on *two* coin flips? Two is better than one, but I think we all will agree you can do a lot better than that.

So you tell your assistant to go back again, which he dutifully does. This time, the records show that for this new date rain has fallen historically on only 10% of the days, which means that there is a 90% chance of sunshine, or, a 1 out of 10 chance. Much better, but still . . . looking at this decision from a Russian roulette perspective (where your job is at stake), choosing that date would be like playing with 10 chambers and one bullet! Would you want to play Russian roulette with that level of confidence?

I think we can all agree that a 90% confidence level is not adequate, even when it is only your job on the line. Can you imagine how much higher that confidence level would need to be if you (or someone you knew) were faced with the electric chair — that is to say, certain death?

Instantly, we can see that the reasonable doubt standard, expressed as a confidence level, *must* be higher than 90%. Of course, it also *must* be lower than 100%, since absolute certainty is not required to convict defendants, because if that were the standard, very, very few defendants, including the guilty ones, would be convicted.

So what is the *right* number? Choosing wisely is critical, because if a mistake is made, we not only send the innocent to jail, we also let the guilty go free, not to mention that we reduce confidence in our overall political system, a very nasty side effect of slipshod procedure.

Between the 90% standard and the 100% standard, there is bound to be some disagreement, but at least this hypothetical has established the parameters:

The reasonable doubt standard, expressed as a confidence level, must be *higher* than 90% and must be *lower* than 100%.

Of course, eternal debate could center on whether the number should *exactly* be 90.0001% or 99.9999%, or any number in between, and since we currently lack an objective way to make this determination, we will simply split the difference for the time being, and provisionally stipulate the number to be 95%, which gives us the following statement:

The reasonable doubt standard, expressed as a confidence level, is 95%.

What does this mean? It means that *in a capital murder case,*

If you are asked to find someone guilty "beyond a reasonable doubt," you need to believe that there is a 95% chance they are guilty!

50% doesn't cut it.
75% doesn't cut it.
And, in fact, 90% doesn't cut it.
When you will be sending someone to the electric chair, you need to be really, really sure!

But, at this stage, someone is likely to ask, "can we really make such a broad determination from one hypothetical situation?" The answer is no: it is going to take more than one benchmark to establish these parameters. Therefore, we need to look at other socially accepted norms to inform our decision.

Our starting point could be based on an *innocent versus guilty conviction ratio*: if 100 people are to be given the death penalty, and some of them turn out to be innocent, what is the number of innocent people murdered by the State that ought to be acceptable in a civilized society? Yes, it turns out that our confidence level will directly translate into innocent deaths (i.e., a confidence level requirement of 50% will result in many more innocent deaths than one of 99%), thus instantly revealing its importance, as the Supreme Court noted in the *Winship* case (*Winship* at 364; emphasis supplied):

It is critical that the moral force of the criminal law not be diluted by a standard of proof that leaves people in doubt whether innocent men are being condemned.

According to the Supreme Court, the moral force of the criminal law comes from its legitimacy, and, if the justice system is seen merely as a high-profile version of Russian Roulette, where the guilty compete for the same electric chair as the unlucky, that legitimacy suffers. Consequently, there are *utilitarian* reasons (if not *moral* ones) to have a standard accepted by the community.

So, as a member of that community, how would you feel about 5 innocent people sentenced to death for every 100 convicted? If you feel that number is too *high*, then you believe that the 95% number is too *low* (kudos to you!). How would you feel if only 1 innocent person was sentenced to death for every 100 people convicted? If that number is acceptable to you, then you believe that the number should be 99%. [1]

I think it ought to be obvious that any argument that can be made against the 95% number from the *innocent-persons-killed* criterion (a criterion mandated as essential by the Supreme Court, not to mention our own morality) would be that it is *too low*, not that it is *too high*, for a society that promises its citizens the right to "life, liberty, and the pursuit of happiness," and therefore ostensibly unwilling to declare that this right wasn't as inalienable as advertised.

Apart from this legal-based utilitarian argument, are there other domains in society that can inform this issue? Yes, the domain of *science*, in evaluating the truth of hypotheses. To this point, Dr. James Fetzer (a PhD in the philosophy of science, author of 20 books in that field, and the Distinguished McKnight University Professor Emeritus at the University of Minnesota) noted in his book *Assassination Science*, that "hypotheses in science are rejected when their

---

[1] This is a theoretical number. In the real world, this number will not translate exactly because people's judgment regarding confidence level can be mistaken. However, theoretically perfect judgment would result in a one-to-one correspondence between confidence determination and outcome. As a real world example, if you are 50% confident that a coin flip will result in *heads*, over a few thousand trials you will be right approximately 50% of the time (assuming a two-sided coin, of course). Note that a confidence level of 95% (assuming a completely accurate observer) results in 5 false convictions for every 100 *convictions*, not every 100 *cases*, according to Dr. Steve Patch, Professor of Statistics at the University of North Carolina in Asheville (e-mail to author, May 11, 2011).

improbability equals or exceeds 1 in 20."(*Assassination Science*, p. 367). In other words, a hypothesis with less than a 95% confidence level is rejected. From this perspective, the 95% confidence level is precisely the demarcation point.

Further proof that this number, or a number extremely close to it, is typically used in science to establish the validity of hypotheses was provided in testimony given to the House Select Committee On Assassinations on December 29, 1978 by Mark Weiss, a professor in the Department of Computer Science of Queens College of the City University of New York. In that testimony, related to the number of shots that were fired in Dealey Plaza on November 22, 1963 (as indicated by an audio recording), Professor Weiss indicated that 95% could be utilized as a demarcation point for the reasonable doubt standard by an attorney (5 HSCA 583):

> Chairman STOKES. Then as a scientist, you are comfortable with the statement to this committee that beyond a reasonable doubt, and to a degree of 95 percent or better, there were four shots in Dealey Plaza?
> Mr. WEISS. Well, I would agree with that, with the somewhat clarification, that since our work concentrated primarily on the third shot, the one from the grassy knoll area, I would imply for the moment, limit the statement to that, with a, again, a confidence level of 95 percent or higher, which I guess if I were a lawyer, I might well express as beyond a reasonable doubt, that shot took place. And then relying upon the corresponding confi-

So science gives us a number right on point.

At this stage of the game, one might be interested in what *the law itself* has to say on the reasonable doubt standard expressed as a confidence level. There have been several articles on this topic, and through a number of surveys that have been done with jurors and judges, a rough consensus has emerged. One survey, performed by Prof. C.M.A McAuliffe, Assistant Professor of Law at Washington and Lee University School of Law, surveyed 171 judges in 1981, and asked them to assign a percentage to "beyond a reasonable doubt" (not confined to capital cases with the death penalty).

Here are the results: [1]

---

[1] C.M.A. McAuliffe, "Burdens of Proof: Degrees of Belief, Quanta of Evidence, or Constitutional Guarantees?", 35 *Vand. L. Rev.* 1293, at 1325 (1982).

Percentage	Number of Judges	Percentage	Number of Judges
50%	1	91%	0
55%	0	92%	1
60%	1	93%	1
65%	0	94%	1
70%	1	95%	31
75%	8	96%	0
80%	14	97%	1
85%	20	98%	6
90%	56	99%	8
		100%	21

If we look at the chart in terms of averages, we find that the average percentage definition assigned to the term "beyond a reasonable doubt" by 171 judges in 1981 for *noncapital* cases was **90.28%**. [1] Based on the results of other surveys,[2] we can assume that the result for capital cases would be higher (although note that *even in these non-capital cases*, 67 of the respondents above indicated that "beyond a reasonable doubt" was 95% or higher).

In 1978, U.S. District Court for the Eastern District of New York in *United States v. Fatico* instantiated a moderately higher standard for *all* cases, and stated that "**If quantified, the beyond a reasonable doubt standard might be in the range of 95+% Probable.**" 458 F. Supp. 388, 406 (E.D.N.Y. 1978), citing *United States v. Schipani*, 289 F.Supp. 43, 57 (E.D.N.Y. 1968), Aff'd, 414 F.2d 1262 (2d Cir. 1969). This is dispositive.

For the purposes of this book, following *Fatico*, the reasonable doubt standard will be stipulated as 95%.

While I have been unable to find a case in which the Supreme Court has provided a quantified number, it is hard to imagine them disagreeing with *Fatico*, since they did write in the *Jackson* case that the reasonable doubt standard demands the prosecution establish "**a subjective state of near certitude** . . . ", and 95% is, if anything, lower than that (*Jackson v. Virginia*, 443 U.S. 307 (1979)).

---

[1] *Ibid.* at 1332.

[2] See, for example, Rita James Simon & Linda Mahan, "Quantifying Burdens of Proof: A View from the Bench, the Jury and the Classroom," 5 *Law & Soc'y Rev.* 319, 322 (1971).

While the domains of science and law might seem to provide all the information we need regarding the standard to be chosen, there is surprising evidence from another domain that the 95% number ought to be at the lower end of the demarcation point for "reasonable doubt," and that domain is . . . *the Bible!*

Don't believe it? Consider the famous story of Abraham bargaining with God which appears in *Genesis*, Chapter 18 (emphasis supplied):

> 22 Then the men turned away from there and went toward Sodom, while Abraham was still standing before the LORD. 23 Abraham came near and said, "Will You indeed sweep away the righteous with the wicked? 24 "Suppose there are fifty righteous within the city; will You indeed sweep it away and not spare the place for the sake of the fifty righteous who are in it? . . . 26 So the LORD said, "If I find in Sodom fifty righteous within the city, then I will spare the whole place on their account." . . . 32 Then he said, "Oh may the Lord not be angry, and I shall speak only this once; suppose ten are found there?" And He said, **"I will not destroy it on account of the ten."**

How can this story be used to derive a standard for reasonable doubt? Very simply. All we need to do is determine the ratio of innocent to guilty (with respect to the population of the cities), and while we do not know the population of Sodom and Gomorrah, we can use a provisional estimate of 50,000, based on an archaeological finding that cemeteries in the area showed the remains of approximately 500,000 buried.[1] Now, while the story of Abraham also does not tell us the threshold number that would result in total destruction (stopping at 10), let's split the difference between zero and ten, and say that the demarcation point is 5 innocent with 49,995 guilty. 5 out of 50,000 is equal to 1 out of 10,000. Now, recall that confidence level can be calculated from the innocent/guilty ratio. If we used that standard to then create a reasonable doubt threshold, *we would deploy a standard that would result in no more than 1 out of 10,000 innocent persons being executed, resulting in a confidence level when translated of 99.9999%!*

If that standard strikes you as ridiculously high, it was in fact way ahead of its time, because an even higher standard is being deployed today by surprisingly enough, *corporate America*.

---

[1] http://www.aish.com/ci/sam/48931527.html (retrieved February 2, 2012).

This standard is used in a strategic movement designed to incorporate confidence level as a means of quality control. The name of the strategy (which achieved popularity in the 1990s, and greater popularity in the 21st century) is *Six Sigma*. For a CEO in Fortune 500 America today, a 95% reliability figure for corporate work product, taking a page out of the Bible, would result in ouster by the Board of Directors, according to this overview of *Six Sigma* from *Wikipedia*:

> The term Six Sigma originated from terminology associated with manufacturing, specifically terms associated with statistical modeling of manufacturing processes. The maturity of a manufacturing process can be described by a sigma rating indicating its yield, or the percentage of defect-free products it creates. **A six sigma process is one in which 99.9999966% of the products manufactured are statistically expected to be free of defects (3.4 defects per million).** Motorola set a goal of "six sigma" for all of its manufacturing operations, and this goal became a byword for the management and engineering practices used to achieve it.[1]

Six Sigma was originally rolled out by Motorola, but these days, numerous Fortune 500 companies utilize the management approach, including General Electric, Lockheed Martin, Xerox, Honeywell, and 3M, to name just a few.[2]

So, if the American justice system were to deploy the same level of quality control in death penalty cases as Fortune 500 companies, we would expect a confidence level of **99.9999966%** to be utilized as a benchmark! And that leads us to this provocative question:

> *Is it too much to expect a standard of* <u>*95% confidence*</u> *in* **death penalty cases** *when corporate America gives us a* <u>*far higher standard*</u> *for the manufacture of* **toaster ovens?**

From the *Six Sigma* perspective, the 95% number is extremely liberal for the prosecution, by no means "too high," [3] a number easily achievable by the vast majority of sellers on *Ebay*.

The final proof that the 95% number is a standard that could certainly be met by the lone assassin theorists (the ones most likely to

---

[1] http://en.wikipedia.org/wiki/Six_Sigma (retrieved April 6, 2011).

[2] http://en.wikipedia.org/wiki/List_of_Six_Sigma_companies (retrieved April 6, 2011).

[3] **50,000** out of 1,000,000 is a much less severe restriction than **3.4** out of 1,000,000.

complain) comes none other from Vincent Bugliosi. In *Reclaiming History*, Bugliosi indicates quite emphatically that meeting the 95% confidence level would be a veritable cakewalk, since, according to Bugliosi, Oswald was guilty *not just* beyond a reasonable doubt (*Reclaiming History*, [hereinafter RH] 592; emphasis supplied):

> Indeed, the evidence against Oswald proves his guilt not just beyond a reasonable doubt, but beyond all doubt, or, as they say in the movies, **beyond a shadow of a doubt**.

In fact, the standard that Bugliosi claims that he can meet is almost ridiculously high, beyond even *Six Sigma* levels (RH 592; emphasis supplied):

> . . . **it is not humanly possible for him to be innocent** . . . Only in a fantasy world could Oswald be innocent and still have all this evidence against him. I think we can put it this way: **If Oswald didn't kill Kennedy, then Kennedy wasn't killed on November 22, 1963**.

So, if anyone is going to claim that the *Fatico* benchmark that we are going to be using in this book (95%) creates a standard of proof far too difficult for the prosecution to meet, it certainly isn't going to be Vincent Bugliosi, the prosecutor who is arguably the one most familiar with the facts of the case. Nor would it be Stephen King, Mr. 98% or 99%. Consequently, while some might follow the lead of the Bible and corporate America and argue that the 95% number is too *low* (and rightfully so), no one can plausibly argue that the number is too *high*, and therefore we will settle on that number, because, contrary to what Mr. Bugliosi and Mr. King claim, the prosecution is going to need all the help it can get.

So, now we have a number to use to evaluate the strength of the evidence for and against claims, and because we do, we are able to translate numerically the impact categories of evidence will have on claims. Naturally, there is going to be room for disagreement on the precise numbers that are going to result from analysis, but luckily absolute precision is not required. If one person argues that he is **50%** confident based on the evidence that a person committed the crime, and another person argues that he is **75%** confident based on the evidence that a person committed the crime, there is some very profound disagreement as to the absolute numbers based on the evidence, but it really doesn't matter, we can see that *both* are well short of the **95%** reasonable doubt standard! And, in fact, essentially the same reasoning applies even if there are *different* reasonable doubt standards. As the U.S District Court noted in *Fatico* (458 F. Supp 388, 411; emphasis supplied):

> The high probability required in criminal cases, however, does not mean that most guilty people who are tried are acquitted. In almost all cases the guilt is so clear or the doubt so great that precise quantification is of no moment. In some few instances which **this court would roughly estimate on the basis of experience as no more than one in ten cases it may make a difference whether the trier's perception of the standard is 80, 90, 95, or 99%.**

As you are going to see later on in this book, the reasoning of this paragraph is particularly apt, and ought to quell any remaining qualms.

So, now that we have a standard by which to evaluate the quality of our evidence, let's see how the quality of our evidence can impact the confidence level of our claims.

Chapter 4: Reasonable Doubt: How Evidence Affects Confidence Level

With our confidence level requirement of 95% firmly established, we are now in a position to determine how the nature of the evidence gathered will affect our ability to achieve that confidence level.

As alluded to in the previous chapter, there are four criteria/decision points the body of evidence must traverse to establish the requisite confidence level. For each element to cross the threshold of reasonable doubt (i.e. to achieve the confidence level of 95%), the body of evidence to be evaluated by a juror must be:

1. Comprehensive
2. Credible
3. Sufficient
4. Consistent

These terms are part of the common threads that are woven throughout the fabric of legal reasoning. Because these criteria are pervasive in the legal record, interested readers should have no problem in pulling up examples, but for documentation purposes I will cite one case (for each criterion) that utilizes that criterion as a potential point of decision, with the key phrase highlighted in every excerpt:

Comprehensive Evidence Needed
(*Jones Stevedoring Company* v. *Paglia*; 2011 U.S. App. LEXIS 21483 at 4-5)
"Because Jones failed to produce specific and **comprehensive evidence** severing the connection between Paglia's covered employment and his hearing loss, the Board properly held that Jones did not rebut the § 20(a) presumption."

Credible Evidence Needed
(*Clean Air Implementation Project, et al.,* v. *Environmental Protection Agency*, 150 F.3d 1200 (1998))
"Before EPA adopted its **credible evidence** rule in February 1997, 62 Fed. Reg. 8314, the agency's air pollution standards specified not only the maximum permissible level of emissions, but also the performance or reference test that should be used as a means of sampling and analyzing air pollutants for the particular standard.

See, e.g., 40 C.F.R. §§ 60.2, 61.02. A reference test is any "generic multi-use test protocol[] that measures whether a source's emissions comply with numeric performance standards." Paul D. Hoburg, "Use of 'Credible Evidence' to Prove Clean Air Act Violations," 25 B.C. ENVTL. AFF. L. REV. 771, 784-85 (1998)."

Sufficient Evidence Needed
(*Quarry Knoll II Corp. et al. v. Planning and Zoning Commission of the Town of Greenwich et al.*, 1999 Conn. Super. LEXIS 3425 at 30-1) "[I]t is the commission that has the burden of marshaling the evidence supporting its decision to persuade the court that there is *sufficient evidence* in the record to support that decision and the reasons given for that decision. An applicant does not have to address concerns that the commission may have by evidence beyond a reasonable doubt."

Consistent Evidence Needed
(*Hayden v. Commonwealth*, 140 Ky. 634 at 636-7; 131 S.W. 521 (1910)) "Besides other ways not necessary to be considered now, a witness may be impeached by showing (1) that he has made statements different from his present testimony, (2) by *contradictory evidence*, and (3) by evidence that his general reputation for untruthfulness or immorality renders him unworthy of belief . . ."

But there is something else to consider in addition to these criteria, a factor which has not yet been mentioned, which is that a jury can only determine how comprehensive, credible, sufficient, or consistent is the evidence which is *before them*; in fact, *not all* evidence is *admissible*, for a whole host of reasons, and to fully discuss those reasons would require a detour that could take us hundreds of pages away from the instant case. Here's the main point:

The *only* evidence which is subject to these criteria is *admissible* evidence.

It is a judge who decides whether or not evidence is admissible. In making his or her decision, there are at least two factors worth mentioning, one that evidence be **relevant**, and another that the evidence **satisfy certain technical protocols** which the legal arena has established as necessary conditions for admissibility, such as the rule that for evidence to be admissible *it must not have a broken chain* *of custody.* These factors are problematic, however, because what is relevant is going to vary with the circumstances, and in some cases, even evidence with a broken chain of custody can be sent to the jury, also depending on the circumstances, the law of the state, and which judge happens to be presiding on the bench that day.

The basic flow can be found in this excerpt from the seventh edition of *Evidence* by Steven Emanuel and Professor Joel Friedman of Tulane Law School (*Emanuel Law Outlines, Evidence*, p. C-1):

I.   FIRST PRINCIPLES

A. Roles of judge and jury: In cases tried to a jury, the judge and the jury divide the responsibility of dealing with the evidence [1]:

  1. Judge's role: The role of the *judge* is to determine *whether the evidence is admissible.*

  2. Role of the jury: Once the judge has decided to admit the evidence, the jury's role is to determine what *weight* the evidence should be given. For instance, it is up to the jury to judge the *credibility* of a witness, and the jury may choose to completely disregard admissible testimony because it believes the witness who is giving that testimony is mistaken or lying.

Luckily, for our immediate purposes, we do not need to worry about the issue of admissibility; all we need to do in this section is focus on the evidence which *has* been admitted, and then use our criteria to analyze the *weight* of that evidence, as determined by how the evidence does or does not satisfy those criteria.

Let's discuss these in turn.

Our first criterion is that the evidentiary record as a whole be **comprehensive**: the record must contain *all* the admissible evidence relevant for any particular charge, conclusion, proposition, premise, or element. In other words, it must include *not only* the evidence presented by the prosecution, but *also* the evidence presented by the defense. If the *only* evidence presented is that by the *prosecution*, and the defense is *prohibited* (by the judge or whatever body relevant to the case) from presenting his or her side of the issue, then obviously the 95% confidence level will not — indeed, *cannot* — be met.

Our second criterion is that the evidence provided by the prosecution in support of a proposition be **credible**: the material evidence which has been gathered, that most critical to the proof of the case, must be *genuine*, not distorted or, worse, *manufactured*. We can easily see how this criterion goes to the heart of the matter: the presumption of innocence can only be defeated with *actual* evidence, and unreliable evidence (lacking credibility) is *not* actual evidence. The importance of this criterion is indicated by the multiple mechanisms and standards established by the law to ensure the reliability of evidence, including the inadmissibility of certain hearsay evidence (i.e., *indirect* testimony, e.g., testimony by Mr. X that Mr. Y made a statement), the inadmissibility of evidence where the pedigree is uncertain (i.e., where the chain of custody for the evidence has not been established), evidence derived from unreliable evaluations such as polygraphs, hypnosis, "harsh interrogations", and so forth. Because the initial burden of proof is on the prosecution, if the prosecution *cannot* come forward with credible evidence, the confidence level remains where it began — **zero**.

Once we are sure that *all* the relevant evidence is in, and the prosecution's evidence is credible, our third criterion is that the evidentiary record be **sufficient** to establish the truth of the charge — the record must consist of *enough* evidence to establish the truth of the conclusion. Because the burden of proof is on the prosecution, this step therefore applies primarily to the prosecution, at this stage. As a brief example, if we assume that *three* witness reports in favor of the prosecution are *required* to establish a 95% confidence level for the charge (or element of the change), and only *one* witness report is given, then obviously the 95% confidence level is *not* met.

Our final criterion is that the evidence must be **consistent**. If we get to this stage, the evidence provided by the defense is subject to analysis for credibility, and once that analysis is performed, we are left with our final evidentiary database. Since we now have **all** the evidence which we need to evaluate the charge's confidence level, and have made sure that all the evidence we have is **reliable**, and have therefore determined that we have a **sufficient** amount of evidence to make our determination, we now need to *compare* our pieces of evidence and make sure that the stories they are telling are broadcasting on the same channel, i.e., are *consistent*. If one witness says the murderer wore a *red* shirt, and another witness says the murderer wore a *blue* shirt, then obviously the evidence is *inconsistent*, and since we have already determined that both witnesses have equally good vision and reliability, the standard of consistency is not met, and consequently, nor is the 95% confidence level.

With these criteria in place, we can create one or more flowchart paradigms for the purpose of analysis. The first flowchart type we will examine can be referred to as a *linear* flowchart. A linear flowchart constructed on the basis of the previous discussion looks like this:

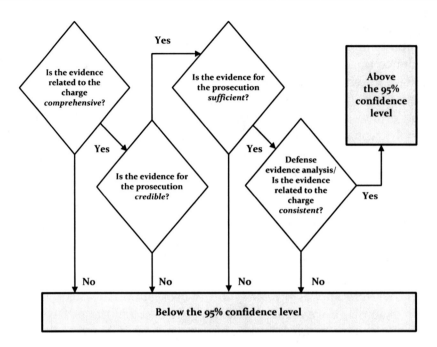

This linear flowchart establishes a flow of confidence level analysis which we can deploy for every elementary factual situation. Note what is critically important about this flowchart:

If there is a "no" at any decision point in the flowchart, then you break out of the flowchart and move to the endpoint where the confidence level falls below 95%!

This is because a "yes" at every decision point is *necessary*: the *only* way a confidence level greater than 95% can be achieved is when *all* the decision points are *positively traversed*.

This analysis of the inevitability breakout flow is based on what is referred to as *tautology*: that is to say, the analysis logically follows based on the *definition of the terms*.

Remember the concept of *presumption of innocence*, where, at the beginning of the presentation of the prosecution's case (before any evidence is in), the confidence level for the charge must be **zero**. Now, the prosecution starting at 0% confidence must climb the mountain to 95%. It can only do that with a sound evidentiary base, which takes us to our first decision point. If the evidence is not **comprehensive**, then by *definition* the evidence required to make the decision that the charge is true *does not exist*, and this will completely abort the ability to increase confidence level above the required 95% threshold. The same goes for the decision points of *credibility, sufficiency,* and *consistency.*

With these criteria in mind, let us analyze a fact pattern to see how this concept of breakout flow works. We will examine a charge, and the evidence for that charge provided by the prosecution and defense:

THE CHARGE

Jim, age 50, has been charged with the crime of *printing* counterfeit bills. The prosecution and defense have introduced the following evidence into the record:

THE EVIDENCE FOR THE CHARGE
Prosecution Evidence

1) Jim tried to pay for a gaming system with counterfeit notes.
2) The police found a printing press in his house, with $7,500 in freshly minted bills next to the printing press.
3) The police also found the following three books in Jim's library: "*The Art Of Counterfeiting,*" "*How To Counterfeit In Five Easy Steps,*" and "*How To Pass Counterfeit Money Without Getting Caught.*"
4) Jim's fingerprints were on the printing press. And the money.
5) A security camera in Jim's house videotaped Jim printing the money just two days before he was arrested.
6) An email sent through his *Gmail* account from Jim to his friend Jack quotes Jim as writing "how easy the counterfeiting racket is."
7) When shown the evidence, Jim admitted to the charge, and explained that he "got into the counterfeiting game" because he "needed the money."

Defense Evidence

1) Jim became an Eagle Scout at the age of 15.

A printing press . . . library books revealing intent . . . fingerprints . . . video . . . and to top it all off, a *confession* . . . evidence doesn't get much better than this!

Still, we do need to run our evidence through the flowchart just to be sure. Our first decision point arises when we ask the question "**is the evidence related to the charge *comprehensive*?**" That is to say, do we have *every* piece of evidence — both for prosecution and defense — we need to make an informed decision regarding the confidence level? For the purposes of this hypothetical scenario, we will assume that we have all of the relevant evidence (even though it appears that the defense was, perhaps understandably, AWOL), and then proceed to the next node in our flowchart.

Our second decision point is perhaps the most important: "**is the evidence for the prosecution *credible*?**" For example, were the books in Jim's library *actually* Jim's books, or did someone plant them there? For the purposes of this evaluation, we will assume that they were his.

To the next decision point: we have gathered all the available evidence, and have stipulated that the evidence for the prosecution is credible, and when we examine that evidence we find that the evidence for the prosecution taken together clearly supports the charge, so therefore we have successfully answered the question "**is the evidence for the prosecution *sufficient*?**", which means that the prosecution has presented enough positive evidence to move to the next step.

Our final decision point is "**is the evidence related to the charge consistent?**" Since we have all the relevant evidence, and all the relevant evidence for the prosecution passes the "smell test," and the evidence presented by the prosecution is sufficient to demonstrate the charge, we now subject the defense evidence to the same credibility tests, and once we determine it passes, we then need to see if *all* the individual pieces of evidence (not just that presented by the prosecution) are consistent with each other (that is to say, that each individual piece of evidence provided by prosecution and defense tells the same story). And in this example, we find out that for the most part it does, although we do have one small piece of evidence (provided by the defense) that does not tell the same story, which is that 35 years before the crime was committed, Jim became an Eagle Scout, and if we assume that all Eagle Scouts are generally of sound moral character, this evidence is somewhat inconsistent.

However, this minor inconsistency is easily dealt with since the inconsistent occurrence occurred 3.5 decades prior to the commission of the crime, and the character of a person can easily change over that period of time. If Jim were 18 years old, the inconsistency of this evidence would present more problems, although that inconsistency would ultimately be defeated by the overwhelming evidence for the charge, and the melancholy recognition that not every Eagle Scout is necessarily 100% pure.

Having run our evidence through these four filters, we find that the evidence makes it through for the most part with ease.

So, now we have the basis for assigning a confidence level, which, according to our flowchart, will be greater than 95%. But what precise number do we assign? Most people, when asked, would now say that it is 100% certain that Jim is guilty, but even if this is not the case, we can certainly say that the confidence level at the high end is above 99%, approaching *Six Sigma* levels. We have all the evidence we need, every item of evidence is legitimate, every item of evidence provided by the prosecution (taken as a whole) is sufficient to prove the charge, and there is no evidence provided by the defense (or prosecution) which substantively contradicts the charge.

Of course, there is always room for a little doubt, especially given Jim's Eagle Scout achievement, so we can reduce our rating somewhat at the lower end of our range. Given this, let's assign a confidence level range with a minimum value of 99, and a maximum value of 99.99 (it is hard to be 100% sure of anything!), which results in the following table:

Minimum Confidence	Maximum Confidence
99	**99.99**

We could average these numbers to give us one number to work with, but for now, let's just stick with the range — a prosecutor's dream. *Our confidence level for the charge is solidly above 95%, therefore Jim is "guilty beyond a reasonable doubt."*

Now let's take a different scenario, an example of an entirely different sort which will give us a *low* confidence level.

THE CHARGE
Jim has been charged with the crime of *printing* counterfeit bills. The prosecution and defense have introduced the following evidence into the record:

EVIDENCE FOR THE CHARGE
Prosecution Evidence
1) Jim tried to pay for a gaming system with counterfeit notes.

Defense Evidence
1)   Jim became an Eagle Scout at the age of 15.

That's it. That's the evidence. So we look at our first criteria, and then ask ourselves the first question which follows from that criteria, **"is the evidence related to the charge *comprehensive*?"** We will assume that it is all the evidence that could reasonably be gathered (meager though it may be), and proceed to the next decision point.

Our next question is **"is the evidence for the prosecution *credible*?"** And the answer is "yes." Jim actually did pass the notes, and he was an Eagle Scout.

Our next question is **"is the evidence for the prosecution *sufficient*?"** And at this point the red light flashes: the answer clearly is "no!" Jim has been charged with the crime of *printing* counterfeit bills, not *passing* counterfeit bills! And, in fact, no other evidence has been produced for the charge; no printing press, no videotape security camera record, no confession, no nothing. A skimpy record that screams "inadequate."

Notice that because the evidence for the prosecution (who has the burden of proof) is not sufficient, we do not even need to move to our final decision point. If the evidence for the prosecution is not sufficient as it stands, we obviously do not need to worry about whether Jim actually was an Eagle Scout, nor whether that evidence is consistent with Jim's Eagle Scout achievement (or any other evidence).

At this point, we now are shuttled down to the end point in the flowchart that says that we should assign a confidence level lower than 95% to this charge. But what specific confidence level is that? Here, there is more room for disagreement. Some might go as low as 1%, others might go as high as 15%, but your author's assessment is as follows:

Minimum Confidence	Maximum Confidence
2	**5**

If you disagree with this assessment, that is fine, and to be expected. Note, however, that relative to the end goal your assessment is probably not *all that far away* from mine, and I think it's safe to say that *both* of our assessments, even though they might be somewhat divergent, are still *well short* of the 95% threshold required; accordingly, even though we disagree as to the exact numbers, we both agree that Jim must be found "not guilty" of this charge, which from the due process perspective is all that counts.

Okay, enough with the elementary examples, prototypes of easy decisions to illustrate how the breakout flow paradigm works. Now let's graduate to a higher level of analysis and muddy the waters somewhat with a more complex example.

THE CHARGE

Jim has been charged with the crime of *printing* counterfeit bills. The prosecution and defense have introduced the following evidence into the record:

EVIDENCE FOR THE CHARGE
Prosecution Evidence
1) Jim tried to pay for a gaming system with counterfeit notes.
2) The police found a printing press in Jim's house, with $7,500 in freshly minted bills (with identical serial numbers) next to the printing press.
3) Jim's fingerprints were on the printing press. And the money.

Defense Evidence
1) A security camera in Jim's house videotaped a person (unknown to Jim, according to Jim's testimony) bringing the printing press into Jim's house while Jim was on vacation, and also videotaped that person printing $7,500 worth of counterfeit bills. Jim is seen on the videotape, upon returning from vacation, apparently surprised that the printing press is in his house. He touches the printing press, and when he sees the money next to the printing press, picks the money up, and then puts some of it into his wallet.
2) Jim's explains to the police after he is arrested for passing counterfeit bills that he had hired a housesitting service to watch his house while he was on vacation, and, unknown to Jim, the person hired to do the housesitting used Jim's home to set up a criminal enterprise.

More complex, but once run through the four decision points, a clear answer should still emerge. Let us assume, for the purposes of this discussion, that the first two decision points are answered in the affirmative; this is **all** the evidence, and the prosecution's evidence is **credible**. But now we have to pause at our third decision point, related to *sufficiency*. Here, we again need only focus on the prosecution's evidence, and ask the question, if this was the *only* evidence offered in this case, would we be 95% confident that the charge was true? If you answer "no," you are done, but if you answer "yes," you still have one more hurdle, and it's a big one. Let's answer "yes," and see why.

We analyze our defense evidence, determine that it is credible, and now ask, "Is the evidence related to the charge **consistent**?" We find out that the answer is **no** — which changes *everything*!

Our confidence level for this charge, whatever it might have been after analyzing just the first three items, now has to be *reduced* because of this contradictory video evidence, and, based on the impact of this evidence (which *positively refutes* the charge), reduced to *a very great extent*. Again, there is going to be some room for disagreement as to how much the confidence level of the charge has been reduced, but that's what jurors are for. If you were a juror, what would you say? Feel free to fill in the blanks!

Minimum Confidence	Maximum Confidence

To my way of thinking, the video is a sledgehammer that shatters the prosecution's case. Therefore, my own personal view (relevant were I a prospective juror) is that, based on the evidence offered by the prosecution and defense (assuming both are equally credible), my *minimum* confidence level for the charge would be 0%, and my *maximum* confidence level for the charge would be 5% (based on the exceptionally slight possibility that the video had been tampered with). Contrast that evaluation with yours.

I assume that some readers would have put a maximum confidence level of 25%, versus my 5%. But again, recall, even with a disagreement as profound as this, the higher confidence level of 25% is still well short of the 95% threshold required; accordingly, Jim must be found "not guilty" of *this* charge (though possibly guilty of the related change of passing counterfeit bills).

So far, our linear model of the flowchart has worked fairly well. But these have been comparatively simple examples. Our next hypothetical is far more complicated — somewhat like the Kennedy case, though by comparison much simpler — and will present extraordinary challenges for our linear model:

THE CHARGE

Jim, age 50, has been charged with the crime of *printing counterfeit bills*. The prosecution and defense have introduced the following evidence into the record:

THE EVIDENCE FOR THE CHARGE

Prosecution Evidence

1) Jim tried to pay for a gaming system with counterfeit notes.
2) The police found a printing press in his house, with $7,500 in freshly minted bills next to the printing press.
3) The police also found the following book in Jim's library: *"How To Forge A New Identity."* Jim claims the book was given to him as a gift.
4) Jim's fingerprints were on the printing press. And the money.
5) A security camera in Jim's house videotaped Jim printing the money just two days before he was arrested, according to the testimony of a detective.
6) An email sent through his *Gmail* account from Jim to his friend Jack quotes Jim as writing "how easy the counterfeiting racket is."
7) When shown the evidence, Jim admitted to the charge, and explained that he "got into the counterfeiting game" because he "needed the money."

Defense Evidence

1) A week before, Jim had advertised his 20-year-old car in a classified ad in the local paper, and 3 days before Jim sold that car to a man named Bill, who paid Jim in cash. Jim used this cash to purchase the gaming system. The ad was definitely placed by Jim, and entered into evidence by the defense. Bill, however, cannot be located by the police force. Still, the title was recorded by the DMV as having been transferred the day before the notes were passed to a person named "Wendy."
2) Jim claims the printing press was used to print flyers for his church. Jim denies that he had $7,500 in his room, and says that if there was any money there, it was planted by

someone. A police log showed that $7,500 was found. A detective testified that he personally only found $2500, and is not sure why the log says $7,500. There is no other testimony by any other policeman that verifies the amount on the log.

3) Jim claims a security videotape would prove the money was planted. Unfortunately for Jim, the police confiscated the tape, and originally refused to release it until a period of 75 years had passed. Eventually, under pressure by the defense, they did. When the tape was run, unfortunately, the defense found a 15 minute gap, and even more unfortunately, *the gap was located precisely in the area that would have exonerated Jim*. Police initially denied that they caused this gap, but later changed their story to this: a new hire at the police force had *inadvertently* erased that part of the tape! "No problem," say the police. One of their detectives testified that he saw the tape *before* it was erased, and in that 15 minute segment, he saw Jim printing the money. The detective who made this allegation had been on the force for 20 years, had received numerous commendations, and had been a member of Jim's church for 20 years. The detective also passed a lie detector test.

4) Jim was going to call five other witnesses for his defense. As luck would have it, though, one witness died of natural causes, two died in an accident before the trial, and the other two who had signed pre-trial affidavits confirming Jim's story then changed their mind and refused to testify in his defense. This left Jim with no witnesses and two discredited affidavits.

5) With regard to the fingerprints on the printing press, Jim said that he handled the printing press in the course of printing the flyers. His fingerprints were on the money because after receiving it from Tom, he counted it.

6) Jim denies sending the e-mail. His friend Jack went on a long-term vacation overseas, and could not be personally contacted, but an affidavit provided by the prosecution, in Jack's handwriting, confirms the receipt of an e-mail without specifically addressing the contents.

7) Jim said that he was coerced into making a confession, but failed a lie detector test administered by the police department. However, the defense found three witnesses to

testify that the person administering the lie detector test had altered the data on three separate occasions. Two of these witnesses, as it so happened, had a prior forgery conviction.

Uh-oh!! A little different, huh? This is the type of devilishly complicated hypothetical situation law school professors provide as fodder for final exam essays, and one that provides a hint of the complexity offered by the Kennedy case. And it is extremely instructive in at least one way; notice, when you saw *only* the prosecution's evidence, you were ready to hang Jim high; but now, this evidence presented by the defense *changes everything*. In addition, and more to the point being made here, you'll notice that due to this complexity, this hypothetical makes the breakout flow model *unworkable*.

Suppose we ask our first question, "is the evidence related to the charge **comprehensive**?" When we analyze the data, we quickly discover that *we can't reliably answer this question!* To take the most obvious example, a key piece of evidence — the tape — was obliterated at the most important point. The evidence could have completely exonerated the defendant! And yet, while we might want to conclude that negligence of this sort on the part of the authorities ought to play the same role in this case as the role the atom bomb played to Nagasaki, we do have the testimony of the detective that Jim was lying. The detective appears to be reliable, and we do not want to believe that a detective would commit perjury. Can this evidence be seen as a legitimate substitute? To ask it another way, since the tape was erased in the worst possible place, can we really say that the detective's "fill-in" testimony — supposedly reliable though it may be — is an adequate substitute for the cold hard evidence the defense would have had had not the police *negligently* handled the evidence?

Now, you might be confused, and consequently undecided at this point, but unfortunately the flowchart really doesn't allow for indecision of this nature. And simply moving forward won't be of much help, because assessing the credibility of the prosecution will require a simultaneous assessment of the credibility of the defense.

At this stage, we can see that the linear model is going to present some difficulties, so let's take a stab at a new model:

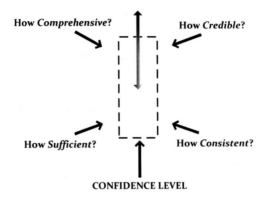

We can refer to this new approach as the *dynamic input model*, a model which allows for a more or less simultaneous analysis (i.e., it need not be analyzed in any particular order). What this model sacrifices in *certainty*, it gains in *flexibility*. Different weights can be assigned to the parameters as warranted by the evidence, and in no particular order.

The center rectangle with broken lines represents a bar indicating confidence level, a bar to be raised or lowered depending on the quality and quantity of the inputs. For example, if the evidence is only 90% comprehensive, the bar can be reduced to a 90% level. If the evidence for the *prosecution* lacks credibility, the height of the bar will be *lowered*, and if the evidence for the *defense* lacks credibility, the height of the bar will be *raised*. If the evidence presented by the prosecution lacks consistency, the height of the bar can be raised or lowered depending on the nature of the inconsistency. And so forth.

Because this model is not linear, our questions change to reflect the reality that they can be asked in any order. Let's try to answer these questions in relation to our latest hypothetical scenario, and see how the answers affect the height of the bar:

How *comprehensive* is the evidence?

The evidence is not nearly as comprehensive as we want it to be. The 15 minute gap is a very serious omission. It is true that the detective has provided substitute testimony, but at the expense of a substantial reduction in the *quality* of testimony; the detective's testimony *functions* almost like hearsay evidence, an evidence of much lower quality, generally considered inadmissible.

BAR *DOWN*

How *credible* is the evidence?

As indicated above, there are serious credibility issues with both prosecution and defense evidence. However, since the burden of proof is on the prosecution, if its credibility issues are not successfully addressed, the credibility issues of the defense are not nearly as important.

One of the major problems the prosecution has is its initial decision to withhold what had the potential to be completely exculpatory evidence. True, eventually the police department did release the evidence, but in withholding the evidence initially it indicated an intent that can only be called *suspicious*. These suspicions are only confirmed by the 15 minute gap.

Yet another serious issue for the prosecution is the anomaly between the amount of money registered on the log and the contradictory testimony. So, either the police department has extraordinary quality control issues, or malicious intent . . . as it so happens, in neither situation is the case for the prosecution improved.

Because of these issues, the credibility issues for the defense do not loom clearly as large. Yes, the name on the title does not reflect the name of the person to whom the car was sold, but that person could be Jim's wife. In any event, the report of title confirms that the car was sold, adding credibility to this claim by the defense.

There are potential problems with the defense allegation regarding the e-mail, in light of the affidavit, but then again, just how reliable is this affidavit given the issues with the gap in the tape, and the fact that it does not really address the content of the letter?

As you can probably guess, the whole case is going to turn on the credibility of the evidence, and at this stage of the game, there seem to be some significant flaws with that presented by the prosecution.

BAR DOWN

How *sufficient* is the evidence?

How this question is answered depends to a great extent on the analysis of credibility. The evidence which is deemed not credible (log entry, detective testimony, lie detector, etc.) can be excluded from consideration, and in the process of exclusion, the case could possibly be decided. At this stage of the game, the prosecution has some very serious issues, and *the more exclusion, the less sufficiency*.

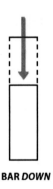

BAR DOWN

How *consistent* is the evidence?

Again, how this question is answered will largely rest on the credibility analysis. However, if we assume that all evidence is equally credible, we see that there are serious problems with consistency (log variation, prosecution vs. defense version of events, etc.) that would radically reduce the confidence level.

The only remedy for this from the perspective of the prosecution is to attack the credibility of the defense, but, considering that it has credibility problems of its own, its attack would itself not be very credible.

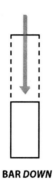

BAR *DOWN*

This is just a very brief, perfunctory analysis, which could go on for many more pages, and could be subject to hours-long debate. In short, this case is a *mess*, and when you have a *mess*, you have a *problem*. Your whole tight-knit case can unravel when even one thread comes loose, particularly if you have *inconsistent* evidence. Follow the thread:

Not **consistent**, not **credible**;
Not **credible**, not **comprehensive**;
Not **comprehensive**, not **sufficient**;
Not **sufficient**, *no case!*

That is one thread, and there are several others possible. In circumstances like the preceding scenario, what do we do? Luckily, complex situations like these can sometimes be resolved by going back to the basics, relying on due process considerations to come to our rescue.

The law of the United States helps us out, especially in regard to the all-important videotape issue. As the Supreme Court pointed out in *Berger v. United States* (295 U.S. 78, 88 (1935); emphasis supplied),

[A prosecutor] is the representative not of an ordinary party to a controversy, but of a sovereignty whose obligation to govern impartially is as compelling as its obligation to govern at all; and **whose interest, therefore, in a criminal prosecution is not that it shall win a case, but that justice shall be done.**

As such, he is in a peculiar and very definite sense the servant of the law, the twofold aim of which is that guilt shall not escape or innocence suffer. He may prosecute with earnestness and vigor — indeed, he should do so. But, **while he may strike hard blows, he is not at liberty to strike foul ones**. It is as much his duty to refrain from improper methods calculated to produce a wrongful conviction as it is to use every legitimate means to bring about a just one.

Indeed, as *Berger* pointed out, one of the primary duties of the law is the disclosure of exculpatory evidence. The standard has been articulated by the *American Bar Association* in 1983, in its *Model Rules Of Professional Conduct*. The primary rule on point is Rule 3.8 (d), which reads as follows: [1]

> The prosecutor in a criminal case **shall . . . make timely disclosure to the defense of all evidence or information known to the prosecutor that tends to negate the guilt of the accused** or mitigates the offense, and, in connection with sentencing, disclose to the defense and to the tribunal all unprivileged mitigating information known to the prosecutor . . .

This standard is exemplified in several cases by the Supreme Court. One of these is *Brady v. Maryland*, in which the Supreme Court discussed the early case of *Mooney v. Holohan*, and stated as follows (373 U.S. 83, 87 (1963) (emphasis supplied)):

> We now hold that the **suppression by the prosecution of evidence favorable to an accused upon request violates due process where the evidence is material either to guilt or to punishment, irrespective of the good faith or bad faith of the prosecution.**
> The principle of *Mooney v. Holohan* is not punishment of society for misdeeds of a prosecutor, but avoidance of an unfair trial to the accused. **Society wins not only when the guilty are convicted, but when criminal trials are fair; our system of the administration of justice suffers when any accused is treated unfairly.** . . . A prosecution that withholds

---

[1] *Model Rules of Prof'l Conduct* R. 3.8(d) (1983) (emphasis supplied).

evidence on demand of an accused which, if made available, would tend to exculpate him or reduce the penalty helps shape a trial that bears heavily on the defendant. That casts the prosecutor in the role of an architect of a proceeding that does not comport with standards of justice . . .

The court also held in *United States v. Bagley* that every defendant has a right to know of **"evidence favorable to the [defendant] that is material to either guilt or punishment."** (473 U.S. 667, 675 (1985) (emphasis supplied)). There are several other cases along the same lines.[1]

Now, it is obvious that these cases are not exactly on point for our hypothetical. For example, what we *do not have* in this case is a videotape demonstrating innocence that has been withheld by the police and/or prosecution (a failure to disclose exculpatory evidence). But what we do have, however, is the *destruction* of that evidence! The tape could have completely shown the innocence of the defendant if it was not destroyed; our hypothetical is less about the *temporary* suppression of evidence and more about the *permanent* suppression of that evidence, which we all must agree is a whole lot worse.

Yes, the prosecution has provided us with the testimony of the detective indicating that the evidence would not operate to exculpate, but in light of the cases above, where there is such an overriding interest in bringing out evidence favorable to the accused, we can see that there has been, at the very least, a dereliction of duty on the part of the prosecution. That *has* to play a role in our decision, because *at a very critical juncture*, the police and prosecution have created something they absolutely do not want to create . . . **doubt!**

Yes, thanks primarily to the issue with the videotape, and the issue with the log, we now have a case *dripping with doubt*!

And doubt does *not* favor the *prosecution*!

To really see the impact of this doubt, contrast this situation with our very first hypothetical, and the extremely high confidence level which resulted. If an extremely high confidence level could be attained with evidence of *high* credibility and *no contradictory evidence*, how much would that confidence level be reduced with evidence of *low*

---

[1] See, the aforementioned *Mooney v. Holohan*, 294 U.S. 103 (1935), *Pyle v. Kansas*, 317 U.S. 213 (1942)., and *United States v. Agurs*, 427 U.S. 97 (1976).

credibility, and a *great deal of contradictory* evidence? The answer essentially speaks for itself. I will let you fill in the blanks, and then I will offer my opinion:

Minimum Confidence	Maximum Confidence

So, here's my opinion: there is *no way* to be confident in a case this doubtful, with so many loose ends. Given all the doubt in this case, I would give a low of 35 and a high of 50. Basically, at its best, to me the case is a coin flip. The primary reason is the 15 minute gap on the tape. This is suspicious! I don't want to believe detectives lie, but even more, I don't want to put an innocent person in jail. As our examination of the law underlying the hypothetical reveals, the police have a *responsibility* to preserve any evidence which can positively exonerate an defendant, and given the overriding assumption of our system that sending innocent people to jail is the *sine qua non* of nadirs to avoid, the failure to execute this responsibility must be met with a severe consequence to the government, sending them the message that if they don't fulfill their responsibility, their power to incarcerate will be reduced or eliminated. If there is a better way to prevent the tyranny of a government manufacturing star chambers that can jail anyone it pleases, I can't think of it.

You will most likely analyze this somewhat differently, and surely give a somewhat different range. And others will give a range different from yours. Ultimately, in an actual case, this decision would not be made just by me, nor just by you, but with other people organized together in a panel of twelve called a *jury*.

And this takes us to another extremely significant point not yet raised:

When a jury makes its decision, the *most significant* opinion is that of the person with the *lowest confidence* level!

One might think that a jury averages out its responses, and reports that average to the judge, but that is not the way it works. If 11 jurors believe that the confidence level is 100%, and one juror believes that the confidence level is 80%, this results in a *mistrial!* Rule 31 of the *Federal Rules Of Criminal Procedure* provides as follows: [1]

> If the jury cannot agree on a verdict on one or more counts, the court may declare a mistrial on those counts. The government may retry any defendant on any count on which the jury could not agree.

In terms of our 95% confidence level, this federal rule takes us to a related rule:

> **In a normal jury trial, *all* the jurors must assign above a 95% confidence level for the charge to go forward. If *even one* juror believes that the case against the defendant is *not proven beyond a reasonable doubt*, there is a *mistrial*, and the government will have to retry the case.**

So, here is the critical takeaway if you have assigned a higher confidence level greater than 95% (and I am not sure that is possible); understand that *if even one person* on a jury disagrees with you, there will be a *mistrial!* Accordingly, it seems extraordinarily unlikely that there would be a successful prosecution based on the fact-pattern above.

At this stage of the game, we have analyzed our evidence using two different models, and we are almost ready to look at the Kennedy evidence in close detail. Before that, however, we need to define the significance of our categories with a few real-world examples, and, following that, discuss one exceptionally important category of evidence, which, if present in the evidentiary database, would be absolutely *toxic* to the case of the prosecution.

[1] *Federal Rules of Criminal Procedure*, Rule 31.
http://www.law.cornell.edu/rules/frcrmp/Rule31.htm (retrieved May 9, 2011)

Chapter 5: Reasonable Doubt: Categories Of Evidence Reducing Confidence Level

In the previous chapter, we analyzed at a high level how four criteria are used to calculate confidence level:

1. How *comprehensive* is the evidence?
2. How *credible* is the evidence?
3. How *sufficient* is the evidence?
4. How *consistent* is the evidence?

Now, evidence can be used (obviously) to increase the confidence level of a proposition, but some evidence can actually *reduce* confidence level in that proposition. In fact, there is a category of evidence (which we can call *meta-evidence*) that throws doubt *on the evidence itself*.

Remember the destroyed videotape in one of our earlier scenarios? The videotape *was* evidence, but that evidence was *destroyed* under the custodial "care" of the police, and that *destruction* now becomes evidence *about* the evidence, i.e., meta-evidence; and certain types of meta-evidence, like *destroyed* evidence, *must reduce confidence level.* Here are the most important categories of evidence reducing confidence level, some of them slightly overlapping, most of them meta-evidence:

A. Altered Evidence
B. Contradictory Evidence
C. Destroyed Evidence
D. Evidence based on data of suspect validity
E. Evidence derived from deviations from accepted procedure
F. Evidence inconsistent with a conclusion
G. Evidence that can support multiple conclusions
H. Evidence which violates the laws of physics
I. Insufficient evidence for the primary proposition
J. Irrelevant evidence (evidence which does not relate to the conclusion [(*non-sequitur*)])
K. Non-evidence: phenomena seen as evidence which are not (i.e., conclusions)
L. Suppressed Evidence

M. Tests not performed which would have the capability to exonerate the defendant

Now, as we examine the evidence in the subsequent chapters, it will not necessarily be clear into which of four criteria these categories fall.

For example, suppose we find an example of evidence *suppressed* by the Warren Commission (which will reduce confidence in one or more elements).

With reference to our four criteria, would this be an example of evidence which is not *comprehensive, credible, sufficient,* or *consistent*? While this is not of great concern for the *dynamic input* model, it is a concern for the *linear flow* model, which may be applicable to future analysis to be performed in this book, and so is included here for those readers who want to use this style of analysis.

So let's take a stab at classification. While *suppressed evidence* could fall under more than one of these categories, depending on how we view it, the most *precise* category would be evidence which is not *comprehensive,* since suppressed evidence by definition prevents a juror from having a comprehensive (complete) view of the evidentiary picture.

But of course we have all of the other evidence categories listed above to contend with, including *destroyed* evidence, *contradictory* evidence, and *irrelevant* evidence. Under which categories should *these* be classified? I have given this some thought, and arrived at the following classification:

Comprehensive
- Tests not performed which would have the capability to exonerate the defendant
- Suppressed Evidence
- Destroyed Evidence

Credible
- Altered Evidence
- Evidence based on data of suspect validity
- Evidence derived from deviations from accepted procedure

- Non-evidence: phenomena seen as evidence which are not (i.e., conclusions)
- Evidence which violates the laws of physics

Sufficient
- Insufficient evidence for the primary proposition
- Irrelevant evidence (evidence which does not relate to the conclusion [(non-sequitur)])
- Evidence that can support multiple conclusions

Consistent
- Contradictory Evidence
- Evidence inconsistent with a conclusion

This categorization is not perfect, but it provides a useful template for a more rigorous version to be created at a future time. In the meanwhile, I am going to explain why I believe these examples relate to the particular criteria.

Comprehensive
Tests not performed which would have the capability to exonerate
Comprehensive evidence is, by definition, a *complete* record. A test that *should* be performed, but is *not*, is by definition a violation of the requirement of comprehensive evidence, which of course, is derived from the due process considerations contained in the Constitution as stated by the Supreme Court. Recall the statement in *Berger v. United States* that the compelling interest "in a criminal prosecution is not that it shall win a case, but that justice shall be done." (*Berger v. United States*, 295 U.S. 78, 88 (1935)). Justice is not done, by definition, when the only tests performed are those which can demonstrate the guilt (versus the innocence) of a party. From the standpoint of keeping the innocent out of jail, the most *important* tests to perform are in fact those which can *exonerate* a defendant. If, for example, the defendant is charged with murder using a rifle, and he argues that he did not fire the rifle, the fact-finding authority reduces confidence (i.e., creates

reasonable doubt) simply by *not testing* the rifle to be sure that in fact it was fired on the day of the shooting.

Suppressed Evidence

For the same reasons listed above, evidence which is suppressed is *by definition* a failure to produce comprehensive evidence. Three examples of suppressed evidence are evidence we never see due to "gag orders" (orders by authorities to potential witnesses that they should not provide testimony), testimony never given because a witness is not called to testify before the relevant tribunal, and evidence said (truthfully or not) to be buried for reasons of "national security."

Destroyed Evidence

To destroy evidence is to *permanently* suppress it! When evidence that could possibly exonerate a defendant is destroyed, it creates the greatest suspicion possible regarding the intent of those destroying the evidence, and a presumption that the evidence destroyed was destroyed because the entity destroying the evidence *did not want it revealed.* As might be expected, examples of this strike a major blow to confidence level for not just one, but two reasons (missing evidence plus evidence of obstruction of justice).

Now let's move on to the categories of evidence reducing confidence level related to *credibility.*

Credible

Altered Evidence

The phrase "credible evidence" is in some sense redundant, because if evidence is not credible, then it doesn't count as evidence at all, in the same way that counterfeit money doesn't count as real money. Again, by definition, when evidence is altered it reduces the credibility of the evidence to the extent of the alteration. To take a simple example, if the goal of a prosecutor is to prove that a person was at a certain location on January 3, and the prosecutor produces a receipt from a store near that location that shows the defendant purchased an item on January 3, the defense irrevocably negates the credibility of the receipt by conclusively showing that the date had been *altered*.

Evidence based on data of suspect validity
Related to the point above, some data may not be altered intentionally, but it might be based on sources that in and of themselves have had demonstrable issues with validity (for example, an uncalibrated radar gun used to justify speeding tickets).

Below are a few examples of suspect data:

- **Witnesses who inherently lack credibility** (*Example*: witnesses who change their stories).
- **Coached witnesses** (*Example*: witnesses led to make a statement by the prosecution or defense).
- **Bribed witnesses** (*Example*: statements made by witnesses who have been paid for the remarks).
- **Intimidated witnesses** (*Example*: statements by witnesses who have been threatened).
- **Tests performed which don't match actual conditions**
  A test designed to demonstrate the viability of an action must duplicate the conditions under which the action was to be performed precisely. If the conditions are dissimilar, the confidence level of the test must be reduced in proportion to the dissimilarity. One example: *repairing* a broken rifle (supposedly used by the defendant) *before* it is first tested for accuracy.

Evidence derived from deviations from accepted procedure
Precisely due to cases such as the above, procedures have been created to help guarantee the authenticity of handled evidence. In certain cases, though, the process by which evidence is handled and gathered deviates *so greatly* from accepted procedure that it raises a doubt as to the validity of the evidence

simply by virtue of the deviation. For example, if the normal procedure when a suspect is interrogated is to have a court reporter or stenographer or tape recorder present, the lack of a court reporter or a stenographer or tape recorder during an interrogation provides *prima facie* evidence of *deviation* from procedure, which reduces confidence because a procedure designed to maintain integrity was *ignored*. Other examples:

- **Oral confirmation rule**
  If a rule of evidence is that no drawing may be admitted which does not have simultaneous oral testimony that the drawing accurately represents reality, any drawing admitted into evidence without that simultaneous oral testimony lacks credibility simply by virtue of the deviation from the established procedure.

- **Hearsay rule**
  According to the *Federal Rules Of Evidence* § 802, hearsay evidence is generally not admissible, with certain well-defined exceptions.[1] Evidence which is admitted which is not part of these categories of exceptions is by definition non-credible evidence.

- **Chain of custody rule**
  An important evidentiary rule regards the *chain of custody*, that a piece of evidence must be able to be directly tracked from its first discovery to its entry into evidence without any gaps in possession, and if that rule is broken, then the evidence is *automatically suspect* due to the deviation from the established procedure.

Non-evidence: phenomena seen as evidence which are not (i.e., conclusions)
You can only convict someone with *evidence*. However, certain phenomena are erroneously characterized as evidence. This general category can capture any examples

---

[1] http://federalevidence.com/rules-of-evidence#Rule802

not listed above, for example, *opinions*, particularly uninformed ones, and particularly opinions as to *conclusions*, which are *not* in and of themselves evidence.

The classical example of this is the phenomenon known as *begging the question*, a close variant of *circular reasoning*. We saw an example of begging the question earlier, when Vincent Bugliosi made the statement (paraphrasing) "since the single bullet theory is true, any conclusions to the contrary based on the Zapruder film must be false." The key problem with Bugliosi's remark is that the statement "the single bullet theory is true" is in fact a *conclusion*, not *evidence*. And if that conclusion is itself *contradicted* by the outstanding evidence (which it is), it's not a particularly legitimate conclusion either.

To give another example, the Warren Commission stipulated the conclusion *Oswald killed Tippit* as evidence supposedly justifying their argument that Oswald killed Kennedy (see WR 20), but since Oswald had never been tried for that crime, that conclusion had not been proven, and therefore could not possibly be legitimately used as evidence.

Evidence which violates the laws of physics

As a final example of evidence which automatically demonstrates what is at times an utter lack of credibility, you can find no finer example than evidence which violates the laws of physics. If, for example, we shoot a bullet into the bone of a human skeleton 500 times, and it comes out deformed every time, then a bullet entered into evidence with no deformity — with the simultaneous claim that it was shot into a human bone — is *automatically suspect* due to the fact that it seemingly contradicts the laws of physics.

One point that should be noted at this stage is that these criteria of *comprehensive* and *credible* evidence do not necessarily exist independently, but in fact can be combined and contrasted with other criteria to magnify their significance.

Let us imagine there is a jurisdiction shown to have an uncalibrated radar gun (no big leap of the imagination here). Suppose in our defense of a client for speeding we ask that jurisdiction for statistics related to arrests for speeding, which they initially resist producing. Suppose that when they *do* eventually produce the statistics, we find the statistics show *far more people* have been arrested for speeding in that jurisdiction than would be expected based on state averages. It is not implausible to expect that the same jurisdiction that could have had an increase in arrests due to a *failure to calibrate* its radar guns (*credibility*) would likewise *suppress the evidence* of this failure (*comprehensiveness*).

This is a classic case of the whole being greater than the sum of its parts, where the *simultaneous* presence of the lack of *credibility* and *comprehensiveness* reduce confidence level even more than each would have done on its own!

There is an inevitable conclusion that one can draw from the previous examples. A fact that many people are not aware of is that *Oswald's defense could now be centered exclusively on the* <u>*inadequacy*</u> *of the evidence offered by the prosecution, and evidence of violations of procedures, and/or manipulation or destruction of evidence, with no need to offer any additional counter-evidence!* This is because the burden of proof is on the prosecution, which can only meet its burden with *legitimate* evidence, and *if it is shown* that that prosecution-generated evidence is for one reason or another *illegitimate*, the case for the prosecution *is not*, and *cannot*, be made, and a verdict of not guilty must be returned solely on that basis.

Now let's look at the remaining categories.

Sufficient
Insufficient evidence for the primary proposition
Due process of law, and, in fact, logic, demand that every proposition be justified by evidence. If the evidence for a proposition is insufficient, then *by definition* there is reasonable doubt, because there is always doubt for propositions without adequate evidence.

There are some surprising implications derived from this requirement. For example, in the Kennedy case, it is said that Governor Connally was struck by a bullet at virtually the same time as President Kennedy, but Connally (unlike Kennedy) did not immediately react, a "delayed reaction" hypothesis postulated to add credence to the single bullet theory. Well, that is one thing to *claim*, but it is another to *prove*.

The need to offer evidence for the alleged delayed reaction by Connally is obvious, but what may not be obvious is that evidence must *also* be offered to prove that *Kennedy* did *not* have a similar delayed reaction, because obviously if they *both* had a reaction identically delayed, the central point would not hold!

Of course, you will quickly note that to prove this latter point regarding Kennedy the prosecution is going to have to enter evidence contradictory to its central point regarding Connally, which will leave the prosecution with completely contradictory testimony, one by one doctor stating that there *was* a delayed reaction, and one by another doctor, stating that there *wasn't*!

Perhaps because of this reason, no evidence for the point was offered, which is a telltale sign that the conclusion is not justified.

Irrelevant evidence (evidence which does not relate to the conclusion [(non-sequitur)])
Some evidence does not relate to a conclusion. For example, offering into evidence the notion that Oswald was a member of the Communist Party supposedly implicates him in the crime of murder. But Oswald was also a Marine. Should that implicate him in the crime of murder as well? If evidence such as this is offered, then the prosecution must also offer evidence that Communists (or Marines) are more likely to assassinate Presidents than other groups of people. As it stands, the evidence on its own is irrelevant.

Evidence that can support multiple conclusions
Some evidence can support multiple conclusions, surprisingly enough. And, when evidence can support *multiple* conclusions, it obviously is not sufficient to support just *one* conclusion. Take this example: a witness sees a man who "looks like Oswald" get into a station wagon. A second witness sees a man who "looks like Oswald" board a bus. These sightings are so close in time that at least one of these

sightings cannot be Oswald himself. From this evidence, we could conclude:

1. Oswald entered a station wagon, and an Oswald *look-alike* boarded a bus.
2. An Oswald *look-alike* entered a station wagon, and Oswald boarded a bus.
3. An Oswald *look-alike* entered a station wagon, and an Oswald *look-alike* boarded a bus.

In supporting *all* these conclusions, the evidence does not truly support any *one* of them.

Having examined these three criteria, let's look at our final criterion.

Consistent
Contradictory Evidence
We have finally arrived at the evidence which undoubtedly provided the rationale for the image of the scales of justice: evidence which is inconsistent with or conflicts with another piece of evidence. *By definition, this situation automatically creates doubt.* Let's say you are accused of shooting a man, and the evidence presented is that you fired *two* bullets. However, *four* bullets are found. That's two bullets more! It's contradictory — and confidence-reducing.

If the case is centered around a *lone* assassin, this discrepancy *automatically* creates reasonable doubt regarding the proposition related to a "lone" assassin.

Other examples of contradictory evidence include:

- **Multiple eyewitness testimony deviating from the proffered conclusion** (*Example*: if the proffered conclusion is that there was only one murderer (located *behind* the victim), and there are multiple witnesses who can testify that they saw shots fired from the *front* of the victim, reasonable doubt is created).

- **Fundamental change in testimony (vacillating testimony)** (*Example*: a doctor testifies that the shot which killed the victim entered in the *chest*, and later *changes* his testimony and now says that the shot which killed the victim entered in the *head*).

Evidence inconsistent with a conclusion

Some evidence positively *disproves* a conclusion (for example, an FBI report says a bullet did not transit, but the conclusion of the investigatory body was that it did). And, though it is extremely rare, you will occasionally find introduced into the record evidence which completely disproves the proposition that it seeks to support!

For example, a ballistic panel reports that a wound *could not* be caused by a pristine bullet, and the conclusion of the investigatory body accepting that report is that the wound *was* caused by a pristine bullet.

Summary

We just seen numerous examples of how categories of evidence and meta-evidence can easily reduce confidence level. While I have attempted to categorize these categories of evidence and meta-evidence in relationship to the criteria I believe are most relevant, the reader should not get too hung up on which category corresponds with which criterion. The bottom line is this:

When you come across *suppressed evidence*, it *reduces* confidence level;

when you come across *destroyed evidence*, it *reduces* confidence level;

when you come across *altered evidence*, it *reduces* confidence level;

when you come across *contradictory evidence*, it *reduces* confidence level;

when you come across *evidence based on data of suspect validity*, it *reduces* confidence level;

when you come across *evidence derived from deviations from accepted procedure*, it *reduces* confidence level;

when you come across *evidence inconsistent with a conclusion*, it *reduces* confidence level;

when you come across *evidence that can support multiple conclusions*, it *reduces* confidence level;

when you come across *evidence which violates the laws of physics*, it *reduces* confidence level;

when you come across *insufficient evidence for the primary proposition*, it *reduces* confidence level;

when you come across *irrelevant evidence (evidence which does not relate to the conclusion)*, it *reduces* confidence level;

when you come across *non-evidence: phenomena seen as evidence which are not*, that *reduces* confidence level;

when you come across *tests not performed which would have the capability to exonerate the defendant*, that *reduces* confidence level!

Remember these categories, because as we proceed through this book, you're going to see further examples of all of them.

Now, as damaging as these categories are to confidence level, they are pikers compared to the next and final category we will discuss, a category so devastating it deserves a chapter all its own.

Chapter 6: Essential Background: Government-Manufactured Reality

We have just seen several examples of categories of evidence that *must* reduce confidence. However, there is one category we did not explore, because its seismic impact raises entirely new issues. The category is that of *manufactured evidence*.

This is another area where the Bible steps in with words of wisdom. The 9th commandment says "Thou shalt not bear false witness against thy neighbor." The manufacturer of evidence says, "try to stop me!"

There is perhaps one thing that everyone can agree on, no matter what their orientation in terms of the Kennedy assassination, and that is when the government is *shown* to have manufactured evidence, it positively *obliterates* the prosecution's case. Because it demonstrates malicious intent, manufactured evidence has a radioactive, toxic quality that spreads to *all* evidence:

**Where there is malicious intent on the part of the prosecution,
how can *any* evidence be trusted?**

Just as a counterfeiter who passes counterfeit money devalues the real money he passes, so do prosecutors who pass along counterfeit evidence devalue any real evidence they happened to possess.

As it turns out, there are two types of manufactured evidence: evidence manufactured *after* a crime has been committed (to make convictions more probable), and, much worse, evidence manufactured *before* a crime has been committed (which demonstrates intent on the part of the fabricators not just to put an innocent person in jail, but also to commit the crime itself!).

Even the least of these is devastating to the prosecution's case. The Supreme Court held in *Napue v. Illinois*, 360 U.S. 264 (1959) that

**[I]t is established that a conviction obtained through use
of false evidence, known to be such by representatives of
the State, must fall under the Fourteenth Amendment,**
Mooney v. Holohan, 294 U. S. 103; *Pyle v. Kansas*, 317 U. S. 213;
Curran v. Delaware, 259 F.2d 707. *See New York ex rel.
Whitman v. Wilson*, 318 U. S. 688, and *White v. Ragen*, 324 U. S.
760. *Compare Jones v. Kentucky*, 97 F.2d 335, 338, with *In re
Sawyer's Petition*, 229 F.2d 805, 809. Cf. *Mesarosh v. United*

States, 352 U. S. 1. **The same result obtains when the State, although not soliciting false evidence, allows it to go uncorrected when it appears.** *Alcorta v. Texas*, 355 U. S. 28; *United States ex rel. Thompson v. Dye*, 221 F.2d 763; *United States ex rel. Almeida v. Baldi*, 195 F.2d 815; *United States ex rel. Montgomery v. Ragen*, 86 F.Supp. 382. See generally annotation, 2 L.Ed.2d 1575.

The law on this point is clear, and requires no further elucidation. But would officers of Government, charged with upholding the constitution, intentionally violate it? The answer, sadly, is *yes*.

Category 1: Manufacturing Reality *After* The Fact

Yes, Virginia, reality can be manufactured, and that's when you know you're not in Kansas anymore, which is why we have a problem, Houston. We are going to look at a few examples at how the criminal justice system takes a page out of the Hollywood playbook, but before we do, let's take a look at how the pros in Hollywood have perfected their dark arts. Consider this example:

You decide to watch a few "reality" shows on TV. The first show you turn to is *The Dating Experiment*. You start watching just in time to see Jennifer say how much she loves Todd. Commercial. You flip the channel, and land on the show *Blind Date*, just in time to see how bored Frank is on his date with Yvette. But will love eventually conquer his temporary torpor? Tune in tomorrow!

You decide to abandon these scintillating narratives for the time being, and choose instead to surf the web, when you land on this eye-opening story, which introduces you to the buzz word of the week, *frankenbiting*:[1]

The heart, Woody Allen said, wants what it wants. For the producers of the ABC reality show *The Dating Experiment*, that was a problem. The heart of one of their female participants did not want what they needed it to want. **She disliked one of her suitors, but it would make a better story if she liked him.**

---

[1] http://www.time.com/time/magazine/article/0,9171,1154194,00.html (retrieved March 19, 2012)

So they sat her down for an interview. Who's your favorite celebrity? they asked. She replied that she really loved Adam Sandler. Later, in the editing room, they spliced out Sandler's name and dropped in audio of her saying the male contestant's name.

That's love, reality-style. This trick, says Todd Sharp, who was a program consultant on the series, is called Frankenbiting. And it happens more often than you may suspect. . . .

[E]ven savvy viewers who realize that their favorite reality shows are cast, contrived and edited to be dramatic may have no idea how brazen the fudging can be. **Quotes are manufactured, crushes and feuds constructed out of whole cloth, episodes planned in multiact "storyboards" before taping, scenes stitched together out of footage shot days apart. . . .**

[D]etails of how these shows manipulate reality have begun leaking out — because of a dispute with the employees hired to do the jiggering. **Those staff members — who create story lines, coach interview answers and cobble together video — say their work amounts to writing, and they are suing their networks and production companies, arguing that they deserve to be covered by the Writers Guild of America. . . .**

It's not that the shows have line-for-line scripts (although reality writers have charged that Paris Hilton was fed lines on *The Simple Life*). But Jeff Bartsch, a freelance reality-show editor, says there are many ways of using footage to shape a story. Bartsch worked on *Blind Date*, a syndicated dating show that features hookups gone right — and comically wrong. If a date was dull or lukewarm, the editors would juice the footage by running scenes out of order or out of context. To make it seem like a man was bored, they would cut from his date talking to a shot of him looking around and unresponsive — even though it was taken while she was in the restroom and he was alone. **"You can really take something black and make it white,"** Bartsch says. . . .

Hooray for Hollywood?

Well, perhaps we expect *false* reality from Hollywood, but we expect *real* reality from our justice system. Unfortunately, when we survey the scene, we quickly learn that the American ideal of justice for *all* is as real as Jennifer's love for Todd.

We can start by looking at a very basic, illustrative case. In 2009, a Georgetown student named Alexandra Torrens-Vilas was arrested in Florida for driving under the influence. But immediately before she was arrested, her car was rear-ended by a patrol car driven by Officer Joel Francisco, who apparently was not much of a Mario Andretti himself, since he collided with her after she had parked her car in the left lane of the roadway to retrieve a cat that had jumped out of her window. As Mike Celizic reported in August 3 of that year for *Today.com*,[1]

> In preparing her defense, Torrens-Vilas' attorneys had requested copies of dash-cam videos from the patrol cars that responded. The videos showed Torrens-Vilas performing sobriety tests, but the attorneys realized there was missing material. Unable to get the missing video from Hollywood police, the attorneys finally obtained it from the state.
>
> What they saw not only resulted in all charges against Torrens-Vilas being dropped, it also led to the suspension of five Hollywood police personnel. **Rather than admit to being responsible for rear-ending the woman's car, police concocted a story that would make everything her fault.**
>
> "It confirmed everything that I thought," Torrens-Vilas told Lauer. "I knew that that's not what happened that night, and it just confirmed everything that I've been saying from the beginning."
>
> According to the tape, Officer Dewey Pressley took the lead in the plot, saying, "Well, I don't lie and make things up ever because it's wrong, but if I need to bend it a little to protect a cop, I'm gonna."
>
> He then tells another officer: **"I will write the narrative out for you. I will tell you exactly how to word it so it can get him off the hook. You see the angle of her car? You see the way it's like this? As far as I'm concerned, I am going to word it she is in the left-hand lane. We will do a little**

---

[1] "Tape reveals cops tried to frame her for crash,"
http://today.msnbc.msn.com/id/32266883/ns/today-today_people/ (retrieved March 24, 2011) (emphasis supplied).

Walt Disney to protect the cop, because it wouldn't matter because she was drunk anyway."

"[D]o a little Walt Disney to protect the cop": now that's what I call *Mickey-Mouse justice*! This tale from the state of Disney (*Pinocchio*) actually teaches us some very important lessons which will be useful as we analyze Oswald's case:

1) Sometimes crimes are "pinned" on defendants on whom the charges can plausibly "stick" due to a seemingly related infraction;

2) Some cops will lie if they feel they are justified, or if it "doesn't matter", or some other reason to which we are not privy;

3) When evidence is missing (like the video in this case), it's not necessarily due to *negligence*; sometimes it's missing to *protect the guilty*.

That tale had a "happy" ending. Unfortunately, the roulette wheel of justice has only one green slot. An article in *The New York Times* in 2011 told a similar tale, unfortunately one far more common, whose "happy" ending was delayed by *decades*: [1]

> During his 30 years in prison, Cornelius Dupree Jr. twice rejected his chance for freedom because an admission of guilt for rape and robbery was the price of parole. "Whatever your truth is, you have to stick with it," Mr. Dupree explained this month after a Texas judge exonerated him of the 1979 crime on the basis of DNA evidence kept in long-term county storage.
>
> Mr. Dupree's freedom highlighted the fact that Dallas County, unlike so many other jurisdictions, bothered to retain DNA samples across decades. No less a factor is an exemplary change in the attitude of the district attorney's office. For the last four years, under the leadership of District Attorney Craig Watkins, it has cooperated in the DNA exoneration of 21 wrongly convicted citizens who lost decades of their freedom. All but one were convicted on the basis of incorrect eyewitness testimony.

---

[2] "A Joy to be Free," http://www.nytimes.com/2011/01/17/opinion/17mon3.html (retrieved March 24, 2011).

30 years in jail for a crime he didn't commit, convicted on false testimony! Mr. Dupree was far less lucky than Ms. Torrens-Vilas, serving decades in prison. However, he at least *was* released. But numerous innocent convicts not nearly as fortunate as Mr. Dupree have *not* been released, and even when there is telling evidence that the evidence which put them in prison was manufactured, they can still lose on appeal.

This latter phenomenon was demonstrated in the case of Kevin Cooper. Cooper was a convict formerly convicted of rape who had escaped from a minimum security prison on June 1. Four days later, on June 5, the family of Douglas Ryen was murdered (with the exception of Mr. Ryen's eight-year-old son, Josh, who survived). Cooper had chosen as his hideout after the escape from prison the house next door to the Ryen's, which made him the most likely suspect. Cooper was, in fact, convicted of the murders. [1]

However, while Cooper would appear at first glance to have been the most likely perpetrator, there were grave issues with the way the trial proceeded, and in fact, it is entirely possible that he was innocent of the charges. Judge W. Fletcher discussed the issues in a dissent published on May 11, 2009 (*Cooper* at 5430):

> The State of California may be about to execute an innocent man.

In his dissent, Judge Fletcher gave numerous examples of how the evidence in the case was *extremely* suspect. For example, testimony by the child had indicated that there were *several* murderers, not just one (*Cooper* at 5436; citations omitted):

> Josh Ryen, the only survivor of the attack, first communicated to SBCSD Deputy Sharp that the murderers were three white men. This statement was the likely source of an entry in the police log during the afternoon of June 5, stating that the suspects were "three young males" driving the Ryens' white station wagon.

---

[1] For details, see *Cooper v. Brown*, 565 F.3d 581 (9th Cir. 2009) , found at http://www.ca9.uscourts.gov/datastore/opinions/2009/05/11/05-990040.pdf. (Retrieved March 25, 2011). Subsequent citations will refer to the PDF which starts at page 5429.

But this obviously exculpating evidence was radically transformed at the time of the trial (*Cooper* at 5449):

> Deputies misrepresented his recollections and gradually shaped his testimony so that it was consistent with the prosecution's theory that there was only one killer.

There was further manipulation related to laboratory tests related to Cooper's genetic profile (*Cooper* at 5449):

> A single drop of blood in the hallway outside the Ryen master bathroom — several feet away from any of the victims — had characteristics consistent with Cooper's genetic profile and inconsistent with the victims'. The crime lab conducted serological testing of this blood drop (entered into evidence as A-41) under suspicious circumstances. The criminologist who conducted the testing arrived at one result, and then altered his records to show a different result that conformed to Cooper's known blood characteristics.

A similar contradiction was found with some extremely incriminating evidence, a green button. However, like many other pieces of evidence in this case (like a hatchet sheath), there was more to the story (*Cooper* at 5452; emphasis supplied):

> Deputies discovered a green, blood-stained button near the closet in [the bedroom where Cooper was hiding out]. It resembled buttons found on certain "camp jackets" issued at CIM. The blood on the button was type A, consistent with Cooper and Doug Ryen. The green button was discovered under the same suspicious circumstances as the hatchet sheath, strongly suggesting it was planted in the . . . bedroom after Cooper had become a suspect. Further, its color showed that it came from a **green** prison-issued jacket. Uncontradicted evidence at trial showed that Cooper was wearing a **brown** or tan prison-issued jacket when he escaped.

The significance of what appeared to be numerous examples of manufactured evidence was pointed out by Judge Fletcher (*Cooper* at 5454):

Cooper claims that the State presented false evidence at trial, in violation of *Mooney v. Holohan*, 294 U.S. 103 (1935), and *Napue v. Illinois*, 360 U.S. 264 (1959). Second, Cooper claims that the State failed to reveal exculpatory evidence, in violation of *Brady v. Maryland*, 373 U.S. 83 (1963). Under both claims, Cooper claims actual innocence under *Schlup v. Delo*, 513 U.S. 298 (1995).

Unfortunately, Judge Fletcher was only writing a dissent. The Circuit Court of Appeals voted to uphold the conviction, and the Supreme Court refused to hear an appeal from that decision. [1]

Let's wind up this discussion of after-the-fact manufacturing of evidence with one final example, from *Ricciuti v. N.Y.C. Transit Authority* (124 F.3d 123 at 126; August 21, 1997). This case, whose subject matter was a bias-related assault by Alfred and Daniel Ricciuti on African-American NYC corrections officer Harlice Watson, was centered around a false confession by Alfred Ricciuti (after an arrest by officer Henry Lopez) to Lieutenant Robert Wheeler, a confession contained in an *unsigned* memorandum (emphasis supplied):

A key piece of evidence in the investigation was a statement contained in an unsigned memorandum typed on Transit Authority letterhead. That memorandum reads:

Lt. Wheeler III interviewed Deft. # 1 [Alfred Ricciuti] at 1725hrs. at District 11.

Deft. states that "I was walking down the street and I bumped into this nigger." "I said I was sorry but I was a little drunk and I don't back down from anybody." "I hit the man and the man punched me back so I hit this guy again and the man hits me and knocks me down." . . . *"I'm not a rowdy guy but I'm not afraid of anyone, even if they have a gun."* . . .

The statement contained in this memorandum found its way verbatim into several subsequent investigation reports prepared in connection with the bias investigation, and

[1] The Supreme Court handed down its decision on November 30, 2009.
http://en.wikipedia.org/wiki/Kevin_Cooper_(inmate) (retrieved May 17, 2011). See also
http://off2dr.com/smf/index.php?topic=2168.0 (retrieved May 17, 2011).

apparently based largely on this statement, the assault was classified as bias-related.

The Ricciutis insist this "confession" was fabricated by Lt. Wheeler. Alfred Ricciuti denies ever making a statement to Lt. Wheeler, and Daniel Ricciuti, who swears he was in his uncle's presence the entire time, avers that no such statement was ever made. Officer Lopez admitted in his deposition that he would have made a notation in his notebook had such a statement been made in his presence, but there was no such notation. Although the statement "admits" Alfred Ricciuti was "a little drunk," none of Officer Lopez's arrest notes indicate that either of the Ricciutis was intoxicated. Both plaintiffs vehemently deny uttering any racial epithets at any time.

The court determined that this was a *false confession*, and noted the constitutional issues (124 F3rd at 130; emphasis supplied):

This argument — an ill-conceived attempt to erect a legal barricade to shield police officials from liability — is built on the most fragile of foundations; it is based on an incorrect analysis of the law and at the same time betrays a grave misunderstanding of those responsibilities which the police must have toward the citizenry in an open and free society. **No arrest, no matter how lawful or objectively reasonable, gives an arresting officer or his fellow officers license to deliberately manufacture false evidence against an arrestee. To hold that police officers, having lawfully arrested a suspect, are then free to fabricate false confessions at will, would make a mockery of the notion that Americans enjoy the protection of due process of the law and fundamental justice. Like a prosecutor's knowing use of false evidence to obtain a tainted conviction, a police officer's fabrication and forwarding to prosecutors of known false evidence works an unacceptable "corruption of the truth-seeking function of the trial process."** *United States v. Agurs*, 427 U.S. 97, 104, 49 L. Ed. 2d 342, 96 S. Ct. 2392 (1976); *Giglio v. United States*, 405 U.S. 150, 153, 31 L. Ed. 2d 104, 92 S. Ct. 763 (1972); *Mooney v. Holohan*, 294 U.S. 103, 112, 79 L. Ed. 791, 55 S. Ct. 340 (1935).

When a police officer creates false information likely to influence a jury's decision and forwards that

information to prosecutors, he violates the accused's constitutional right to a fair trial, and the harm occasioned by such an unconscionable action is redressable in an action for damages under 42 U.S.C. § 1983. *United States ex rel Moore v. Koelzer*, 457 F.2d 892, 893-94 (3d Cir. 1972); see also *Smith v. Springer*, 859 F.2d 31, 34 (7th Cir. 1988); *Geter v. Fortenberry*, 849 F.2d 1550, 1559 (5th Cir. 1988). **Here, a reasonable jury could find, based on the evidence, that defendants Lopez and Wheeler violated the plaintiffs' clearly established constitutional rights by conspiring to fabricate and forward to prosecutors a known false confession almost certain to influence a jury's verdict.**

We have now seen several examples of reality manufactured by the government after the fact. Just isolated incidents? Only a few bad apples? I guess that would depend on how you define "few." In any event, these "few" are only a few examples of a much larger problem. If you want to see how pervasive this problem is, the small sampling of law review articles below related to the topic will give an indication of its depth. The interested reader is referred to these articles, and the many cases and articles to which they subsequently refer:

- Rodney Uphoff, "Convicting The Innocent: Aberration Or Systemic Problem?", 2006 *Wis. L. Rev.* 739 (2006).

- Simon A. Cole, "Forensics Symposium: The Use And Misuse Of Forensic Evidence; Fingerprinting: The First Junk Science?," 28 *Okla. City U.L. Rev.* 73 (2003).

- Tamara F. Lawson, "Can Fingerprints Lie?: Re-Weighing Fingerprint Evidence In Criminal Jury Trials," 31 *Am. J. Crim. L.* 1 (2003).

- Richard H. Underwood, "Perjury: An Anthology," 13 *Ariz. J. Int'l & Comp. Law* 307 (1996).

- Steven P. Ragland, "Using The Master's Tools: Fighting Persistent Police Misconduct With Civil Rico," 51 *Am. U.L. Rev.* 139 (2001).

- Richard A. Leo, Steven A. Drizin, Peter J. Neufeld, Bradley R. Hall & Amy Vatner, "Bringing Reliability Back In: False Confessions And Legal Safeguards In The Twenty-First Century," 2006 *Wis. L. Rev.* 479 (2006).

- Mitchell P. Schwartz, "Compensating Victims of Police-Fabricated Confessions," 70 *U. Chi. L. Rev.* 1119 (2003).

- Gabriel J. Chin, Scott C. Wells, "The "Blue Wall Of Silence" As Evidence Of Bias And Motive To Lie: A New Approach To Police Perjury," 59 *U. Pitt. L. Rev.* 233 (1998).

- Jeffrey L. Kirchmeier, Stephen R. Greenwald, Harold Reynolds, and Jonathan Sussman, "Vigilante Justice: Prosecutor Misconduct In Capital Cases," 55 *Wayne L. Rev.* 1327 (2009).

- "Prosecutors Must Disclose Exculpatory Information When The Net Effect Of The Suppressed Evidence Makes It Reasonably Probable That Disclosure Would Have Produced A Different Result - *Kyles v. Whitley,* 115 *S. Ct.* 1555 (1995)," 26 *Seton Hall L. Rev.* 832 (1996).

- Nadia Soree, "When the Innocent Speak: False Confessions, Constitutional Safeguards, and the Role Of Expert Testimony," 32 *Am. J. Crim. L.* 191 (2005).

- Brandon L. Garrett, "Innocence, Harmless Error, And Federal Wrongful Conviction Law," 2005 *Wis. L. Rev.* 35 (2005).

- Myrna Raeder, "What Does Innocence Have To Do With It?: A Commentary On Wrongful Convictions And Rationality," 2003 *Mich. St. L. Rev.* 1315 (2003).

Now, most of the cases in these law review articles refer to the *least* obnoxious side of evidence manufacturing, which is that some branches of government will on occasion manufacture reality "after the fact" to secure the unjust convictions of those who lost the American justice lottery.

But would any branch of government dare to manufacture reality "before the fact" to achieve likewise unjust objectives? The surprising answer is *yes* . . .

Let's turn to that next.

Category 2: Manufacturing Reality *Before* The Fact

The "dirty little secret" of government is that on occasion it will not only *frame* people for crimes they did not commit, it will on occasion *create crimes out of thin air,* as Samuel Gross and Barbara O'Brien reported in 2008 in the *Journal of Empirical Legal Studies,* summarizing data also contained in the *Frontline* documentary *LAPD Blues:* [1]

> We do know about a substantial number of exonerations of innocent defendants who pled guilty and received comparatively light sentences in one particularly disturbing factual context. In the past decade, several systematic programs of police perjury have been uncovered, which ultimately led to exonerations of at least 135 innocent defendants who had been framed for illegal possession of drugs or guns in Los Angeles, Dallas, and Tulia, Texas. **These are not cases in which the wrong person was convicted for a real crime, but ones where the police lied about crimes that had never happened at all.** Most of these innocent drug and gun defendants pled guilty and had been released by the time

---

[1] Samuel R. Gross and Barbara O'Brien, "Frequency and Predictors of False Conviction: Why We Know So Little, and New Data on Capital Cases," *Journal of Empirical Legal Studies* Volume 5, Issue 4, 927–962, December 2008. In footnotes to the above, the authors noted "The Los Angeles cases were discovered when a major scandal in the Rampart Division of the Los Angeles Police Department unraveled, beginning in September 1999. Ultimately, at least 100 defendants were exonerated. For an in-depth look at the Rampart scandal, including links to official reports and reviews and a summary of the scandal's aftermath, see PBS Frontline, L.A.P.D. Blues, available at http://www.pbs.org/wgbh/pages/ frontline/shows/lapd/bare. html; see also *Report of the Rampart Independent Review Panel* (Nov. 16, 2000), available at http://www.ci.la.ca.us/oig/rirprpt.pdf; Lou Cannon, "One Bad Cop," *N.Y. Times Magazine,* Oct. 1, 2000, at 32; Anna Gorman, For Some, it's Too Late to Overturn Convictions: Judges Are Refusing to Review Cases Involving Tainted Officers if Inmate Is No Longer in Custody, L.A. Times, May 19, 2002, at B1 (nearly 150 convictions overturned); David P. Leonard, Policing the Criminal Justice System: Different Worlds, Different Realities, 34 Loy. L.A. L. Rev. 863, 872-79 (2001) (Rampart residents overwhelmingly Latino); Stephen Yagman, Bada Bing, L.A. City Hall Has a Rico Ring, L.A. Times, Apr. 25, 2001, at B9 (more than 110 convictions overturned); Texas Scandal Throws Doubt on Anti-Drug Task Forces, USA Today, Mar. 31, 2004, at 3A; Adam Liptak, $5 Million Settlement Ends Case of Tainted Texas Sting, N.Y. Times, Mar. 11, 2004, at A14; Polly Ross Hughes, Perry Pardons 35 in Tulia Sting, Houston Chronicle, Aug. 23, 2003, at A1."

they were exonerated two to four years later. These cases do demonstrate that some innocent defendants who are not facing the death penalty or very long terms of imprisonment will plead guilty in return for greatly reduced sentences.

Notice the drop. We first started with examples of how a crime can be "pinned" on the innocent. This paragraph now shows us how a "non-crime" can be pinned on the innocent. Can it get any worse? Yes.

Manufacturing reality after the fact to put a person in jail for a crime not committed is one thing — but actually *committing* a *crime* and then attempting to "pin" it on an innocent party is quite another — and doubly sinister.

As you might gather, any evidence of government misconduct of this magnitude would normally be destined for the shredder, but a few accounts and documents detailing these disturbing schemes have miraculously survived.

Some of them have survived because they are not documenting manufactured *crimes*, only manufactured *reality*; however, once we realize that government can manufacture reality, it takes no great leap of the imagination to realize that government can manufacture the "reality" that a crime *they* committed was perpetrated by "X".

So, let's begin this journey of discovery by starting with two comparatively benign examples from World War II, *Operation Mincemeat* and Hitler's Jig.

Operation Mincemeat was a plan devised by the British to deceive Hitler that the Allies planned to invade Greece and Sardinia instead of Sicily. The method of operation was to make sure that a body with "top secret" Allied war plans washed up on shore; when the Germans read the plans, they would think that they were viewing reality of the real variety, and act accordingly.

To create the illusion of reality, a body first had to be found. The team behind *Operation Mincemeat* charged with finding the body was headed by Lieutenant Commander Ewen Montagu, a Royal Navy intelligence officer: [1]

With the help of the renowned pathologist Sir Bernard Spilsbury, Montagu and his team determined what kind of body they needed: a man who appeared to have died at sea by hypothermia and drowning, and then floated ashore after

[1] http://en.wikipedia.org/wiki/Operation_Mincemeat (retrieved March 26, 2012).

several days. However, finding a usable body seemed almost impossible, as indiscreet inquiries would cause talk, and it was impossible to tell a dead man's next of kin what the body was wanted for. Under quiet pressure, Bentley Purchase, coroner of St. Pancras District in London, obtained the body of a 34-year old Welsh man named Glyndwr Michael, on the condition that the man's real identity would never be revealed. The man had died after ingesting rat poison which contained phosphorus. After being ingested, the phosphide reacts with hydrochloric acid in the human stomach, generating phosphine, a highly toxic gas. Coroner Purchase explained, "This dose was not sufficient to kill him outright, and its only effect was so to impair the functioning of the liver that he died a little time afterwards", leaving few clues to the cause of death. Montagu later claimed the man died from pneumonia, and that the family had been contacted and permission obtained, but none of this was true. The dead man's parents had died and no known relatives were found.

Once the body had been found, the next step was to build up the story with layer upon layer of verisimilitude. The brilliance of *Operation Mincemeat* was in the level of details used to create the illusion of reality (Wikipedia, *Operation Mincemeat*):

> The next step was creating a "legend": a synthetic identity for the dead man. He became "Captain (Acting Major) William "Bill" Martin, Royal Marines", born 1907, in Cardiff, Wales, and assigned to Headquarters, Combined Operations. . . . The rank of acting Major made him senior enough to be entrusted with sensitive documents, but not so prominent that anyone would expect to know him. The name "Martin" was chosen because there were several Martins of about that rank in the Royal Marines . . .

And numerous props were used to prop up the "legend" (Wikipedia, *Operation Mincemeat*):

- In keeping with his rank, he was given some good quality underwear, at the time extremely difficult to obtain due to rationing.

- He also had a pompous letter from his father, a letter from the family solicitor, and a letter from Ernest Whitley Jones, joint general manager of Lloyds Bank, demanding payment of an overdraft of £79 19s 2d (£79.96). There were a book of stamps, a silver cross and St Christopher's medallion, a pencil stub, keys, a used twopenny bus ticket, ticket stubs from a London theatre, a bill for four nights' lodging at the Naval and Military Club, and a receipt from Gieves & Hawkes for a new shirt (this last was an error: it was for cash, and officers never paid cash at Gieves; but the Germans did not catch it). All these documents were on authentic stationery or billheads.

- To make the Major even more believable, Montagu and his team decided to suggest that he was a bit careless. His ID card was marked as a replacement for one that had been lost, and his pass to Combined Operations HQ had expired a few weeks before his departure and not been renewed.

- While the cover identity was created by Montagu and his team, the false documents were also being created. Montagu and his team insisted that these must be at the very highest level, so that there would be no question of the supposed senders being misinformed. The main document was a personal letter from "Archie Nye" (Lt. General Sir Archibald Nye, Vice Chief of the Imperial General Staff) to "My dear Alex" (General Sir Harold Alexander, commander of 18th Army Group in Algeria and Tunisia). The letter covered several "sensitive" subjects, such as the (unwanted) award of Purple Heart medals by U.S. forces to British servicemen serving with them, and the appointment of a new commander of the Guards Brigade. This explained its being hand-carried rather than sent through regular channels.

Operation Mincemeat was "swallowed whole" by the Germans, and resulted in reducing German combat strength against the Russians. Now, while some of the British military had successfully manufactured fiction designed for consumption by a German audience, another division was manufacturing fiction for the people back home.

In a newsreel that was shown in movie theaters in 1940, Hitler was said to have danced a jig after descending from a railway car in which France had surrendered. But the "dance" was illusory. Using an optical printer, British film editors took an image of Hitler raising his leg and looped it over and over, making him appear to dance a ludicrous jig: [1]

These two examples are fairly well-known, and few would argue that these were not justifiable deceptions. All's fair in love and war, as the saying goes.

But when we get to the story of Pearl Harbor, we find a deception that makes you begin to question the saying: apparently, America was *not surprised* by the attack on the Hawaiian naval base (*Towers Of Deception*, p. 274):

> The most painstakingly researched book on Pearl Harbor is Robert B. Stinnett's *Day Of Deceit: The Truth About FDR And Pearl Harbor*. Based on 17 years' research and tens of thousands of previously unreleased documents, US Navy veteran Stinnett proves that Roosevelt successfully arranged for Japan to strike US facilities at the cost of 2,460 US lives.
>
> Roosevelt secretly assigned a top aide to draw up what became an eight-point plan to provoke Japan. Cutting down Japan's oil supplies was part of the plan and was carried out, as were the other seven points. The keys to the plan were that "the US should not fire the first shot" and that US losses should be great enough to inflame public opinion. By August 6, 1941, Japanese forces were poised to attack the CS naval base at Pearl

---

[1] http://www.museumofhoaxes.com/hoax/archive/permalink/hitlers_silly_dance/ (retrieved March 26, 2012).

Harbor in Hawaii, where the Pacific fleet had been purposefully exposed to them. The Franklin Delano Roosevelt US high command had broken all the Japanese codes (although the Japanese did not know this) and could have prevented the attack, but Roosevelt made sure it was unopposed.

Here is the memo containing the eight-point plan designed to inflame Japan, authored by Lieutenant Commander Arthur McCollum, head of the Far East desk of Navy intelligence (*Day Of Deceit*, p. 275):

9.   IT IS NOT BELIEVED THAT IN THE PRESENT STATE OF POLITICAL OPINION THE UNITED STATES GOVERNMENT IS CAPABLE OF DECLARING WAR AGAINST JAPAN WITHOUT MORE ADO; AND IT IS BARELY POSSIBLE THAT VIGOROUS ACTION ON OUR PART MIGHT LEAD THE JAPANESE TO MODIFY THEIR ATTITUDE. THEREFORE, THE FOLLOWING COURSE OF ACTION IS SUGGESTED:

    A. MAKE AN ARRANGEMENT WITH BRITAIN FOR THE USE OF BRITISH BASES IN THE PACIFIO, PARTICULARLY SINGAGPORE.

    B. MAKE AN ARRANGEMENT WITH HOLLAND FOR THE USE OF BASE FACILITIES AND ACQUISITION OF SUPPLIES IN THE DUTCH EAST INDIES.

    C. GIVE ALL POSSIBLE AID TO THE CHINESE GOVERNMENT OF CHIANG-KAI-SHEK.

    D. SEND A DIVISION OF LONG RANGE HEAVY CRUISERS TO THE ORIENT, PHILIPPINES, OR SINGAPORE.

    E. SEND TWO DIVISIONS OF SUBMARINES TO THE ORIENT.

    F. KEEP THE MAIN STRENGTH OF THE U.S.FLEET NOW IN THE PACIFIC IN THE VICINITY OF THE HAWAIIAN ISLANDS.

    G. INSIST THAT THE DUTCH REFUSE TO GRANT JAPANESE DEMANDS FOR UNDUE ECONOMIC CONCESSIONS, PARTI- CULARLY OIL.

    H. COMPLETELY EMBARGO ALL U.S. TRADE WITH JAPAN, IN COLLABORATION WITH A SIMILAR EMBARGO IMPOSED BY THE BRITISH EMPIRE.

10.   IF BY THESE MEANS JAPAN COULD BE LED TO COMMIT AN OVERT OF WAR, SO MUCH THE BETTER. AT ALL EVENTS WE MUST BE FULLY PREPARED TO ACCEPT THE THREAT OF WAR.

A.H. McCOLLUM ✓

CC-OP-16
  OP-16-F
  FILE

Justifiable? Considering that it brought America into a war it might well have entered too late, we have to say "yes." At the same time, other books show a more disturbing side to that war, which if true may initiate yet another reassessment on our part.

Interested readers are urged to follow this thread off-line, starting with the books *Wall Street And The Rise Of Hitler* by Antony C. Sutton and *IBM And The Holocaust: The Strategic Alliance Between Nazi Germany And America's Most Powerful Corporation* by Edwin Black, as well as other books by those authors, and similar books on the same topic. If the thread truly leads in the direction these authors have pointed to, the following picture might emerge: one group of Americans finance Hitler, forcing another group of Americans to provoke an attack on Pearl Harbor, which means that these two groups of Americans, if it turned out they were *coordinating* their actions, *were manufacturing a global war.* A thesis this provocative, needless to say, requires an extraordinary amount of evidence for justification, but research this important must be gathered.

All that at a later time: as we return to the main point, it is clear the direction in which we are headed. Eventually we are going to be crossing the line of justifiability: is there ever a time when military deception *cannot* be justified?

I believe the answer must be "yes": the line in the sand is the *false-flag* operation, where a government commits a crime posing as an enemy, then uses the crime to justify an attack on that same enemy (*Towers Of Deception*, p. 262):

What Is a False Flag Operation?

A false-flag operation is a contrived, staged event, usually shocking, planned by its actual perpetrators to appear to have been done by others. The term comes from naval history: a ship flying a flag not of its true nationality is flying a "false flag." For purposes of this chapter we categorize an event as false flag if it:

(a) Involves significant destruction of life and/or property, or

(b) Is fairly spectacular. The Gunpowder Plot is an example. Although there was no loss of life (until the alleged plotters were executed), it qualifies because of the stunning impact on the England of that time, and

(c) Is used by the perpetrators for a major political purpose, such as to launch or justify war, stage a coup, destabilize a society, subvert a popular movement, round up "undesirables" or cause a major change in policy. Most false-flag ops enable the deceitful rulers who order them to accomplish several aims among those listed.

The *Gunpowder Plot* was one example, and the *Reichstag Fire* created by Nazi Germany was another. And there is evidence that even America contemplated such an operation, in a memo written for a false-flag op known as *Operation Northwoods.* [1]

---

[1] http://en.wikipedia.org/wiki/Operation_Northwoods. Other URLS are
http://www.smeggys.co.uk/operation_northwoods.php,

This memo was sent to President Kennedy, having been authored by the Joint Chiefs of staff. This memo was ordered destroyed along with numerous other documents related to the "Bay of Pigs", but was the "one that got away," and with the mask ripped off provides a peek into how the federal government attempted to do a "Walt Disney" on Cuba.

The basic concept outlined in the March 13, 1962 *Northwoods* memo was to create a series of incidents that would falsely implicate Cuba in an attack on an American plane, thereby "justifying" an invasion of the United States on that country.

One of the main goals of this plan was to "camouflage the ultimate objective" of making a phony reality credible by enabling "a logical build-up of incidents to be combined with other seemingly unrelated events" to "develop an international image of a Cuban threat to peace":

3. This plan, incorporating projects selected from the attached suggestions, or from other sources, should be developed to focus all efforts on a specific ultimate objective which would provide adequate justification for US military intervention. Such a plan would enable a logical build-up of incidents to be combined with other seemingly unrelated events to camouflage the ultimate objective and create the necessary impression of Cuban rashness and irresponsibility on a large scale, directed at other countries as well as the United States. The plan would also properly integrate and time phase the courses of action to be pursued. The desired resultant from the execution of this plan would be to place the United States in the apparent position of suffering defensible grievances from a rash and irresponsible government of Cuba and to develop an international image of a Cuban threat to peace in the Western Hemisphere.

http://www.gwu.edu/~nsarchiv/news/20010430/doc1.pdf, and
http://media.nara.gov/media/images/36/15/36-1469a.jpg (retrieved 3/28/2011).

The Joint Chiefs planned to achieve the desired "legitimate provocation" on the part of U.S. with "harassment plus deceptive actions":

1. Since it would seem desirable to use legitimate provocation as the basis for US military intervention in Cuba a cover and deception plan, to include requisite preliminary actions such as has been developed in response to Task 33 c, could be executed as an initial effort to provoke Cuban reactions. Harassment plus deceptive actions to convince the Cubans of imminent invasion would be emphasized. Our military

The slogan "Made in America" was given a new spin by the *Northwoods* memo: to give the "genuine appearance" that attacks on a U.S. base in Guantanamo were perpetrated by "hostile Cuban forces," incidents should be manufactured to make the attack "credible":

2. A series of well coordinated incidents will be planned to take place in and around Guantanamo to give genuine appearance of being done by hostile Cuban forces.

a. Incidents to establish a credible attack (not in chronological order):

(1) Start rumors (many). Use clandestine radio.

(2) Land friendly Cubans in uniform "over-the-fence" to stage attack on base.

(3) Capture Cuban (friendly) saboteurs inside the base.

(4) Start riots near the base main gate (friendly Cubans).

Then the *Northwoods* team contemplated a series of actions that that can only be described as treasonous, including *blowing up a United States ship* and creating *terrorist actions on United States soil!!*

The military would then exploit the national indignation resulting from their actions through "casualty lists" published in United States newspapers:

3. A "Remember the Maine" incident could be arranged in
several forms:

.   a. We could blow up a US ship in Guantanamo Bay and
blame Cuba.

        b. We could blow up a drone (unmanned) vessel anywhere
in the Cuban waters. We could arrange to cause such incident
in the vicinity of Havana or Santiago as a spectacular result
of Cuban attack from the air or sea, or both. The presence
of Cuban planes or ships merely investigating the intent of
the vessel could be fairly compelling evidence that the ship
was taken under attack. The nearness to Havana or Santiago
would add credibility especially to those people that might
have heard the blast or have seen the fire. The US could
follow up with an air/sea rescue operation covered by US
fighters to "evacuate" remaining members of the non-existent
crew. Casualty lists in US newspapers would cause a helpful
wave of national indignation.

        4. We could develop a Communist Cuban terror campaign in
the Miami area, in other Florida cities and even in Washington.

Pay close attention to this last paragraph! The Joint Chiefs claimed that they could "develop a communist Cuban terror campaign" in Miami and even Washington. But how, pray tell, could they do that? How could they be so confident that the aforementioned "Communists" would cooperate? Here's one theory:

Maybe that was because the supposed "Communists" were actually Americans paid to *pose* as "Communists" by the United States government!

Wow. I need to catch my breath here. Is this really Walt Disney's "America"?

After hinting in the broadest possible terms that they would mobilize Uncle Sam's military might to murder Americans on a ship, the Joint Chiefs next indicated they had no problem executing innocent Cuban refugees, refugees who risked their lives to flee the gray and gloomy skies of Cuban dictatorship for the red white and blue opportunities of America — a country which neglected to tell them that the famous Emma Lazarus poem on the *Statue of Liberty* had an asterisk:

> **Give me your tired, your poor,**
> **Your huddled masses yearning to breathe free,**
> **The wretched refuse of your teeming shore.**
> **Send these, the homeless, tempest-tost to me . . . ***

> *** *So we can use them as pawns in a Pentagon-created false-flag operation. It's how we keep the shores of America safe for freedom and democracy.***

After this, with absolutely no trace of irony, the Joint Chiefs of Staff indicated that the "terror campaign" they created to murder innocent Cubans and frame Cuba would project to the international community Cuba's illegitimacy, with the Chiefs showing their deep regard for human life by stipulating that they would only be "wounding" Cuban refugees already in America (unlike their cousins in the boats), closing with what must be one of the least self-aware statements in the history of the universe:

The terror campaign could be pointed at Cuban refugees seeking haven in the United States. We could sink a boatload of Cubans enroute to Florida (real or simulated). We could foster attempts on lives of Cuban refugees in the United States even to the extent of wounding in instances to be widely publicized. Exploding a few plastic bombs in carefully chosen spots, the arrest of Cuban agents and the release of prepared documents substantiating Cuban involvement also would be helpful in projecting the idea of an irresponsible government.

As if this wasn't enough, the *Operation Northwoods* memo indicated the pursuit of a more elaborate conspiracy, extremely deep and sophisticated, utilizing American college students:

8. It is possible to create an incident which will demonstrate convincingly that a Cuban aircraft has attacked and shot down a chartered civil airliner enroute from the United States to Jamaica, Guatemala, Panama or Venezuela. The destination would be chosen only to cause the flight plan   route to cross Cuba. The passengers could be a group of college students off on a holiday or any grouping of persons with a common interest to support chartering a non-scheduled flight.

Perhaps novices in this line of work (considering the fact that this memo was not folded, spindled, drawn, quartered, shredded, sliced, diced, dissected, chopped, mashed, pounded, puréed, burned, bulldozed, or otherwise mutilated), the Joint Chiefs of Staff indicated they would deploy the branch of "government" far more experienced in covert operations like these — the CIA — to create fake identities for the college students, who would be transported in a counterfeit plane (what, you didn't know there were such things?) belonging to a CIA front organization (known as a "proprietary"):

a. An aircraft at Eglin AFB would be painted and numbered as an exact duplicate for a civil registered aircraft belonging to a CIA proprietary organization in the Miami area. At a designated time the duplicate would be substituted for the actual civil aircraft and would be loaded with the selected passengers, all boarded under carefully prepared aliases. The actual registered aircraft would be converted to a drone.

Because killing American college students (unlike passengers on a U.S. ship and refugees from Cuba) would be going too far, the Joint Chiefs of Staff decided to disembark the college students at an Air

Force Base, curiously exposing themselves to the risk that someone would expose the worst-laid plan of mice and men:

b. Take off times of the drone aircraft and the actual
aircraft will be scheduled to allow a rendezvous south of
Florida. From the rendezvous point the passenger-carrying
aircraft will descend to minimum altitude and go directly
into an auxiliary field at Eglin AFB where arrangements will
have been made to evacuate the passengers and return the
aircraft to its original status. The drone aircraft

As I stated, this would have been an amazing risk for the Joint Chiefs. College students would have been duped into participating in an act of treason against the United States, and surely one of them would have gone to the press once they learned how they were used. Why were the Joint Chiefs so sure they could control this leak? You'll see why soon.

In the meantime, with our college students safely disembarked at the base, the main plan would continue. The Chiefs would fly the plane into Cuban airspace, and to mitigate any risk that the Cuban government would not shoot down an airplane with American college students (completely defeating the purpose of showing the American people how dangerous and uncivilized was the Cuban government), the American military would remotely destroy the plane by radio signal:

aircraft to its original status. The drone aircraft
meanwhile will continue to fly the filed flight plan. When
over Cuba the drone will being transmitting on the international distress frequency a "MAY DAY" message stating he
is under attack by Cuban MIG aircraft. The transmission
will be interrupted by destruction of the aircraft which will
be triggered by radio signal. This will allow ICAO radio

To render implausible the inevitable claims of "conspiracy theorists" (i.e. people who can spot a lie a mile off) that this was a terrorist action "Made in the USA", the Joint Chiefs would draw independent radio stations affiliated with the International Civil Aviation Organization (ICAO) into the scheme to add to its credibility:

be triggered by radio signal. This will allow ICAO radio stations in the Western Hemisphere to tell the US what has happened to the aircraft instead of the US trying to "sell" the incident.

Phew!

The *Operation Northwoods* memo: a devastating revelation, an official government document that confirms the worst fears we could have about "our" government.

The Joint Chiefs were well aware of the explosive nature of their memo, as indicated by their recommendations for transmittal:

RECOMMENDATIONS

8. It is recommended that:

a. Enclosure A together with its attachments should be forwarded to the Secretary of Defense for approval and transmittal to the Chief of Operations, Cuba Project.

b. This paper NOT be forwarded to commanders of unified or specified commands.

c. This paper NOT be forwarded to US officers assigned to NATO activities.

d. This paper NOT be forwarded to the Chairman, US Delegation, United Nations Military Staff Committee.

The memo was then forwarded to the only authorized recipient, Secretary of Defense McNamara, who in all likelihood discussed the plan with President Kennedy. Needless to say, Kennedy and/or McNamara, at least one of whom did not have the ethics of a cobra (probably Kennedy), deep-sixed the outlined operations, which was distributed only one year and eight months before President Kennedy's assassination . . .

The *Northwoods* memo offers a breathtaking view into the seamy underside of only *one* American covert operation; and there most likely have been *hundreds*. Power like this gives the green light to the "government" (or, perhaps, a rogue group which has hijacked the government) to manufacture "terrorist incidents" the same way McDonald's manufactures Chicken McNuggets, with no fear of discovery.

We don't often get a look at memos like this, so learn well!

But, given that we *do* have the memo, what *have* we learned? Many, many valuable things, most of which contribute to an understanding of the Kennedy assassination:

- The American government, in this case, represented by the Joint Chiefs of Staff, would perpetrate a scheme of deception to achieve an end, even though the means would be immoral, illegal, and un-American to the core.
- To the people running the show (and as you can see, in this case it literally was a "show"), "War is hell": murdering and wounding innocent people is part of the game, and "collateral damage" is the price others pay when the military decides to flex its muscles.
- To some of the people running the show (the ones at the top, unfortunately), framing an innocent government with a crime it did not commit was *A-OK* and *SOP*.
- The military had the *ability* to create this deception.
- The military was *immoral enough* to create this deception.
- The military had media assets they knew would publicize their plan.
- The military believed that innocent college students would not reveal their plan, or, if they would, that their comments could be somehow bottled up.

As mentioned, this final point was the potential Achilles heel of the entire enterprise. Recall that college students have been recruited. One of the arguments against conspiracy "theories" is that "someone would have talked" (and that therefore since no one talked, there was no conspiracy), yet obviously this was no concern for the *Northwood* authors. What did they know that we don't?

Perhaps they knew they had *control of the media*, and therefore the ability to control leaks. Perhaps they were aware that agencies such as FBI and CBI had "counterintelligence" programs with the ability and experience to manufacture *news* in the same way the Joint Chiefs could manufacture a *geopolitical crisis*!

Recall that the Military and the CIA are working hand-in-hand. If the Military and the CIA had control of the media, then their scheme was safe from prying eyes.

Control of this nature would, by its nature, involve a good deal of coordination from network to network, from magazine to magazine, from newspaper to newspaper. Hugh Wilford wrote a book on this very topic. The title says it all:

the mighty wurlitzer
HOW THE CIA PLAYED AMERICA

The genesis of the term, according to Wilford, was as follows (*Mighty Wurlitzer*, p. 7; footnote omitted):

> The CIA constructed an array of front organizations that Frank Wisner, the Agency's first chief of political warfare, liked to compare to a "Mighty Wurlitzer" organ, capable of playing any propaganda tune he desired.

If you don't have time to read the Wilford book, but still want to know how the pipes of the organ work in concert, all you need to do is read the following excerpts from a report created by the Church Committee in 1975 and 1976 to investigate the intelligence agencies, a committee which, apart from including Frank Church, included political luminaries from both sides of the political spectrum such as Walter Mondale, Gary Hart, Howard Baker, Barry Goldwater, and Richard Schweiker.

Data describing the operation of the Wurlitzer was found in Book 1 of their report, titled *Foreign And Military Intelligence*, in particular Chapter 10 titled "The Domestic Impact Of Foreign Clandestine Operations: The CIA And Academic Institutions, The Media, And Religious Institutions," to be cited hereinafter as 1 CCR.

The basic concept of the Wurlitzer (or *matrix*, to use another, related term), is to *control the flow of information* through a network of academics, foundations, publishers, and mass media in general, information flowing downhill and eventually resulting in a "hall of mirrors", echo chamber effect where people only report what other people are reporting. As we learned from the Asch effect, if multiple sources report the *same* false information, people see that false information as *reality*. If reality is defined as what people *report*, defining *what* people report is all you need to do.

Here is how the Wurlitzer might look today:

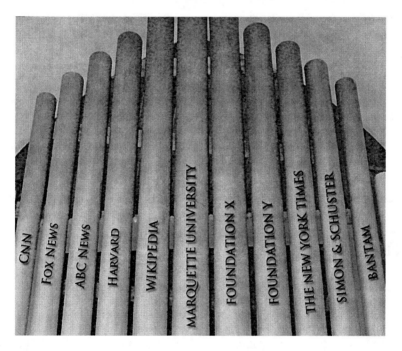

Unfortunately, that metaphor is *linear*, when the actual information path would most likely be *hierarchical* (bottom-up or top-down, depending on your orientation). The best way to control the flow of information is to first control the *source* of information, academics located at universities, the fountainhead from which our knowledge well bubbles, and the role of these academics is to not only *report* the information which is "approved", but also to *lend prestige* to that information, to legitimize it: information which is *not* discussed appears illegitimate because it seems to be a minority, "fringe" view not worthy of discussion by the best and the brightest (1 CCR 189-90):

The Central Intelligence Agency is now using several hundred American academics [11], who in addition to providing leads and, on occasion, making introductions for intelligence purposes, occasionally write books and other material to be used for propaganda purposes abroad. Beyond these, an additional few score are used in an unwitting manner for minor activities.

These academics are located in over 100 American colleges, universities, and related institutes. At the majority of institutions, no one other than the individual concerned is aware of the CIA link. At

While academics generally knew of CIA involvement (and most likely signed "nondisclosure" agreements to not disclose the source of their funds), on other occasions academics could receive grants to do "approved" work without knowing that the CIA was the source (1 CCR 181):

The relationships have varied according to whether made with an institution or an individual, whether the relationship is paid or unpaid, or whether the individuals are "witting"—i.e. aware—of CIA involvement. In some cases, covert involvement provided the CIA with little or no operational control of the institutions involved; funding was primarily a way to enable people to do things they wanted to do.

The grants designed to steer the academics in the "right" direction were provided by numerous foundations: as the Committee reported, of 700 large grants, at least 108 involved "partial or complete CIA funding" (1 CCR 182):

The CIA's intrusion into the foundation field in the 1960s can only be described as massive. Excluding grants from the "Big Three"— Ford, Rockefeller, and Carnegie—of the 700 grants over $10,000 given by 164 other foundations during the period 1963–1966, at least 108 involved partial or complete CIA funding. More importantly, CIA funding was involved in *nearly half* the grants the non-"Big Three" foundations made during this period in the field of international activities. In the same period more than one-third of the grants awarded by non-"Big Three" in the physical, life and social sciences also involved CIA funds.

With the *source* of information controlled, the next step would be to control the *output* of that source, which could be op-ed pieces in newspapers, articles in journals or magazines, or simply books (1 CCR 192-93):

Covert propaganda is the hidden exercise of the power of persuasion. In the world of covert propaganda, book publishing activities have a special place. In 1961 the Chief of the CIA's Covert Action Staff, who had responsibility for the covert propaganda program, wrote:

> Books differ from all other propaganda media, primarily because one single book can significantly change the reader's attitude and action to an extent unmatched by the impact of any other single medium . . . this is, of course, not true of all books at all times and with all readers—but it is true significantly often enough to make books the most important weapon of strategic (long-range) propaganda.

This was no Mickey Mouse operation: well over 1000 books were produced by the CIA's "knowledge" factory (1 CCR 193):

> Well over a thousand books were produced, subsidized or sponsored by the CIA before the end of 1967. Approximately 25 percent of them were written in English. Many of them were published by cultural organizations which the CIA backed, and more often than not the author was unaware of CIA subsidization. Some books, however, involved direct collaboration between the CIA and the writer.
>
>> The advantage of our direct contact with the author is that we can acquaint him in great detail with our intentions; that we can provide him with whatever material we want him to include and that we can check the manuscript at every stage. Our control over the writer will have to be enforced usually by paying him for the time he works on the manuscript, or at least advancing him sums which he might have to repay . . . [the Agency] must make sure the actual manuscript will correspond with our operational and propagandistic intention. . . .

These books could be authored on nearly any topic, depending on the need of the day.

Say some renegade JFK assassination author finds evidence implicating your organization, the CIA, in the assassination of President Kennedy. Because the author has evidence, you cannot implicate him directly as a "nut job", but what you can do is lump him in the same category as an author with an identical thesis on that point, as well as an additional discredited "nut job ready" thesis.

So, let's say you want to discredit this line of JFK research; all you have to do is find an author who postulates viable thesis X and ridiculous thesis Y, and then give *that* author a book contract (not the other guy). There is no need to work with author NJ directly, because you know what he or she is going to say in advance. For example, you might even publish a book like this:

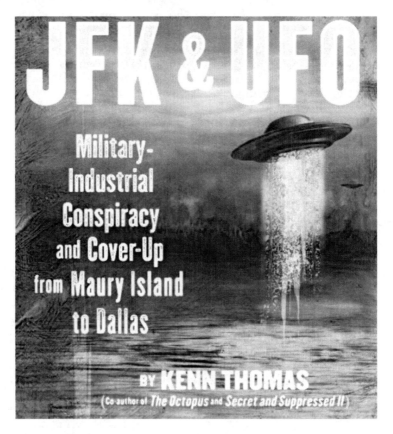

Now, *was* this book published in 2011 sponsored by the CIA in some way, shape or form for the purpose I described? We have no idea. However, what we *do* know is numerous books authored in the 1960s and 70s *were* sponsored by the CIA, without the knowledge of the Americans reading them. One such book was supposedly written by a "Chinese defector" (1 CCR 199):

An American who reads one of these books which purportedly is authored by a Chinese defector would not know that his thoughts and opinions about China are possibly being shaped by an agency of the United States Government. Given the paucity of information and the inaccessibility of China in the 1960s, the CIA may have helped shape American attitudes toward the emerging China. The CIA considers such "fallout" inevitable.

Now, with a ready, willing, and able team of certain eager beaver academics salivating for the chance to get a grant to publish approved writings, and well over 1000 books consequently published with your "ready for prime-time" content, how do you make sure that the content of those books *makes* it to prime time? Well, if you control the media, you can make sure that those books are *reviewed*, and that the topics of those books also become *newsworthy* items. In this regard, it would be important to have a slew of media contacts, and with a secret program in place called *Operation Mockingbird*, the CIA had no shortage there (1 CCR 195):

> Although the variety of the CIA relationships with the U.S. media makes a systematic breakdown of them almost impossible, former CIA Director Colby has distinguished among four types of relationships.[19] These are:
>   (1) Staff of general circulation, U.S. news organizations;
>   (2) Staff of small, or limited circulation, U.S. publications;
>   (3) Free-lance, stringers, propaganda writers, and employees of U.S. publishing houses;
>   (4) Journalists with whom CIA maintains unpaid, occasional, covert contact.

The largest category of the above was "stringers" and "employees", the vast majority of whom were well aware of their CIA relationships. That article by Tom Wicker, that story by James Reston, an *Op-Ed* piece in the *Times* by Errol Morris: a genuine piece, or was this a story planted and/or commissioned and/or approved by the CIA? I have no idea; do you? (1 CCR 196)

> (3) The third, and largest, category of CIA relationships with the U.S. media includes free-lance journalists; "stringers" for newspapers, news magazines and news services; itinerant authors; propaganda writers; and agents working under cover as employees of U.S. publishing houses abroad. With the exception of the last group, the majority of the individuals in this category are bona fide writers or journalists or photographers. Most are paid by the CIA, and virtually all are witting; few, however, of the news organizations to which they contribute are aware of their CIA relationships.

Of course, with all that false "information" floating around out there, you might think that this would have a negative impact on the ability of United States to construct an intelligent domestic and foreign policy. After all, for our policymakers, this false information would be as dangerous as false alarms on the screen of an air traffic

controller. No need to worry though, the senior officials in charge
were well aware of the subterfuge — well, at least *some* of the
subterfuge (1 CCR 201):

> estimates. Regular coordination between the CIA and the State De-
> partment's INR has been instituted to prevent the self-deception of
> "senior U.S. officials" through black propaganda. It should be noted
> that this procedure applies only to black propaganda and only to
> "senior U.S. officials." No mechanism exists to protect the U.S. public
> and the Congress from fallout from black propaganda or any other
> propaganda.

Now, this may strike you as bizarre, but there are some people out
there who don't see a problem with actions of this nature, perhaps due
to some dubious "national security" rationale that functions like a
white blood cell of the mind to diffuse the implications of facts like
these.

My advice to these people is to take a look at how far out that
chain-link fence is from the center of your camp; the farther away
from the center, the more you can call it "security"; the closer to the
center, the more you should call it "prison wire."

The Church Committee, like anyone else whose EEG had not flat-
lined, was well aware of implication of the facts we have seen (1 CCR
179):

> munist ideological and institutional threat. Time and experience would
> also give increasing currency to doubts as to whether it made sense for
> a democracy to resort to practices such as the clandestine use of free
> American institutions and individuals—practices that tended to blur
> the very difference between "our" system and "theirs" that these
> covert programs were designed to preserve.

The bad news, as the Church Report noted, is that what we think
has occurred is different from what can *possibly* occur, and as
Murphy's law tells us, anything that *can* go wrong *will* go wrong, so the
question is, *if* there was a military *coup d'état* in America (unlikely
though we wish that possibility to be), could any such *coup* possibly be
recognized if the military would have *control* over how that coup was
perceived? And if the CIA (or more precisely, one or more handfuls of
highly placed officials in the CIA) was *also* behind a *coup d'état*, that
would not be very good news, due to their control of the media.

That is why the following prediction in the *Times* that any *coup
d'état* in the United States would be CIA-driven was particularly

unwelcome, particularly since it appeared in an article in *The New York Times* on October 3, 1963, just *six weeks* before President Kennedy's assassination![1]

The C.I.A.'s growth was "likened to a malignancy" which the "very high official was not sure even the White House could control . . . any longer." "If the United States ever experiences [an attempt at a coup to overthrow the Government] it will come from the C.I.A. and not the Pentagon." The agency "represents a tremendous power and total unaccountability to anyone."

Now, folks, that is some wake-up call. Note that the source was a "very high official" in the federal government. What official would leak something as provocative as that to *The Times* without approval from President Kennedy himself?

Connect the dots: coup . . . CIA . . . media.

We need to follow this line a little further. Edward Luttwak, a professor at Georgetown University, told us in 1969 that Presidents could be put into power without the benefit of a general election (*Coup D'Etat*, p. ix):

---

[1] "In the Nation: The Intra-Administration War In Vietnam," *The New York Times*, October 3, 1963.

Evolgato imperii arcano, wrote Tacitus: "The secret of empire was out—an Emperor could be made elsewhere than in Rome." Nowadays the secret of empire is that a president can be made otherwise than by a general election and the key to that secret is the subject of this book. It is the coup d'état. In the last ten years, on my individual

Luttwak stated later in his book that an excellent public relations team would be just as effective in maintaining the public order as a legion of black-helmeted SWAT infantry equipped with pepper spray, rubber bullets, and tasers (*Coup D'Etat*, p. 173):

The masses have neither the weapons of the military nor the administrative facilities of the bureaucracy, but their attitude to the new government established after the coup will ultimately be decisive. Our immediate aim will be to enforce public order, but our long-term objective is to gain the acceptance of the masses so that physical coercion will no longer be needed in order to secure compliance with our orders. In both phases we shall use our control over the infrastructure and the means of coercion, but as the coup recedes in time, political means will become increasingly important, physical ones less so.

Seizing the control over the flow of information would be an absolutely critical tool to maintain power (*Coup D'Etat*, p. 117):

Control over the flow of information emanating from the political center will be our most important weapon in establishing our authority after the coup. The seizure of the main means of mass communication will thus be a task of crucial importance. One, though only one, of the

The media that would be best suited in this regard would be *mass* communications, particularly radio and television, which allows you to control the uncritical masses, who would rather watch *Blind Date* than read Luttwak's *Coup D'Etat*; *Blind Date*, admittedly, is probably a lot more entertaining, but *Coup D'état* tells you where the cancer is, and thus gives you a means to fight it (*Coup D'Etat*, p. 174):

Our second and far more flexible instrument will be our control over the means of mass communications; their importance will be particularly great because the flow of all other information will be affected by our physical controls. Moreover, the confused and dramatic events of the coup will mean that the radio and television services will have a particularly attentive and receptive audience. In broadcasting over the radio and television services our purpose is not to provide information about the situation but rather to affect its development by exploiting our monopoly of these media. We will have two principal objectives in the information campaign that will start immediately after the coup: (*a*) to discourage resistance to us by emphasizing the strength of our position; and (*b*) to dampen the fears which would otherwise give rise to such resistance.

Not a touchy-feely guy, this Luttwak. Can't believe what you're reading? Well, since I can't believe what I'm writing, I guess we're on the same page. That, however, is the beauty of evidence; it gives you permission to think any thought naturally flowing from the evidence, including the formerly unthinkable ones.

Now, do we know, based on the information that has so far been presented, that the CIA (or, far more likely, a group of insiders who hijacked the CIA) was behind the assassination of President Kennedy? No, we do not.

We do know this though: if Oswald *was* the assassin of Kennedy, we *don't* necessarily need to worry about that possibility. Conversely, if the evidence shows that Oswald was *not* the assassin of Kennedy, we *do*.

That being the case, don't you wish this book was called *Improbable: The Case Against Lee Harvey Oswald*?

Well, it's not, so let's continue to unwind this intriguing thread.

We know there is a Wurlitzer mechanism, but how does the player of the organ coordinate the pipes? Through memos distributed to "media assets" under contract. As luck would have it, we not only have the *Northwoods* memo that tells us by *implication* there is some mechanism of media control, and the Church Report that *in fact* there was in place a mechanism of media control, we also happen to have one of the memos distributed to CIA station chiefs as *direct evidence* of media control, in a memo related to, of all things, the Kennedy assassination!

This memo was inspired by the Jim Garrison investigation of Clay Shaw, an investigation which could have led directly to the CIA had that investigation not been sabotaged, and an investigation which provided the perfect opportunity to produce a "damage control" memo. On April 1, 1967, the CIA produced a memo that we desperately wish was an April Fool's joke on America, but no luck there.

Eventually declassified in 1998, the memo began as follows:[1]

In the case of the Kennedy assassination, one of the nasty rumors that the Central Intelligence Agency had to squash was the legitimacy of any ideas that then-President Johnson was involved in the

---

[1] Those with a membership to *maryferrell.org*, the premier JFK assassination research website, can access the following document by going to the following URL:
http://www.maryferrell.org/mffweb/archive/naraSearch.do, and typing in the following record number: **104-10404-10376**. Alternatively, you can go to the main webpage, and type the record number into the search results field there. The following URL pulled up the document as of March 30, 2011: http://www.maryferrell.org/mffweb/archive/viewer/showDoc.do?mode=searchResult&absPageId=214533

assassination, and/or that Oswald worked for the CIA, and/or that the CIA was otherwise involved:

American society. Moreover, there seems to be an increasing tendency to hint that President Johnson himself, as the one person who might be said to have benefited, was in some way responsible for the assassination. Innuendo of such seriousness affects not only the individual concerned, but also the whole reputation of the American government. Our organization itself is directly involved: among other facts, we contributed information to the investigation. Conspiracy theories have frequently thrown suspicion on our organization, for example by falsely alleging that Lee Harvey Oswald worked for us. The aim of this dispatch is to provide material for countering and discrediting the claims of the conspiracy theorists, so as to inhibit the circulation of such claims in other countries. Background information is supplied in a classified section and in a number of unclassified attachments.

    3. _Action_. We do _not_ recommend that discussion of the assassination question be initiated where it is not already taking place. Where discussion is active, however, addressees are requested:

The memorandum requested that "friendly elite contacts" (the ones mentioned in the Church report) be informed that the charges of the critics "are without serious foundation", and that certain conspiracy discussions would "appear to be deliberately generated by communist propagandists" (even though there was absolutely no evidence to support either of these allegations):

a. To discuss the publicity problem with liaison and friendly elite contacts (especially politicians and editors), pointing out that the Warren Commission made as thorough an investigation as humanly possible, that the charges of the critics are without serious foundation, and that further speculative discussion only plays into the hands of the opposition. Point out also that parts of the conspiracy talk appear to be deliberately generated by Communist propagandists. Urge them to use their influence to discourage unfounded and irresponsible speculation.

The memo suggested employing "propaganda assets" (i.e., journalists and editors with a previous affiliation with the CIA paid to write or publish articles on demand) to launch unsubstantiated counter-framing memos into the media ether:

b. To employ propaganda assets to answer and refute the attacks of the critics. Book reviews and feature articles are particularly appropriate for this purpose. The unclassified attachments to this guidance should provide useful background material for passage to assets. Our play should point out, as applicable, that the critics are (i) wedded to theories adopted before the evidence was in, (ii) politically interested, (iii) financially interested, (iv) hasty and inaccurate in their research, or (v) infatuated with their own theories.

Notice how just these two memos, the _Northwoods_ memo of March 13, 1962, and the CIA memo of April 1967, along with the revelations of the Church Committee, reveal the amazing power of

government, which *not only* had the will and the way to launch a
military operation with a self-created pretext, but also had the power
to bury these plans as "classified" documents somehow involved in
"protecting" America's "national security," even though in fact they did
just the opposite! They also had the power to enlist the media to tout
the cover story and bury the back-story as well. So, along with the
power to manipulate reality, and the power to *disguise* their
manipulation of reality, they also had the power to use their
"propaganda assets" to discredit anyone who dared to rip off their
mask, dipping into the defamation well and pulling out as many
phrases as needed.

Now, in the case of *Operation Northwoods*, it could be argued that
we should all relax. After all, the plan was presumably vetoed by
McNamara and Kennedy. Can we relax? No!

While the *Northwoods* plan was never put into effect, the
COINTELPRO operation was. That plan was executed by a different
branch of government, the FBI. This massive operation, with roots in
the earliest part of the 20th century, became especially prominent in
the 60s. Memos taken from FBI offices in Media, Pennsylvania in
March 1971 were published in the book *The Cointelpro Papers* for all
the world to see. And what we see in these memos is *Northwood*-style
activity actually carried out.

Take, for example, the well-named "Operation Hoodwink", which
was designed to promote a dispute between the Communist Party and
the Mafia (*The Cointelpro Papers*, p. 42):

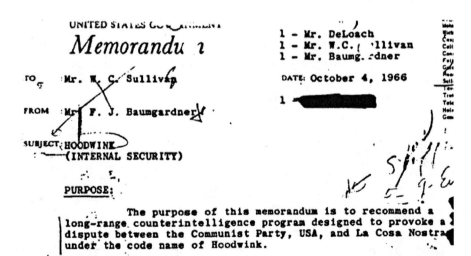

The FBI would provoke the dispute between these groups by anonymously forwarding a counterfeit leaflet supposedly attacking Mafia "labor practices" (*The Cointelpro Papers*, p. 42):

> The New York Office has recommended a specific technique to initiate this program. This technique consists of anonymously forwarding one leaflet to a local La Cosa Nostra leader attacking the labor practices of one of his enterprises. The leaflet would ostensibly be published by a local Party unit. A note with the leaflet would give the impression that it has received wide circulation.

Hoodwink was used against the Communist Party and the Mafia, two organizations not generally held in high esteem. Because of this, some would erroneously conclude a *Hoodwink*-type operation was justified (as confined to these groups). But history shows that when the Pandora's box is opened, the virus inside spreads wide. Yes, alas, it wasn't just the Communist Party and the Mafia hoodwinked. The web of deceit would eventually spread beyond these groups, and other Americans not nearly as deserving would soon find themselves caught in that web. For example, a fake leafleting attack was used, later, to cause disruption in the peace movement against the Vietnam War (*The Cointelpro Papers*, p. 58):

> Enclosed for the Bureau is a copy of an unsigned leaflet entitled "Fly United?", mailed this past week to some 230 selected individuals and organizations in New Left and related groups under the CCINTELPRO at New York with prior Bureau authority.
>
> The leaflet is designed to cause disruption in the peace movement, primarily in the New Mobilization Committee to End the War in Vietnam, and to minimize the growing influ-

A similar approach was used to attack a Puerto Rican pro-independence movement, this time to be distributed through FBI propaganda assets at a newspaper (*The Cointelpro Papers*, p. 70):

> As an alternative, it is suggested San Juan prepare a brief article which would be in the nature of alerting Puerto Ricans to the dangerousness of the various segments of the independence movement in Puerto Rico. Such an article would, of course, have to be interesting enough to interest a newspaper contact to utilize the same and sufficiently informative to develop hostility in the minds of readers towards the elements engaged in the independence movement. The article should be self-sustaining in interest and informative without using confidential information received from our sources, and it should not embarrass the Bureau.

The net began to cast wider; eventually the COINTELPRO net was used not just against the Vietnam Antiwar Movement and the Puerto Rican Pro-independence Movement, but even against the winner of the 1964 Nobel Prize for peace, Dr. Martin Luther King! The FBI decided to celebrate Dr. King's prestigious win in a memo (issued six weeks later) which looked for ways to address the "problem" of removing Dr. King "from the national scene" (*The Cointelpro Papers*, p. 98):

Date: December 1, 1964

To: Mr. W. C. Sullivan

From: J. A. Sizoo

Subject: MARTIN LUTHER KING, JR.

> Reference is made to the attached memorandum DeLoach to Mohr dated 11/27/64 concerning DeLoach's interview with ▮▮▮▮ ▮▮▮▮ and to your informal memo, also attached.
>
> ▮▮▮▮▮▮▮ stated to DeLoach that he was faced with the difficult problem of taking steps to remove King from the national picture. He indicates in his comments a lack of confidence that he, alone, could be successful. It is, therefore, suggested that consideration be given to the following course of action:
>
> That DeLoach have a further discussion with ▮▮▮▮▮ and offer to be helpful to ▮▮▮▮▮ in connection with the problem of the removal of King from the national scene;

You thought that the "I" in "FBI" stood for "investigation" and not "infiltration" or "intimidation" or "instigation"? Think again!

One way the memo proposed to remove King from the national scene was to send Dr. King an anonymous letter that would induce him to commit suicide (!), the suggested content of which follows (*The Cointelpro Papers*, p. 99):

> The American public, the church organizations that have been helping - Protestant, Catholic and Jews will know you for what you are - an evil, abnormal beast. So will others who have backed you. You are done.
>
> King, there is only one thing left for you to do. You know what it is. You have just 34 days in which to do (this exact number has been selected for a specific reason, it has definite practical significant. You are done. There is but one way out for you. You better take it before your filthy, abnormal fraudulent self is bared to the nation.

What, you weren't aware that "giving peace a chance" to the extent that you won a Nobel Peace prize was a federal crime deserving of a self-inflicted death penalty? Since *the FBI is only authorized to investigate violations of federal law*, they obviously thought so. Unless there is some sort of subterranean law we haven't been permitted to examine, you might want to go back to the statute books on that one, guys.

King wasn't the only antiwar activist targeted. Another memo, issued in 1968, was used to create potential violence against comedian Dick Gregory (who was outspoken against the Vietnam war), using the Mafia as its involuntary intermediary (*The Cointelpro Papers*, p. 104):

> Chicago airtel and LHM dated 5/2/68 and captioned "Richard Claxton Gregory" concern a speech by Gregory on 4/28/68 where he noted that "Syndicate hoods (are living all over. They are the filthiest snakes that exist on this earth." Referenced Bulet instructed you to develop counter-intelligence action concerning militant black nationalist Dick Gregory.
>
> Consider the use of this statement in developing a counterintelligence operation to alert La Cosa Nostra (LCN) to Gregory's attack on LCN. It is noted that other speeches by Gregory also contain attacks on the LCN. No counterintelligence action should be taken without Bureau authority.

These latter efforts were comparatively primitive. But an August 5, 1968 memo detailed a propaganda project in southern Florida aspiring to the level of *Operations Northwoods* sophistication, a project designed to suck some of the sunshine out of the Sunshine State.

Working with their "propaganda assets," local COINTELPRO specialists oversaw the creation of a television "documentary" on both the black liberation movement and the new left in the Miami area, a documentary anything but "news": the basic idea was to take the least media-savvy representatives of the "New Left", and shine the spotlight on them instead of their more articulate brethren (*The Cointelpro Papers*, p. 119):

> As you are aware publicity about New Left and black nationalist groups, especially television coverage, sometimes enhances the stature of these groups. At the same time, Miami has demonstrated that a carefully planned television show can be extremely effective in showing these extremists for what they are. Local New Left and black nationalist leaders were interviewed on the show and seemed to have been chosen for either their inability to articulate or their simpering and stupid appearance.

The program, viewed by a large Florida television audience not aware that the FBI was doing a "Walt Disney" on them, was edited to take the statements of key activists out of context in such a way as to make them appear to *advocate gratuitous violence* and, in addition (and inconsistently) *seem cowardly*. To add to the professionalism, the documentary made sure to de-contextualize the comments of the activists, thus turning potentially plausible claims into inherently absurd claims, utilizing camera angles deliberately selected to make those interviewed come off like "rats trapped under scientific observation" (*The Cointelpro Papers*, p. 119):

> Miami furnished a film of this show for Bureau review and it was apparent that the television source used the very best judgment in editing comments by these extremists. He brought out that they were in favor of violent revolution without their explaining why. But he also brought out that they, personally, would be afraid to lead a violent revolution, making them appear to be cowards. The interview of black nationalist leaders on the show had the leaders seated, ill at ease, in hard chairs. Full-length camera shots showed each movement as they squirmed about in their chairs, resembling rats trapped under scientific observation.

The FBI leadership called upon "[e]ach counterintelligence office [to] be alert to exploit this technique both for black nationalists and New Left types," which was extremely effective in framing those who were on the show in "a most unfavorable light" (*The Cointelpro Papers*, p. 119):

> Each counterintelligence office should be alert to exploit this technique both for black nationalists and New Left types. Miami learned from sources that those who appeared on the show realized that it presented them in a most unfavorable light. One even complained to the television station about it. This counterintelligence operation will be of great value in the South Florida area and the Bureau hopes these results can be duplicated in other offices. Success in this case resulted from hard work and acumen on the part of the Agents who handled the matter. Especially important was the choice of individuals interviewed as they did not have the ability to stand up to a professional newsman. The fine job of interviewing and editing done by the news people involved was also most important.

Shows like this obviously played a role in accounting for much of the negativity with which the New Left and black liberation movements came to be publicly viewed by the end of the 1960s. Unfortunately, the FBI made sure that the agents in charge would not alert the American public that they were the well from which the geyser of disinformation was spurting, so that government-manufactured reality would appear to be the natural order of things (*The Cointelpro Papers*, p. 119):

> Each office should be alert to the possibility of using this technique. No counterintelligence action should be taken without Bureau authority. For your information operations of this type must be handled through reliable, established sources and must be set up so that the FBI is not revealed as the source.

This particular COINTELPRO operation could have probably gone on indefinitely, but the memos you have seen were distributed to news agencies. Having their cover blown, Director Hoover declared that this flavor of COINTELPRO was deep-sixed (at least until the heat was off).

However, while the official program supposedly was ended, the program was unofficially continued by changing the name of activists to "terrorists," which then opened the door to re-frame further organizations. The FBI started with the Mafia, and ended with . . . nuns? (*The Cointelpro Papers*, p. 306; footnotes omitted; definition of acronym added in brackets):

> This was accomplished in the immediate aftermath of COINTELPROs alleged demise, as is shown in the accompanying April 12, 1972 Airtel from Director L. Patrick Gray to the SAC, Albany. The word selected was "terrorist". . . The public, which experience had shown would balk at the idea of the FBI acting to curtail political diversity as such, could be counted on to rally to the notion that the Bureau was now acting only to protect them against "terror." Thus, the Bureau secured a terminological license by which to pursue precisely the same goals, objectives and tactics attending COINTELPRO, but in an even more vicious, concerted and sophisticated fashion.
>
> The results of such linguistic subterfuge were, as was noted in the introduction to this book, readily evidenced during the 1980s when it was revealed that **the FBI had employed the**

rubric of a "terrorist investigation" to rationalize the undertaking of a multi-year "probe" of the nonviolent CISPES [*Committee In Solidarity With The People Of El Salvador*] organization — **extended to encompass at least 215 other groups, including Clergy and Laity Concerned, the Maryknoll Sisters, Amnesty International, the Chicago Interreligious Task Force, the U.S. Catholic Conference, and the Virginia Education Association — opposed to U.S. policy in Central America.** Needless to say, the CISPES operation was attended by systematic resort to such time-honored COINTELPRO tactics as the **use of infiltrators/provocateurs, disinformation, black bag jobs, telephone intercepts, conspicuous surveillance (to make targets believe "there's an agent behind every mail box"),** and so on.

If the FBI can on a limited budget and with limited motivation frame people of little notoriety who, being alive, could defend themselves, just imagine what they could do to a person dead, with no defense, a national pariah to boot, and with resources and motivation unlimited.

A person like Lee Harvey Oswald.

Conclusion

What have we learned? That the Land of Oz and the Magic Kingdom may be home not-so-sweet-home, and that you may not have to look so hard to find "A CRIME" in "AMERICA".

The relevance of the foregoing to the Kennedy assassination is clear:

The <u>Military</u>, whose *Northwoods* plan was rejected by Kennedy, and which showed conclusively it would manufacture reality to commit acts of treason against the United States, had control of President Kennedy's *autopsy*;

The <u>CIA</u>, which was fingered as a potential suspect for a *coup d'état* by "a very high official" in the Kennedy administration in a news article six weeks before President's Kennedy's assassination, and whose ex-director Allen Dulles (fired by Kennedy) served on the Warren Commission (which had top-

down responsibility for the investigation into Oswald), had control of the *media*;

The <u>FBI</u>, which authored a memo that set the "removal of [Dr. Martin Luther] King from the national scene" as a national priority, and which manufactured reality to thwart the goals of groups opposed to the Vietnam war — had bottom-line control of the *investigation* into the assassination of a President ready to wind down that war.

Didn't find reading this chapter that enjoyable, did you? Well, I can't really say I enjoyed writing it either.

But this chapter had to be written, because if you've learned just one thing, it's this:

HERE is where you can stick the epithet "wacky conspiracy theorist"!

(I had another image in mind, but I discarded the idea when I decided to make this a family-friendly book.)

We now know that governments can, and do, manufacture reality, and with that key observation proven, we are now ready to take a look at The Case Against Lee Harvey Oswald in detail.

Chapter 7: The Case Against Lee Harvey Oswald

Let's sum up what we have learned so far.

1. There can be no conviction in any case where there is *reasonable doubt* (which can be seen in terms of *confidence level*).
2. A *case* consist of *propositions* dividable into *elements*.
3. The confidence level for a proposition can, at best, be *no stronger than the confidence level for the weakest element associated with that proposition.*
4. The confidence level for an element is affected by *evidence*, and not just the *quantity* of evidence, but also the *quality* of evidence, using the criteria of *comprehensiveness, credibility, sufficiency,* and *consistency.*
5. Certain kinds of evidence can *reduce* confidence level.
6. Some evidence, particularly *manufactured* evidence, can positively *obliterate* the prosecution's case by its mere presence.
7. Various arms of government *have*, from time to time, manufactured evidence.

With this background in mind, we now turn to The Case Against Lee Harvey Oswald. At the outset, you should know that The Case Against Oswald is *not* simply "Lee Harvey Oswald killed President Kennedy." That is not the "case", that is simply a general *conclusion related to* the case. Being too simple, it does not allow for a precise examination of how the evidence relates to the case's specific components.

When we define the case specifically, we find it can most concisely be described as being comprised of four statements:

1. The **Legal Assumption** underlying two propositions and a conclusion.
2. **Proposition One**, related to the *number* of gunmen (1).
3. **Proposition Two**, related to the *identity* of the gunman (Oswald).
4. The **Conclusion**, which naturally follows if the legal assumption is true and the evidence establishes the truth of the propositions beyond a reasonable doubt.

We can see The Case Against Oswald from this bird's eye view:

THE CASE AGAINST LEE HARVEY OSWALD

LEGAL ASSUMPTION
All the evidence in The Case Against Lee Harvey Oswald stipulated as admissible is *authentic*. This admissible evidentiary record is *comprehensive, credible, sufficient,* and *consistent* to the extent that it precludes reasonable doubt regarding *both* of the following propositions regarding the assassination of President John F. Kennedy:

PROPOSITION ONE
There was one and only one gunman in Dealey Plaza on November 22, 1963, and that gunman was neither aided nor abetted by any person or group.

PROPOSITION TWO
Lee Harvey Oswald was the lone gunman in Dealey Plaza on November 22, 1963.

CONCLUSION
Therefore, it is proven beyond a reasonable doubt that Lee Harvey Oswald fired the shot that killed President John F. Kennedy.

Remember, if reasonable doubt is established for *even one* of the first 3 statements above, then the conclusion cannot be supported!

Along these lines, I need to make two important points: Reasonable doubt applies to the legal assumption as well; if the legal assumption is invalid, the propositions must fail by *definition*. What is also interesting is that if the *first* proposition is not demonstrated, the case for the *second* proposition *also* falls apart, and the conclusion therefore must fall as well, for reasons we will detail shortly.

Let's discuss these in turn.

LEGAL ASSUMPTION

All the evidence in The Case Against Lee Harvey Oswald stipulated as admissible is authentic. This admissible evidentiary record is comprehensive, credible, sufficient, and consistent to the extent that it precludes reasonable doubt regarding both of the following propositions regarding the assassination of President John F. Kennedy:

Underlying the entire case is the legal framework within which it is analyzed. The United States Constitution refers to the concept of "due" process, and there are numerous protocols which are due. If these protocols are absent and/or violated, they can result in a "not guilty" verdict purely on what someone may refer to as "technicalities," but in fact are constitutional safeguards designed to make sure that innocent people do not go to jail. Millions of American soldiers have risked their lives in a defense of these "technicalities," if that's the word you want to use. But if so, it's the *wrong* word: at the risk of stating what ought to be obvious, the Constitution isn't a "technicality," it's *the supreme law of the land*. And the officers of government take an oath of office that they will follow that law.

One of the key protocols defining the process that is "due" is known as the *Federal Rules Of Evidence*, and its chief reason for being is to mandate, as close as possible, the satisfaction of the above. Underlying these Federal Rules are, of course, the laws of logic, which inspired not only the Federal Rules but all the other rules of evidence in United States.

With that in mind, we start with the most basic concept of all, that any evidence offered to prove a case be *authentic*. This *authenticity requirement* is a *sine qua non* parameter for any case to go forward.

A key case in this area is *Miller v. Pate* (386 U.S. 1, 87 S. Ct. 785), which was argued before the Supreme Court on January 11, 1967, and decided October 13, 1967.

In that case, a prisoner (Lloyd Miller) was appealing his conviction for murder. Key evidence securing his conviction was underwear shorts covered with reddish-brown stains. The prosecution said that Miller was wearing the shorts when he committed the murder, and referred repeatedly to bloody shorts, as well as a scientific analysis showing that the stains were *blood*. The jury even heard *expert* testimony that the stains were, in fact, blood (*Miller* at 3-4):

Against this background the jury heard the testimony of a chemist for the State Bureau of Crime Identification. The prosecution established his qualifications as an expert, whose "duties include blood identification, grouping and typing both dry and fresh stains," and who had "made approximately one thousand blood typing analyses while at the State Bureau." His crucial testimony was as follows:

"I examined and tested 'People's Exhibit 3' to determine the nature of the staining material upon it. The result of the first test was that this material upon the shorts is blood. I made a second examination which disclosed that the blood is of human origin. I made a further examination which disclosed that the blood is of group 'A.'"

Now, an "expert" said that, and not just any expert, but an expert who had approximately 1000 blood typing analyses to his credit. Experts wouldn't lie, would they? We certainly would hope not, especially since *false testimony could send an innocent man to his death.*

Because we don't want to believe that anyone would do anything so malicious and for apparently no good reason, we naturally are more likely to believe the "expert" than the "murderer," and as a result, this evidence was extremely important in securing the conviction against Miller (*Miller* at 4-5):

The "blood stained shorts" clearly played a vital part in the case for the prosecution. They were an important link in the chain of circumstantial evidence against the petitioner, and, in the context of the revolting crime with which he was charged, their gruesomely emotional impact upon the jury was incalculable.

But then, at a later proceeding, Miller was permitted to have the shorts examined by a different expert, a chemical microanalyst. What was discovered was shocking (*Miller* at 5):

What the microanalyst found cast an extraordinary new light on People's Exhibit 3. **The reddish-brown stains on the shorts were not blood, but** *paint*. . . . The witness said that he had tested threads from each of the 10 reddish-brown stained areas on the shorts, and that he had found that all of them were encrusted with mineral pigments ". . . which one commonly uses in the preparation of paints." **He found "no traces of human blood."** . . . It was further established that counsel for the prosecution had known at the time of the trial that the shorts were stained with paint. The prosecutor even admitted that the Canton police had prepared a memorandum attempting to explain "how this exhibit contains all the paint on it."

Needless to say, this discovery of inauthentic evidence completely obliterated the case of the prosecution (*Miller* at 7; footnotes omitted):

> **More than 30 years ago this Court held that the Fourteenth Amendment cannot tolerate a state criminal conviction obtained by the knowing use of false evidence.** *Mooney v. Holohan*, 294 U.S. 103. There has been no deviation from that established principle. *Napue v. Illinois*, 360 U.S. 264; *Pyle v. Kansas*, 317 U.S. 213; cf. *Alcorta v. Texas*, 355 U.S. 28. **There can be no retreat from that principle here.**

Once again, at the risk of repeating myself, this is no isolated phenomenon. Readers interested in this area of law are referred to the following articles available at a county law library near you:

- Conviction on testimony known to prosecution to be perjured as denial of due process. 2 L ed 2d 1575, 3 L ed 2d 1991.

- Conviction of criminal offense without evidence as denial of due process of law. 80 ALR2d 1362.

- Suppression of evidence by prosecution in criminal case as vitiating conviction. 33 ALR2d 1421.

Thus, in the legal assumption I have broken out the authenticity requirement separately, when it could be considered to be a subset of either *admissible* or *credible* evidence. However, as I stated, this is a special category, because if you can show that the prosecution has admitted into evidence that which he could have reasonably been expected to know was inauthentic evidence, it taints all the other evidence that has been admitted, and with the essential cornerstone of the case removed — a belief that the evidence-gathering authority is *itself* credible — the entire structure erected by the prosecution must fall.

If the evidence *is* authentic, we can then move to the other criteria: conclusions must have *admissible* evidence behind them, and we are not entitled to see conclusions as true without an evidentiary base that satisfies the *four* criteria discussed in the earlier chapter.

Now that we have a better understanding of the legal assumptions, let's move to a discussion of the propositions, and the sources stipulating them.

PROPOSITION ONE

There was one and only one gunman in Dealey Plaza on November 22, 1963, and that gunman was neither aided nor abetted by any person or group.

What is the source of the content of this proposition? We have several sources, two official government investigations, and two notable books which are proponents of the *Lone Assassin Theory*:

Warren Report, Page 21
"The Commission has found **no evidence that anyone assisted Oswald** in planning or carrying out the assassination."

Warren Report, Page 22
"On the basis of the evidence before the Commission it concludes that Oswald **acted alone**."

Warren Report, Page 375
"THE EVIDENCE reviewed above identifies Lee Harvey Oswald as the assassin of President Kennedy and indicates that he **acted alone** in that event. There is no evidence that he had accomplices or that he was involved in any conspiracy directed to the assassination of the President."

Reclaiming History, Page xxvi
"[A] tenacious, indefatigable, and, in many cases, fraudulent group of Warren Commission critics and conspiracy theorists have succeeded in transforming a case very simple and obvious at its core — Oswald killed Kennedy and **acted alone** — into its present form of the most complex murder case, by far, in world history."

Case Closed, **Page 413**
"None of the early critics created a cogent alternate account to compare to the one set forth of Oswald **acting alone**."

The record, however, is not completely unanimous. In 1978, the *House Select Committee on Assassinations* (HSCA) stated "**[t]he committee believes, on the basis of the evidence available to it, that President John F. Kennedy was probably assassinated as a result of a conspiracy.**" (HR 95) However, the HSCA did so exclusively on the basis of acoustical data (HR 93) which some commentators later (accurately or inaccurately) claimed to be of suspect validity. Consequently, if the validity of the acoustical data was somehow to be impeached, the HSCA also would have concluded that Oswald acted alone since their belief was based on no other evidence.

In addition to this "escape clause" for the primary conjecture, the HSCA stated that the nature of the conspiracy they were considering was in any event functionally identical to the lone assassin scenario:

House Select Committee on Assassinations Final Report, **Page 98**
"If the conspiracy to assassinate President Kennedy was limited to Oswald and a second gunman, its main societal significance may be in the realization that agencies of the U.S. Government inadequately investigated the possibility of such a conspiracy. In terms of its implications for government and society, an assassination as a consequence of a conspiracy composed solely of Oswald and a small number of persons, possibly only one, and possibly a person akin to Oswald in temperament and ideology, would not have been fundamentally different from an assassination by Oswald alone."

Based on the preponderance of data identified above, the two government documents and two primary lone assassin books, I conclude that the statement

There was one and only one gunman in Dealey Plaza on November 22, 1963, and that gunman was neither aided nor abetted by any person or group.

is *Proposition One* in The Case Against Lee Harvey Oswald.

At first glance, the idea that there was *one and only one* assassin of the President would seem to be a tangential consideration in assessing the guilt of Oswald. After all, couldn't Oswald have been the assassin who shot President Kennedy even if there were multiple shooters?

Perhaps, but then again, *perhaps not*, and if it can be shown that the first proposition cannot be demonstrated true beyond a reasonable doubt, the validity of the second proposition is *automatically* thrown into doubt! Of the severest possible kind! How can *Proposition Two* ("Lee Harvey Oswald was the **lone** gunman in Dealey Plaza on November 22, 1963") possibly be true if there was **more than one** gunman?!

Vincent Bugliosi was well aware of the consequences for the case if *Proposition One* was demonstrated to be, from the legal perspective, false. In *Reclaiming History*, regarding the mock trial he conducted with Gerry Spence in London in 1986, Bugliosi related the reason he had to hammer home the point that Oswald was the lone assassin, and in the relation of that reason showed why the death of *Proposition One* would *automatically* lead to the death of the *entire case* (RH Endnotes, p. 553; emphasis supplied):

> [I]f the jury believed or suspected that others were involved, this would inevitably generate in their minds a number of unanswered questions about who these people were and the nature of their involvement. These thoughts in turn could cause the jurors to conclude that they simply did not know the whole story, what really happened, **hurting the credibility of my whole case** against Oswald **and** *raising a reasonable doubt* **of his guilt** in their minds.

Read that well: if others *were* involved in the assassination of Kennedy, "reasonable doubt" as to the guilt of Oswald would *automatically* be raised in the minds of the jurors!

Bugliosi re-related the point yet again in a separate context in his book (RH 833; emphasis supplied):

> A few Dealey Plaza witnesses gave statements of observing men on the upper floors of the Book Depository Building, which, if true, would support the conclusion that whoever shot Kennedy from the building may have had someone else with him. Since this would conflict 100 percent with the Warren Commission's

conclusion of no conspiracy, **it arguably spills over and throws into question the Commission's main conclusion that Oswald killed Kennedy, and I am therefore including this discussion under the "evidence of Oswald's innocence" rubric.**

Read that well: if there *was* a conspiracy to kill Kennedy, it would throw into question the Commission's main conclusion, so much so that it should be considered evidence of Oswald's innocence!

These twin admissions by Bugliosi are absolutely key: if anyone would know how devastating the existence of a conspiracy would be to the primary conclusion, it would be a prosecutor with decades of experience, twenty of them studying the Kennedy assassination.

As Bugliosi has noted, the *mere evidence* of conspiracy *itself* raises reasonable doubt, particularly in light of the fact that the commission found *no evidence* that Oswald was tied to a conspiracy (WR 374):

CONCLUSION

Based upon the investigation reviewed in this chapter, the Commission concluded that there is no credible evidence that Lee Harvey Oswald was part of a conspiracy to assassinate President Kennedy. Examination of the facts of the assassination itself revealed no indication that Oswald was aided in the planning or execution of his scheme. Review of Oswald's life and activities since 1959, although productive in illuminating the character of Lee Harvey Oswald (which is discussed in the next chapter), did not produce any meaningful evidence of a conspiracy. The Commission discovered no evidence that the Soviet Union or Cuba were involved in the assassination of President Kennedy. Nor did the Commission's investigation of Jack Ruby produce any grounds for believing that Ruby's killing of Oswald was part of a conspiracy. The conclusion that there is no evidence of a conspiracy was also reached independently by Dean Rusk, the Secretary of State; Robert S. McNamara, the Secretary of Defense; C. Douglas Dillon, the Secretary of the Treasury; Robert F. Kennedy, the Attorney General; J. Edgar Hoover, the Director of the FBI; John A. McCone, the Director of the CIA; and James J. Rowley, the Chief of the Secret Service, on the basis of the information available to each of them.[1296]

In other words, if there *was* a conspiracy, according to the Warren Commission, we must assume that Oswald was *not a part of it!* So in and of itself, curiously enough, the prosecution's case does indeed rest on what first glance appears to be an unrelated proposition.

This point is so critical, let's analyze it further to see why conspiracy automatically creates doubt.

Remember the final conclusion to be established: "Lee Harvey Oswald *fired the shot that killed* President John F. Kennedy." Note that the crime is:

murder of a President

but not

shooting at a President and *missing*

nor

shooting at a President and *wounding* without killing

So, if there *was* a conspiracy to assassinate President Kennedy, to prove the conclusion that "Lee Harvey Oswald fired the shot that killed President John F. Kennedy," it would *not only* be necessary to show that Oswald was one of the shooters, but it would *also* be necessary to show that Oswald fired the *fatal* shot, which would automatically be assumed if he was the only gunman, but would be extremely difficult to show if he was not. This is because only *one* of the three shots claimed to be fired that day in Dealey Plaza by the Warren Commission was a fatal shot — the bullet which struck Kennedy in the back was not fatal, and one bullet *missed completely*. It was only the headshot which resulted in the death of President Kennedy.

Therefore, if Oswald *did* fire a shot, and there were multiple shooters, perhaps Oswald fired the shot that missed, and *only* that shot, which would mean obviously that he did not fire the shot that killed President Kennedy.

So, from a probability perspective, even if Oswald *did* fire a shot, there would be a 66% probability that he did not fire the shot that killed the President, and if he fired two shots, a 33% chance, which in both cases falls well short of the reasonable doubt standard.

Of course, if the evidence ultimately showed that *more* than three shots were fired, then the probability would drop even more.

In the face of this argument against the main conclusion, some would argue that the *vicarious liability* rule in criminal law would result in Oswald's guilt. As Bugliosi himself noted (RH Endnotes 552),

> Oswald's defense attorneys wouldn't argue . . . that Oswald was a part of a conspiracy, because if they did, under the vicarious liability rule of conspiracy (which makes each conspirator criminally responsible for all crimes committed by his co-conspirators in the furtherance of the object of the conspiracy), they would be arguing Oswald's guilt.

There are at least two points to note about Bugliosi's observation: if Oswald *was* part of a conspiracy (as a murderer or one aiding and/or abetting a murder), he would indeed be guilty from the perspective of vicarious liability, but the conclusion of the Warren Commission and every other entity that advocates the *Lone Assassin Theory* is *not* that Oswald was guilty from a vicarious liability perspective, but that he *actually* fired the shot that killed the President!

And so, therefore, there is a further point, far more critical. Oswald's attorneys would not necessarily argue that Oswald was a part of a conspiracy, as Bugliosi claims. To the contrary, what they would more likely have argued was that there **was** a conspiracy of which Oswald was **not** a part![1]

Unfortunately for the vicarious liability theory, Oswald's *motivation* must also be factored in, for the purpose of establishing what in criminal law is known as *mens rea* (Latin for "guilty mind"[2]); in other words, *intent*.

Without the proper *intent* to commit the crime, Oswald could not be found guilty of that crime. [3]

---

[1] At least knowingly.

[2] http://www.duhaime.org/LegalDictionary/M/MensRea.aspx (retrieved April 5, 2011).

[3] See select provisions of the *Model Penal Code*, http://www1.law.umkc.edu/suni/CrimLaw/ MPC_Provisions/model_penal_code_default_rules.htm (retrieved April 5, 2011). See also *United States v. Staples*, 511 U.S. 600, 605 (1994); *Liparota v. United States*, 471 U.S. 419, 426 (1985); *Morissette v. United States*, 342 U.S. 246, 250-51 (1952).

This is one of the most elemental principles in criminal law, and Oswald's defense could have rested on this necessary principle. As Jessica Kozlov-Davis wrote in the *Michigan Law Review*, [1]

> Most commentators agree that the *mens rea* for conspiracy is purpose, or a specific desire to further the criminal enterprise. No federal statute explicitly prescribes a *mens rea* for conspiracy. The Supreme Court has consistently held that, based on the Model Penal Code, **the appropriate *mens rea* is intent to further the aims of the conspiracy.** According to the Model Penal Code, a person is guilty of conspiracy if, with the purpose of promoting the commission of a crime, he agrees with another person to engage in such conduct as constitutes a crime, or agrees to help another person plan or commit a crime. **The prosecution must meet two burdens in a conspiracy case. First, it must establish that the defendant knew of the unlawful goals of the conspiracy. Second, it must establish that the defendant had the purpose or intent to further its goals, and thus intended to be member of the conspiracy.**

In the *Creighton Law Review*, Ryan Grace additionally noted that there were *two* types of intent required to establish conspiracy, "intent to *achieve the objective* of the conspiracy, and "intent to *agree to commit* a conspiracy." [2] Considering that the Warren Commission found no evidence that Oswald had any intent to agree to commit a conspiracy, *that evidence simply does not exist,* and so any vicarious liability theory must fall.

But let's take this further: if there *was* a conspiracy, there are at least two possibilities that would lead to a "not guilty" verdict for Oswald:

1.   There was a conspiracy, but Oswald was completely unaware of, did not participate in, and had no foreknowledge of it.
2.   There was a conspiracy, and Oswald had some awareness and foreknowledge of the events that were the subject of the conspiracy, but Oswald was not made aware of the true nature

---

[1] "A Hybrid Approach to the Use of Deliberate Ignorance in Conspiracy Cases," Jessica Kozlov-Davis, 100 Mich. L. Rev. 473 (2001).

[2] "Casenote: Defining The Sprawling Arms Of Conspiracy: The United States Court Of Appeals For The Eighth Circuit Correctly Addressed The "Clean Breast" Doctrine As It Affects Withdrawal From A Conspiracy In United States v. Grimmett", Ryan Grace, 35 Creighton L. Rev. 433 (2002).

of the conspiracy, nor of his role in it, and did not participate in any way that could be construed as "participation in a conspiracy."

If the possibility is the first one, then obviously Oswald has no guilt whatsoever. He is *completely* cleared. Not guilty.

What is more likely based on the evidence that has been developed in dozens of books and articles is Possibility Two, that Oswald had some awareness of what was going on, but was given a "cover" story leading to actions used to implicate him later on, and if there was such a "cover" story, this could likewise lead to a "not guilty" verdict. The plausibility of this hypothesis would be a function of any evidence introduced to show that Oswald was acting as an undercover agent for the United States government in the five years previous.

From the standpoint of probability alone, there was an excellent chance of this, as Mark North related in his book, quoting a press report of 1962 (*Act Of Treason*, p 213):

> "The Federal Bureau of Investigation has nearly 1500 informants in the 8500-member Communist party, according to a former agent who also made public a report criticizing the 'autocratic' way the bureau is run. The former agent is Jack Levine. . . . The bureau, Mr.Levine said, had found that the informants payroll had become a 'severe drain,' and that 'through its dues-paying FBI contingent it had become the largest single financial contributor to the coffers of the Communist party.'"

In other words, with 1500 informants out of 8500 Communists, there was a 17% chance in 1962 that Oswald worked for the government, with no more evidence than that!!

This excerpt from North's book provides another interesting historical takeaway: that the biggest single *supporter* of the Communist Party in 1962, considered at the time one of the greatest *threats* to the United States government was (drum roll) . . . *the United States government*!

And, there is a 17% chance that at least one of the "subversive" actions conducted at the time by some of those "communists" was in fact the actions of . . . *the United States government*!

File that one away for the time being.

Returning to the main point at hand, this program had a long history, certainly pre-dating the "red scare" of the 50s. The agents sent to infiltrate the Communist party in these earlier days exposed themselves to at least two kinds of risk; the risk of being found out by the Communists, and the risk of falsely being accused as a Communist by those out of the loop.

One such individual was Robert Ronstadt, who, like Oswald, was an ex-marine, recruited by the government to go undercover and become a "communist." An affidavit was prepared in his behalf by Joseph McCarthy: [1]

COLD WAR AGAINST INVESTIGATION OF SUBVERSION **1499**

RONSTADT EXHIBIT No. 1

February 10, 1961

TO WHOM IT MAY CONCERN:

During 1946, while engaged in private investigation in Los Angeles, California, I first met Robert C. Ronstadt. At that time, much of my work was devoted to combating internal and external Communism. I had been an F.B.I. agent for several years; however, immediately prior to 1946, I had spent six years with Naval Intelligence and O.S.S. in combating Communism.

In order to infiltrate the Communist Party of the United States, I located areas in which known Communists lived and places where they worked. The next project was in the selection of the right man to infiltrate the Communist Party.

Experience had proven that too frequently this effort was thwarted by the philosophy of the Party, causing the undercover man to lean sympathetically toward Communism. Therefore, extreme care was exercised to find a man of high courage, fine intelligence, and complete devotion to Democracy.

The man selected for the mission was Ronstadt, who went on to live his double identity for a total of ten years, from 1946 to 1956:

Robert Ronstadt was that man. He had just returned from the war as an officer in the Marine Corps. He realized the risk and sacrifice such an assignment would entail, but he also recognized the enormous contribution he might make to our way of life. In remarkably short time, he became the object of interest of local Communists. He was screened and tested by them for months and was finally invited to become a Party member.

During all of this time, Bob Ronstadt lived in danger of exposure. It became necessary for him to change his entire pattern of living. His associates were largely Fellow Travelers and Party members.

While I was not employed by the F.B.I. at that time, nevertheless, all pertinent information gathered by Ronstadt was furnished the Bureau.

At the end of a two-year period, Ronstadt was deeply entrenched in the Communist Party and had become an extremely valuable source of information. The F.B.I. requested that he continue his assignment as a counterspy. Ronstadt was destined, because of his love of country, to lead this double life for an additional eight years.

Joseph P. McCarthy

[1] "The Communist Party's Cold War Against Congressional Investigation of Subversion: Report and Testimony of Robert Carillo Ronstadt," Committee on Un-American Activities, House Of Representatives, 87th Congress, 2nd session (October 10, 1962), p. 1499, found at http://www.archive.org/details/communistpartyscoounit (retrieved May 3, 2011).

Ex-marine Ronstadt himself indicated that when he was accepted into the Communist Party he reported directly to the FBI, and the FBI was keenly interested in that information not getting out (Ronstadt testimony, p. 1497):

At the time I was accepted into the Communist Party and at that time, I reported directly to the FBI.

In other words, the FBI didn't want to particularly share information with anyone, and although all the reports up until this point had been accessible to them, they felt that they wanted to have direct access at all times.

Undercover work can be extremely dangerous when people think that you are a Communist, and you actually are not! In Ronstadt's case, it got out that he was both a Communist and an FBI informer, except the media got the order reversed, and accused him of being a communist-turned-FBI-informer, instead of what he was, an ex-Marine FBI informer who had infiltrated the Communist Party and who never was truly a Communist to begin with. Ronstadt explained what happened when his cover was blown (Ronstadt testimony, p. 1510):

Mr. Doyle. When did they discover that you were a phony Communist?

Mr. Ronstadt. I don't think that they ever really discovered that until probably January of this year when I started campaigning for Congress—I am running for Congress in the 27th Congressional District, and I felt that in order to let the people there know, and in order to avert, for instance, a last-minute accusation that I was a Communist, I felt that it would be wise to tell the various Democratic groups where I spoke some of my background. This I did, and one of the newspapers, unfortunately picked it up, and got the thing twisted.

In other words, they came out with a statement that Robert C. Ronstadt, former Communist, turned FBI informer—was running for Congress. Well, this created kind of a bad impression, so I turned around and I sued them.

Could what we learned about Ronstadt have applied equally well to Oswald? If so, Oswald's actions as a "Communist" pre-dating the assassination would have been *under the orders of the U.S. government*, and we know that the *Northwoods* memo anticipated using similar false communists in one of their phony "terror" campaigns.

In addition, some have argued that Oswald could have been not only an agent of the FBI, but also the CIA, even though the CIA disavowed any knowedge of his actions (CE 870: 17 H 866):[1]

> JOHN A. McCONE, being duly sworn, deposes and says that he is the Director of Central Intelligence, and that based on his personal knowledge of the affairs of the Central Intelligence Agency and on detailed inquiries he caused to be made by the officers within the Central Intelligence Agency who would have knowledge about any relationship Lee Harvey Oswald may have had with that Agency, he certifies that:
>
> Lee Harvey Oswald was not an agent, employee, or informant of the Central Intelligence Agency;
>
> the Agency never contacted him, interviewed him, talked with him, or received or solicited any reports or information from him, or communicated with him, directly or indirectly, in any other manner;
>
> the Agency never furnished him any funds or money, or compensated him, directly or indirectly, in any fashion; and
>
> Lee Harvey Oswald was never associated or connected, directly or indirectly, in any way whatsoever with the Agency.
>
> _(signature)_ (L.S.)
> JOHN A. McCONE
>
> Subscribed and sworn to this 18 day of May,

The CIA says, "he's not our man." But then again, if the man accused of killing the President of the United States *was*, would they have admitted to it?

Of course not, not only in that circumstance, but even in less controversial circumstances, especially if Oswald was what was referred to as a "long-range-asset," an individual either given a new identity or one who had an old identity extensively redefined. Allen Dulles, the ex-CIA director fired by Kennedy (who served on the Warren Commission), explained how the CIA went about creating these "long-range-assets" (*The Craft of Intelligence*, pp. 54-5):

> If you are really born in Finland but are supposed to have been born in Munich, Germany, then you must have documents showing your connection to that city. You have to be able to act like someone who was born and lived there.

---

[1] http://www.history-matters.com/archive/jfk/wc/wcvols/wh17/html/WH_Vol17_0446b.htm (retrieved March 21, 2012).

Arrangements have to be made in Munich to confirm your
origin in case an investigation is ever undertaken. . . .
Obviously, an intelligence service will go to all this trouble
only when it is intent upon creating deep-set and long-range
assets.

Having created a cover for agents of this nature, the government
would then, if questioned, write a letter similar to the affidavit above
signed by McCone and deny any connection, even to the extent of not
paying individuals for the covert operations in those cases when the
lawsuit would reveal the identity of the covert operative, preserving
the intelligence community Holy Grail of "plausible deniability."

We think of this spycraft as a modern phenomenon, but it's as
least as old as the 19th century. We know this because a case on just
this point went to the Supreme Court in . . . 1875!

In that case, *Totten v. United States* (92 U.S. 105), Enoch Totten
claimed to have been hired by President Lincoln for a "secret service"
(the word "covert" not in vogue at the time) at the then-whopping
salary of $200 per month for a military intelligence mission.

This case established the precedent that an intelligence agent
could not compel the government by court action to pay for covert
actions rendered. For our purposes, what we learn from the case is that
government will *always* deny the existence of covert operations. As the
Court stated, [1]

The service stipulated by the contract was a secret service; the
information sought was to be obtained clandestinely, and was
to be communicated privately; the employment and the service
were to be equally concealed. **Both employer and agent
must have understood that the lips of the other were to
be forever sealed respecting the relation of either to the
matter.** This condition of the engagement was implied from
the nature of the employment, and is implied in all secret
employments of the government in time of war or upon
matters affecting our foreign relations where **a disclosure of
the service might compromise or embarrass our
government** in its public duties . . .

---

[1] *Totten v. United States*, 92 U.S. 105 at 106 (1875), found at
http://supreme.justia.com/us/92/105/case.html. See *The Craft Of Intelligence*, pp. 127-8 for a
discussion of the case.

So, if anyone expects the CIA to reveal that Oswald was an agent of the CIA (if he was), don't hold your breath.

But if Dulles wouldn't talk, others would. A former finance officer for the CIA, Jim Woolcott, claimed that Oswald was a CIA double agent to the Soviet Union. Woolcott had issued the paychecks for a counterespionage project in which Oswald was involved (*JFK And The Unspeakable*, p. 366).

Wilcott provided an interview in March 22, 1978 for the HSCA. In that interview, Wilcott not only linked Oswald to the CIA, but also the CIA to the assassination, provocatively suggesting as a possibility Warren Commissioner Dulles' involvement in the murder (Wilcott interview, p. 12; JFK Record Number 180-10116-10096): [1]

```
branches all night.  Much was said at these meetings about observing
the "need-to-know" principle.  The mood had changed from the elation
of the previous day to a more serious one.  That was when I first
heard about CIA somehow being involved.  Not long before going off
duty, talk about Oswald's connection with CIA was making the rounds.
While this kind of talk was a jolt to me, I didn't really take it
seriously then.  Very heavy talk continued up to about the middle of
January.  Based solely on what I heard at Tokyo Station, I became
convinced that the following scenario is true:

             THE ASSASSINATION SCENARIO
    CIA people killed Kennedy.  Either it was an outright project
of Headquarters with the approval of McCone or it was done outside,
perhaps under the direction of Dulles and Bissell.  It was done in
retaliation to Kennedy's renegging on a secret agreement with Dulles
to support the invasion of Cuba.  The other political factors prev-
```

Coming from a CIA insider, this is information that can't be ignored. Furthermore, we *know* Wilcott was privy to insider information.

Take a look at the second paragraph in the screen capture below, where Wilcott predicts an operation similar to *Operation Northwoods*. This is extremely significant, because the Wilcott statement was

[1] http://www.history-matters.com/archive/jfk/hsca/secclass/Wilcott_3-22-78/html/Wilcott_0013a.htm (retrieved March 23, 2012).

prepared in 1978, over 20 years before anyone knew the *Northwoods* memo existed! (Wilcott interview, p. 15) [1]

As Bissell pressured his top lieutenants, they in turn pressured the case officers, intelligence officers and project officers who in turn pressured the field agents to turn in reports that the Cuba Desk wanted to hear. This was not simply a question of poor management. It was a contrived plot to secure a minimum basis to claim support after it was realized that truly valid minimum popular support could not be had. The original invasion plans were then changed to include the creation of an incident that would call for an all out attack by the US military. Kennedy was not to know of this change, and it was not discussed at the November.1960 meeting of the invasion briefing.

One such plan was to somehow get Castro to attack Guantanamo by making him believe that rebels were attacking from there. Another was to interpose a ship in a rebel attack and get it blown up. This was said to have been discarded when ONI (Office of Naval Intelligence) got wind of it and became very angry, and perhaps was the source of some of the snitching on the Cuba foul ups to Kennedy. Just prior to

Willcott also said that several CIA personnel — "at least six or seven" — knew that Oswald had been a CIA agent (Wilcott interview Executive Session, p. 8; this screen capture is from the original transcript): [2]

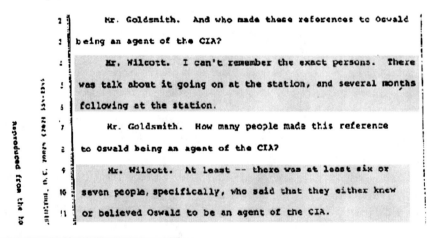

Mr. Goldsmith. And who made these references to Oswald being an agent of the CIA?

Mr. Wilcott. I can't remember the exact persons. There was talk about it going on at the station, and several months following at the station.

Mr. Goldsmith. How many people made this reference to Oswald being an agent of the CIA?

Mr. Wilcott. At least -- there was at least six or seven people, specifically, who said that they either knew or believed Oswald to be an agent of the CIA.

---

[1] http://www.history-matters.com/archive/jfk/hsca/secclass/Wilcott_3-22-78/html/Wilcott_0016a.htm (retreived March 28, 2012).

[2] *Harvey and Lee CD ROM*, Image *nov_22-23-17.jpg*.

Wilcott was not the only CIA insider to connect the CIA to the assassination. Several members of the CIA participated in a conspiracy to murder Kennedy, according to a deathbed confession by E. Howard Hunt which was given most likely in January 2007, a confession which *still* had not been reported in the major media as of April 10, 2012 (based on a *Nexis* search by the author [only one story found in the *Eureka Times Standard*]), in an operation which Hunt referred to as "the big event," which reads in pertinent part as follows (names of CIA personnel in bold italic): [1]

> I heard from ***Frank*** [BK: Sturgis] that LBJ had designated ***Cord Meyer Jr.*** to undertake a larger organization while keeping it totally secret. Cord Meyer himself was a rather favorite member of the Eastern aristocracy. . . .
>
> As for ***Dave Philips***, I knew him pretty well at one time. He worked for me during the Guatemala project. He made himself useful to the agency in Santiago, Chile where he was an American businessman. In any case, his actions, whatever they were, came to the attention of the Santiago station chief and when his resume became known to people in the Western Hemisphere division he was brought in to work on Guatemalan operations.
>
> ***Sturgis*** and ***Morales*** and people of that ilk, stayed in apartment houses during preparations for the big event. Their addresses were very subject to change so that where a fellow like Morales had been one day, you'd not necessarily associated with that address the following day. In short it was a very mobile experience. . . .
>
> What is important in the story is that we backtrack the chain of command up through Cord Meyer and laying the doings at the doorstep of LBJ. He in my opinion, had an almost maniacal urge to become President. He regarded JFK, as he was in fact, an obstacle to achieving that. He could have waited for JFK to finish out his term and then undoubtedly a second term. So that would have put LBJ at the head of a long list of people who were waiting for some change in the executive branch.

---

[1] http://www.saintjohnhunt.com/testament.html (retreived March 28, 2012).

Of course, this maps on perfectly to the prediction in the *Times* we saw earlier that any *coup d'état* in the United States would be CIA-driven:[1]

> **The C.I.A.'s growth was "likened to a malignancy" which the "very high official was not sure even the White House could control . . . any longer." "If the United States ever experiences [an attempt at a coup to overthrow the Government] it will come from the C.I.A. and not the Pentagon." The agency "represents a tremendous power and total unaccountability to anyone."**

This article is especially significant, because it was written by a reporter so close to Kennedy that he helped Kennedy edit *Profiles In Coverage*, and therefore had excellent access to Kennedy, which could have meant that this story originated from Kennedy himself (for even more background on this relationship, see the post-1992 edition of Mark Lane's *Rush To Judgment*, p. viii-x).

Another provocative statement linking the CIA to the assassination was uttered by another CIA insider, James Angleton (chief of the CIA's counterintelligence (CI) staff from 1954 to 1975), who made a curious statement in some parting remarks (after resigning) to *The New York Times* on December 25th, 1974:[2]

> **"A mansion has many rooms, and there were many thing going on during the period of the [antiwar] bombings. I'm not privy to who struck John."**

---

[1] "In the Nation: The Intra-Administration War In Vietnam," *The New York Times*, October 3, 1963.

[2] "Helms Disavows 'Illegal' Spying By The CIA In US," *The New York Times*, December 25th, 1974.

Another CIA insider who linked Oswald to the CIA was former executive assistant to the Deputy Director, Victor Marchetti. In the book *JFK And The Unspeakable*, James Douglass described Marchetti's theory about a phone call placed by Oswald from prison to a "John Hurt" in Raleigh, North Carolina. There were two John Hurts in Raleigh. One of them had a military intelligence background: John David Hurt served as U.S. Army counterintelligence Special Agent. Marchetti explained why (*JFK And The Unspeakable*, p. 365):

> Marchetti said he thought Oswald was following the standard intelligence practice of trying to contact his case officer through a "cut-out," a "clean" intermediary with no direct involvement in an operation. As to why Oswald's call was made to North Carolina, Marchetti pointed out that the Office of Naval Intelligence had an operations center in Nags Head, North Carolina, for agents who had been sent as fake expatriates to the Soviet Union — corresponding to Oswald's background.
>
> In an interview, Marchetti said, "[Oswald] was probably calling his cut-out. He was calling somebody who could put him in touch with his case officer. He couldn't go beyond that person. There's no way he could. He just had to depend on this person to say, 'Okay, I'll deliver the message.' Now, if the cut-out has already been alerted to cut him off and ignore him, then . . ."

However, contacting this "cutout," if that is indeed what happened, would have been an extremely risky business, if he was the wrong person to contact.

One indication is a *Termination Secrecy Oath* CIA personnel were required to sign in the early '60's. Here is one example from August, 1963, an oath signed by Ross Crozier. Notice what it says: "in the event I am called upon . . . to testify or provide information which I am pledged hereby not disclose, *I will notify the Organization immediately.*" Note that violation would have exposed the person signing the oath to prosecution under espionage laws: [1]

---

[1] http://www.maryferrell.org/mffweb/archive/viewer/showDoc.do?docId=14454 (retrieved April 10, 2012).

5. I have been advised that, in the event I am called upon by the properly constituted authorities to testify or provide information which I am pledged hereby
not to disclose, I will notify the Organization immediately; I will also advise
said authorities of my secrecy commitments to our government and will request that
my right or need to testify be established before I am required to do so.

6. I am aware of the provisions and penalties of the espionage laws of our government and am fully aware that any violation on my part of certain matters sworn
to by me under this oath may subject me to prosecution under the terms of these
laws, and that violation of other portions of this oath are subject to appropriate
action, including such dissemination of the violation as the circumstances warrant.

I have read and understand the contents of this oath and voluntarily affix my
signature hereto with the full knowledge that this oath was executed for the
mutual benefit of myself and our government, and that it will be retained in the
files of the Organization for its future use or for reference by me at any time
in the future that I may be requested or ordered to testify or disclose any of
the matters included within the scope of this oath.

IN WITNESS WHEREOF, I have set my hand and seal this_____ **30th** _____day of

____**August**____ 19 **63**.

_____(SEAL)
                            Signature

Any CIA personnel threatening to expose the relationship to the
wrong individual could have been killed for doing that, and Marchetti
had no problem admitting that he himself would do the killing! (*JFK
And The Unspeakable*, p. 366)

INTERVIEWER: "Okay, if someone were an agent, and they
were involved in something, and nobody believes they are an
agent. He is arrested, and trying to communicate, let's say, and
he is one of you guys. What is the procedure?"
MARCHETTI: "I'd kill him."
INTERVIEWER: "If I were an agent for the Agency, and I was
involved in something involving the law domestically and the
FBI, would I have a contact to call?"
MARCHETTI: "Yes."
INTERVIEWER: "A verification contact?"
MARCHETTI: "Yes, you would."
INTERVIEWER: "Would I be dead?"
MARCHETTI: "It would all depend on the situation. If you get
into bad trouble, we're not going to verify you. No how, no
way."
INTERVIEWER: "But there is a call mechanism set up."
MARCHETTI: "Yes."
INTERVIEWER: "So it is conceivable that Lee Harvey Oswald
was . . . "

MARCHETTI: "That's what he was doing. He was trying to call in and say, 'Tell them I'm all right.' "
INTERVIEWER: "Was that his death warrant?"
MARCHETTI: "You betcha. Because this time he went over the dam, whether he knew it or not, or whether they set him up or not. It doesn't matter. He was over the dam. At that point it was executive action."

So, here we have four CIA personnel — Wilcott, Angleton, Hunt, and Marchetti — indicating, in one way or another, Oswald's connection to the CIA, and a CIA connection to the assassination!

If these statements by CIA insiders weren't enough, there is also evidence in this December 2, 1963 FBI memo that connects the bullets said to have been used in the assassination with the CIA: [1]

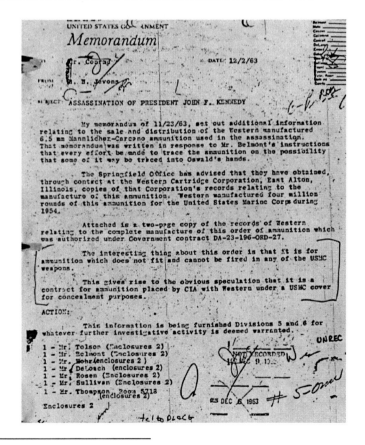

[1] http://contentdm.baylor.edu/cdm4/document.php?CISOROOT=/15p0age-arm&CISOPTR=34855&REC=9, 124-10018-10305 (retrieved March 21, 2012)

In case that is too difficult to read, let us zoom in on the key paragraphs here:

> The interesting thing about this order is that it is for ammunition which does not fit and cannot be fired in any of the USMC weapons.
>
> This gives rise to the obvious speculation that it is a contract for ammunition placed by CIA with Western under a USMC cover for concealment purposes.

We also have the following memo related to Oswald's intelligence history, which looks like an answer to this Zen Koan: "what memo tells *nothing*, while at the same time tells *everything?*" (*Searching the Shadows*, p. 213):

Building from evidence like what we have seen above, Craig Roberts, a former police officer and a trained sniper with extensive combat experience (he was part of the first Marine battalion landing team to see action in Vietnam), summarized the line of research developed in this area (*Kill Zone*, pp. 69-70; footnotes omitted):

Entire books have been written describing Oswald's past and links to the intelligence community. Some say he was recruited by the CIA, others the FBI and still others, the KGB. The most logical assumption is that Oswald was originally ONI — Office of Naval Intelligence. He was recruited while stationed at Atsugi, Japan, as a Marine radar operator working air traffic control. Atsugi was an operational center for "spook" operations such as the U-2 spy planes that overflew China and Russia. Sometime during his tour he, along with Roscoe White, was recruited by the intelligence community, and sometime later — probably just before "defecting" to Russia — he became a shared asset. [90 days after Oswald defected to Russia, an obsolete SAM-2 missile shot CIA U-2 pilot Francis Gary Powers out of the sky over Russian territory. This incident effectively cancelled the arms summit between Eisenhower and Kruschev scheduled to occur in Switzerland. In the past, the SAM-2 could not knock down the U-2s because the Russians did not know what altitude the Lockheed spy planes flew at.]

According to Victor Marchetti, Deputy Assistant to the Director of the CIA, Richard Helms, "Oswald was likely a 'dangle,' an American intelligence agent put out there for the Soviets to recruit in the hope that he could penetrate the Soviet intelligence network. [He probably worked for] the Office of Naval Intelligence, the Navy's CIA."

Regarding Oswald's status at the time of his defection to Russia, Marchetti said, "I believe Oswald was working with Naval Intelligence, but the FBI was coordinating on the operation, as was the CIA when he was in Russia."

What is known is this: Oswald had a CIA "201" file. A 201 file is a personnel file which contains all records regarding an employee. In Oswald's case, his 201 file took up two entire file drawers. He also had an FBI registered informant number, S-179, and drew a monthly paycheck from the Bureau of $200.00.

Marchetti and others say that Oswald was a CIA agent, and there is some evidence that the CIA was involved in the assassination. On the surface, that looks bad for Oswald, but before we automatically jump to the conclusion that Oswald, a CIA agent, was part of a CIA-led conspiracy, we need to dig a little deeper.

Assume for the moment that some employees of the CIA *were* implicated in the assassination of Kennedy, and that Oswald worked for the CIA, either with or without some foreknowledge of the assassination.

Would that have *automatically* made Oswald guilty from the perspective of vicarious liability? Not necessarily. To make that determination, we would have to know the answer to the following absolutely key question:

"Prior to the assassination, what were Oswald's orders?"

The whole case would rest on this missing piece of information, because there are a whole host of possibilities that do *not* involve Oswald in the assassination as a *witting* participant, but might involve him as an *unwitting* participant, one directed to take actions A, B, and C by his superiors, actions which seemed innocent enough to Oswald enough at the time (given his undercover role), but which in retrospect laid down a trail of evidence designed to anchor his "legend" as a future assassin.

Let us take one simple example. In New Orleans on August 9, 1963, Oswald was passing out pro-Cuba pamphlets in front of the *International Trade Mart*, and a television camera just happened to be around to record that activity. Perhaps Oswald was told that, as an undercover agent, he should pass out the pamphlets so that the television camera could record people taking the pamphlets, so that they could later be tracked by the FBI as potential Communists.

If this was the case, Oswald would have thought he was playing the role of the good mole, but in fact the *real* purpose of the episode would have been to capture *his* activities on film so that he could be linked after the assassination not only as a communist, but also a supporter of Castro.

The orders to enact this COINTELPRO-like scheme could have originated at the highest levels, and only those at the highest levels would have known the true purpose of the orders, getting lower-echelon levels involved in the conspiracy without their knowledge.

As we consider the universe of possibilities, there is no end to scenarios that could exonerate Oswald. According to one hypothesis related to Oswald's role as an undercover agent, Oswald could even have been informed of plans to assassinate President Kennedy, but only because he was simultaneously told that he was part of a CIA "abort team" that would attempt to *stop* the assassination, and he might have been asked to carry a rifle into the building for the purpose of handing it off to someone else who would try to stop the assassination.

This is not to say that the evidence shows that Oswald *was* carrying a rifle into the building, only that *even if* he was, if *Proposition One* was not proven true beyond a reasonable doubt, that action could be explained in a way that would not implicate him as a guilty party in the assassination (an explanation that would be unavailable if *Proposition One* were true). [1]

This is because if that scenario were true, Oswald obviously lacked the intent necessary for the crime of murder, as can be easily seen in the following hypothetical situation:

> *Suppose someone asks you to deliver a package for them to an attorney's office because their car has run out of gas. Being the good Samaritan, you do that. 30 minutes after you deliver the package, it explodes.*

A crime has been committed. Arguably, by a conspiracy. But are *you* part of the conspiracy? No: you lack the *intent* to commit the crime.

The same would be true in Oswald's case, for exactly the same reasons. Consequently, evidence regarding Oswald's possible background as an undercover agent, if indeed he was one, would have to have been explored and developed to discover his intent and foreknowledge of the assassination (if any). Without this key evidence establishing his intent and foreknowledge, a case against him could not move forward.

Here is yet another scenario in which Oswald would not be implicated, mentioned by Walt Brown in his book *Treachery In Dallas*, a scenario again developed from evidence indicating that Oswald had been an undercover agent, specifically, that as a marine, Oswald was also an "asset" stationed at the Atsugi Naval Air Station in Japan, working for the Office of Naval Intelligence or the CIA, or both, in an undercover role as a "communist" (developing the credibility that would enable him to infiltrate Castro's Cuba in lines with his earlier "defection" to the Soviet Union).

From Brown's perspective, Oswald may have been informed that a *fake* assassination attempt would be launched on the President, much in the manner of the *Operation Northwoods* scheme, and the only

---

[1] For discussion of this possibility, see *Files On JFK*, pp. 112 and 138 and 303, testimony of James Files and Tosh Plumlee and Senator Bob Bennett (R-UT), respectively.

purpose of that attempt would be to provide a pretext for the invasion of Cuba. As Brown speculates,

> Oswald had been told that the purpose of the fake attempt was that once a bullet or a blank was fired over the limousine into the expanse of lawn in the plaza, the Secret Service would swarm over the President, law-enforcement people would find the Mannlicher as planned, trace it to "Hidell" and hence to pro-Cuban forces, and the United States would clean out Castro's rats' nest once and for all. Oswald, who would have to leave town until the noise cleared down, was told that when all was said and done, he would be the hero of the piece, and no blame could attach to him . . .

In this line of analysis developed by Brown, the Kennedy assassination was a fully-contrived plot, *a la* Northwoods, complete with a full set of bogus incidents and motivations.

Recall that the Northwoods plan began with a downed American plane destroyed remotely by radio transmitter, to be blamed on Cuba. Coincidentally, just two days before Kennedy was assassinated, there happened to be a downed American plane possibly designed to provide an Oswald/Cuban nexus (*The New York Times*, 11/21/63):

U-2 Airplane Is Believed Down Over Gulf of Mexico

KEY WEST, Fla., Nov. 20 (UPI)—A U-2 airplane of the type that makes reconnaissance missions over Cuba appeared to have crashed today in the Gulf of Mexico 40 miles northwest of here.

Military sources in Washington said that the U-2 pilot had not radioed any indication of trouble before the crash, and that the plane had presumably gone down because of mechanical trouble. But they said the crash could have been the result of a Cuban attack.

The announcement of the crash was made at Strategic Air Command headquarters in Omaha. SAC said that the sleek, black jet vanished from land-based radarscopes at 10:32 A.M. and that eight minutes later a pilot in the area observed an oil slick.

The pilot of the U-2 was identified as Capt. Joe E. Hyde Jr., 33 years old, of La Grange, Ga.

U-2 planes have repeatedly flown surveillance over Cuba. It was their discovery of So-

Cross denotes spot where the U-2 plane crashed

viet missile sites in Cuba that touched off the Cuban crisis of October, 1962. The planes fly at extremely high altitudes on their photographic missions.

An air-sea search was under way for the U-2.

And these are just some of a whole host of scenarios in which Oswald could have had some possible foreknowledge without the requisite intent.

Of course, whether or not any of these scenarios are true can only be determined through an analysis of any evidence that miraculously escaped the shredder, but the fact remains is that these scenarios are certainly *possible*, and, being possible, provide a potential means for Oswald's exoneration of the charge of the murder of the President.

In fact, all we really need to do from an evidentiary perspective to cast reasonable doubt on Oswald's guilt is to show that there was *some* conspiracy: because the hypotheses just discussed are *possible*, he must be now presumed innocent in a second (conspiracy-related) case, *even in light of the evidence presented against him*, based on the very distinct possibility that this evidence could *itself* be a part of the conspiratorial matrix!

This is why the death of *Proposition One* is also the death of The Case Against Oswald, and any attempt to prove Oswald's guilt would have to be a *new* case entirely, built on entirely *different* premises, using evidence that according to the Warren Commission simply does not exist.

That would be a bad case too. But that's not this case. That is a *future* case that would *apparently* be doomed. With *Proposition One* doomed, *this* case would be doomed in the here and now.

And this is why so much effort has been expended to claim that Oswald, if he acted at all, acted *alone*. For the parties responsible for erecting and maintaining *The Oswald Wall*, establishing the validity (or lack thereof) of the "lone gunman" hypothesis is important because the lone gunman scenario itself is a weathervane that, unlike the conspiracy scenario, can point *only* to Oswald.

Think about it: if there is only ONE gunman, and ALL the evidence gathered points to that gunman, who else could it be, besides Oswald? The propositions are mutually confirming.

On the other hand, with *multiple* gunmen (or even a lone gunman supported by a network of accomplices), we have to ask *this* question:

If there are MULTIPLE gunmen, why does ALL the evidence gathered point to only *one* gunman — Oswald?

Just this question alone automatically gives us a free pass into the world of reasonable doubt, as Bugliosi himself noted above. Additionally, the observation gives us not only a presumption of innocence on the charge of conspiracy from a vicarious liability perspective, but also a presumption that would be impossible to overcome given the *total absence of evidence* that Oswald knowingly and willingly participated in the conspiracy.

And this concludes the discussion of our first proposition, "**There was one and only one gunman in Dealey Plaza on November 22, 1963, and that gunman was neither aided nor abetted by any person or group.**" With this proposition in mind, let us move to the statements that enable us to formulate our second proposition.

PROPOSITION TWO
Lee Harvey Oswald was the lone gunman in Dealey Plaza on November 22, 1963.

Again, we have several sources for this proposition, 2 official government records, and the two books previously cited which are proponents of the *Lone Assassin Theory*:

Warren Report, Page 19
"The shots which killed President Kennedy and wounded Governor Connally were **fired by Lee Harvey Oswald**."

Warren Report, Page 195
"On the basis of these findings the Commission has concluded that Lee Harvey **Oswald was the assassin** of President Kennedy."

HSCA Report, Page 51
"**LEE HARVEY OSWALD FIRED THREE SHOTS AT PRESIDENT JOHN F. KENNEDY**; THE SECOND AND THIRD SHOTS HE FIRED STRUCK THE PRESIDENT; THE THIRD SHOT HE FIRED KILLED THE PRESIDENT."

Reclaiming History, Page 952
"[I]t is not humanly possible for him to be innocent . . . **Only in a fantasy world could Oswald be innocent** . . . If Oswald didn't kill Kennedy, then Kennedy wasn't killed on November 22, 1963."

Case Closed, **Page 472**
"Lee Harvey Oswald, driven by his own twisted and impenetrable furies, was the only assassin at Dealey Plaza on November 22, 1963. To say otherwise, in light of the overwhelming evidence, is to absolve a man with blood on his hands, and to mock the President he killed."

While there are disagreements among these sources in terms of exactly when the bullets were fired, and which bullet hit President Kennedy or Governor Connally, these sources are unanimous: the gunman who killed President Kennedy was Lee Harvey Oswald.

With this proposition determined from these sources, and no further discussion necessary, we finally reach our conclusion.

CONCLUSION

Therefore, it is proven beyond a reasonable doubt that Lee Harvey Oswald fired the shot that killed President John F. Kennedy.

Being a conclusion, this statement itself requires no evidence, or any justification other than the truth of the propositions. If all the evidence which is required to establish the truth of the propositions has been presented, and that evidence is comprehensive, credible, sufficient, and consistent, then this conclusion naturally follows from these propositions.

But evidence is required to support the propositions. And, since the propositions themselves are subdividable into necessary components, evidence is required for *those* components.

This takes us to our next chapter, the *elements* of propositions of The Case Against Lee Harvey Oswald.

We will turn to those next.

Chapter 8: Elements Of The Case Against Lee Harvey Oswald

As noted in the previous chapter, propositions can be divided into *subpropositions*, to be subsequently referred to more elegantly in this book as *elements* (note to attorneys: this usage, as a synonym for subproposition, is more *fact*-oriented than the *law*-oriented manner in which you are used to hearing the term).

As used in this book, the term *element* refers to a fact subsidiary to the proposition which *must* be true for the proposition to be true.

Suppose you wanted to prove the general conclusion "men have walked on the moon." You could start by creating this proposition:

"The first man walked on the moon on July 20, 1969."

You could then analyze the proposition and determine the necessary subsidiary factual assumptions (i.e. elements) which also have to be true for the proposition to be considered true. Some of these are as follows:

- **"America had the capacity to launch a rocket into outer space by July 20, 1969."**
- **"America did in fact launch a rocket into outer space before July 20, 1969."**
- **"The rocket launched into outer space by America before July 20, 1969 was capable of carrying and sustaining astronauts."**
- **"The capacity to keep a man alive on the moon had been achieved before July 20, 1969."**

At that point, you could choose one of the elements (for example, **"America had the capacity to launch a rocket into outer space by July 20, 1969."**), and gather all the relevant evidence, whether it supports or contradicts your element. This evidence could be comprised of the following evidence types:

- Witness testimony (e.g., witnesses who saw a rocket take off from the launchpad, testimony of astronauts, testimony of engineers in the control room, etc.)
- Photographs (of the launching pad, taken from outer space, taken on the moon, etc.)

- Audio records
- Taped video
- Physical Evidence
- Documentation (e.g., internal memoranda prepared by NASA)

You would then implement the same procedure for all the other elements. As would soon readily become apparent, a massive amount of evidence supporting the elements would be gathered, and the sheer weight of this evidence, along with its quality and consistency, would demonstrate the truth of the elements, and therefore the proposition, beyond a reasonable doubt.

Note that with reference to the proposition "the first man walked on the moon on July 20, 1969," a number of subpropositions could be formulated that are *not* necessary, and are therefore *not* elements. For example, "**America had the greatest desire of any country to put a man on the moon by July 20, 1969.**" While this might have been true, even if false, it would not reduce the confidence level of the proposition. This would *not* be true of the elements: if even *one* of them was false, then the proposition would be *disproven*.

This same general approach is especially necessitated in law, which requires the meticulous organization of facts into categories to add clarity to the case ("WTO Case Review 2004", 22 Ariz. J. Int'l & Comp. Law 99 at 215; emphasis supplied):

> **[A] judge ought not to fail at the task of organizing the elements of a case into widely understood cognitive categories, and the starting point of any case, in any country, at any time, is the category of "Facts."** A statement at the outset of the opinion of what exactly transpired yields a document that is more by virtue of its clarity and efficiency. In turn, the interest of justice — for the parties to the case and for lawyers advising clients in the future based on the jurisprudence of the case — is served.

With this proviso in mind, let's once again look at the factual propositions comprising The Case Against Lee Harvey Oswald:

THE CASE AGAINST LEE HARVEY OSWALD

LEGAL ASSUMPTION
All the evidence in The Case Against Lee Harvey Oswald stipulated as admissible is *authentic*. This admissible evidentiary record is *comprehensive, credible, sufficient,* and *consistent* to the extent that it precludes reasonable doubt regarding *both* of the following propositions regarding the assassination of President John F. Kennedy:

PROPOSITION ONE
There was one and only one gunman in Dealey Plaza on November 22, 1963, and that gunman was neither aided nor abetted by any person or group.

PROPOSITION TWO
Lee Harvey Oswald was the lone gunman in Dealey Plaza on November 22, 1963.

CONCLUSION
Therefore, it is proven beyond a reasonable doubt that Lee Harvey Oswald fired the shot that killed President John F. Kennedy.

The validity of the **legal assumption** will be determined as we analyze the evidence adduced for the propositions. Nor do we have to provide separate evidence for the **conclusion**; if the legal assumption and the propositions are true, then the conclusion will *automatically* be true via the laws of deductive reasoning (if there is only *one* gunman, and Oswald *is* that gunman, then obviously Oswald fired the fatal shot). Consequently, all we need to do for each proposition is to determine its component elements, and then *analyze* the evidence justifying each of the elements.

At the risk of being redundant, *all* of the elements must be considered as true for the proposition to be supported. "True," in this case, must be seen in the context of reasonable doubt, which of course is a primary component of our legal assumption. Again, as noted earlier (and worth repeating), if there is reasonable doubt regarding the truth of even *one* of the elements (that is to say, if there is a confidence level of less than 95% for *any one* element), then the proposition *itself* cannot be proven beyond a reasonable doubt (that is to say, there is a confidence level of less than 95% for the proposition).

This primary directive related to *every* element having to achieve the threshold is drawn directly from the key holding determined by the Supreme Court in the *Winship* opinion discussed earlier (*In Re Winship*, 397 US 358 at 364 (1970); emphasis supplied):

> Lest there remain any doubt about the constitutional stature of the reasonable doubt standard, we explicitly hold that the Due Process Clause protects the accused against conviction except upon **proof beyond a reasonable doubt of** *every* **fact necessary to constitute the crime** with which he is charged.

Note that the Supreme Court is unequivocal on this point: proof beyond a reasonable doubt must be achieved for *every* fact necessary to constitute the crime: *every* element of *every* proposition.

In fact, this is the *minimum* criterion to be deployed. From a probability assessment perspective, the correct procedure is to actually *multiply* the confidence level of the elements to arrive at the ultimate confidence level of the proposition. Thus, the Supreme Court directive would posit a *necessary*, but not a *sufficient* condition. This point will be discussed at length further in this book when we analyze *Element One* of *Proposition One* in detail.

With this critical protocol of due process in mind, let us look at the *factual* elements comprising *Proposition One*.

PROPOSITION ONE
There was one and only one gunman in Dealey Plaza on November 22, 1963, and that gunman was neither aided nor abetted by any person or group.

ELEMENT ONE
Exactly three shots were fired from the sixth-floor southeast window of the Texas School Book Depository at Dealey Plaza on November 22, 1963 — no more, no less — and the three shells found on the floor of the Depository — in the possession of the Warren Commission — were fired from Lee Harvey Oswald's rifle, to the exclusion of all other weapons in the world.

ELEMENT TWO
All of the shots fired at Dealey Plaza on November 22, 1963 were fired from the sixth-floor southeast window of the Texas School Book Depository, and from no other location.

ELEMENT THREE
Lee Harvey Oswald was the *only* person on the sixth floor of the Texas School Book Depository at 12:30 p.m. on November 22, 1963.

ELEMENT FOUR
The shots fired at Dealey Plaza on November 22, 1963 were fired from no other weapons besides Lee Harvey Oswald's Mannlicher-Carcano.

ELEMENT FIVE
A rifleman could plausibly have fired 3 separate shots from the Mannlicher-Carcano within the elapsed time of the shooting and corresponding with the keyframes of the Zapruder film.

ELEMENT SIX
There was one and only one bullet which struck Governor Connally, and that bullet (identified as CE 399) first passed through the body of President Kennedy.

Remember, these factual elements are all *necessary* — they *must* be true for the proposition to be true. For most, the necessity of these elements will be obvious, but there is no harm in a little analytical redundancy to achieve clarity.

ELEMENT ONE

Exactly three shots were fired from the sixth-floor southeast window of the Texas School Book Depository at Dealey Plaza on November 22, 1963 — no more, no less — and the three shells found on the floor of the Depository — in the possession of the Warren Commission — were fired from Lee Harvey Oswald's rifle, to the exclusion of all other weapons in the world.

The Warren Commission stated that *only* three shots were fired in Dealey Plaza. Indeed, no more than three cartridges were ever claimed to have been found on the sixth floor of the Texas School Book Depository. However, if there is other evidence that demonstrates that there were *more* than three shots fired, or evidence that Oswald fired *fewer* than three shots, then obviously there was more than one gunman, and the proposition is disproven.

Vincent Bugliosi, in *Reclaiming History*, agreed with the logic of this line of analysis in his discussion of the assassination of Robert Kennedy, and noted the importance of ancillary evidence in making a determination regarding the number of shots fired, such as additional bullet holes. As he stated in relation to that case (RH Endnotes 551):

[A]ny bullet holes observed in addition to those accounted for . . . would constitute evidence of a second gun being fired.

Bugliosi reiterated the point regarding statements he received on the number of bullets fired (including one from Thomas Noguchi, the coroner of Los Angeles) (RH Endnotes 551):

[I]n the absence of a logical explanation, these statements, by simple arithmetic, add up to too many bullets and therefore, the probability of a second gun.

He then discussed his conclusion as he stated to the media at the time, first indicating that if he was "forced to the wall" he would conclude that there was no conspiracy because bullet holes could be explained with an alternative hypothesis (even though this contradicts the first statement quoted above), but on the other hand, that that conclusion would not necessarily be the final word (RH Endnotes 551):

> If I were forced to the wall, I'd say there was no conspiracy, that the additional bullets and bullet holes can be accounted for by the existence of fragments and ricochets . . . I reiterated that in the absence of official contravening evidence, we were talking about too many bullets for Sirhan to have fired them all.

While Bugliosi most likely did not believe in a conspiracy in the assassination of Robert Kennedy (notwithstanding his contradictory statements), his central point stands: *if* the evidence demonstrates that more bullets were fired than *could* have been fired by the assassin — and there is no plausible alternative explanation or evidence to the contrary — then this would be *proof* of conspiracy, and one's beliefs should be modified accordingly.

ELEMENT TWO
All of the shots fired at Dealey Plaza on November 22, 1963 were fired from the sixth-floor southeast window of the Texas School Book Depository, and from no other location.

The Warren Commission claimed that at the time of the assassination, Oswald was at the sixth floor southeast window of the Texas School Book Depository. Since Oswald could not be in two places at one time, if there *were* shots fired from another location, the element would positively be disproven, and likewise the *Lone Gunman* proposition with which it is irrevocably associated.

ELEMENT THREE
Lee Harvey Oswald was the *only* person on the sixth floor of the Texas School Book Depository at 12:30 p.m. on November 22, 1963.

The Warren Commission claimed that Oswald was the only person on the sixth floor of the Texas School Book Depository at the time of the assassination. If another person was on the southern side of the sixth floor, this individual could have aided Oswald, and also could have fired the shots. An accomplice = conspiracy.

ELEMENT FOUR
The shots fired at Dealey Plaza on November 22, 1963 were fired from no other weapons besides Lee Harvey Oswald's Mannlicher-Carcano.

According to the Warren Commission, Oswald had one and only one weapon, a 40" Mannlicher-Carcano. Even if Oswald had more than one weapon, he would not have had time (and obviously no inclination) to switch back and forth between weapons in the time within which the shots were fired. Accordingly, if there is evidence to show that other weapons besides Oswald's Mannlicher-Carcano were used, the element would be positively disproven, and so would the proposition.

ELEMENT FIVE
A rifleman could plausibly have fired 3 separate shots from the Mannlicher-Carcano within the elapsed time of the shooting and corresponding with the keyframes of the Zapruder film.

The Mannlicher-Carcano allegedly owned and used by Oswald was not a rapid-fire machine gun. Before a bullet could be fired, the bolt had to be manually operated to place the bullet in the chamber before firing. This could only be done at a certain speed.

The Warren Commission estimated that the rifle could be fired no faster than 2.3 seconds between shots. Accordingly, all the shots that Oswald allegedly made had to be physically possible within the beginning and end of the shooting sequence. Moreover, the Zapruder film shows the relative timings of the shots to President Kennedy and Governor Connally. If Kennedy and Connally were struck by separate bullets faster than the 2.3 seconds, the element, and therefore the proposition, would be positively disproven.

ELEMENT SIX
There was one and only one bullet which struck Governor Connally, and that bullet (identified as CE 399) first passed through the body of President Kennedy.

The Warren Commission created a concept known as the *Single Bullet Theory* because it was not physically possible (based on the Zapruder film) for Oswald to make two separate shots in the time frame established by the film. The bullet which ostensibly achieved this feat was allegedly found on a stretcher at Parkland Hospital, and was identified by the Warren Commission as Commission Exhibit 399, abbreviated as CE399. If it can be shown that the *Single Bullet Theory* is invalid because no bullet passed through the body of President Kennedy, subsequently striking Governor Connally, the proposition would positively be disproven.

The foregoing analysis has demonstrated why these elements of *Proposition One* are necessary. Now let's move to the elements of *Proposition Two*.

Note to the reader: As of this writing in 2012, the volume that will contain the analysis on Proposition Two, Volume 4, has yet to be written. Consequently, the elements for Proposition Two are subject to change.

PROPOSITION TWO
Lee Harvey Oswald was the lone gunman in Dealey Plaza on November 22, 1963.

ELEMENT ONE
The key evidence in the case actually connects Lee Harvey Oswald to the assassination.

ELEMENT TWO
Lee Harvey Oswald, at the time of the assassination, was present at the window from which it was alleged that the shots were fired (the sixth floor of the southeast window of the Texas School Book Depository), and the weapon purported to be Oswald's Mannlicher-Carcano 6.5 mm Italian rifle was in Oswald's possession at the time it was fired.

ELEMENT THREE
A rifleman of Lee Harvey Oswald's capabilities could plausibly have fired 3 separate shots using the Mannlicher-Carcano within the elapsed time of the shooting and with the requisite accuracy required.

ELEMENT FOUR
Lee Harvey Oswald was not framed for the murder of President John F. Kennedy.

ELEMENT ONE
The key evidence in the case actually connects Lee Harvey Oswald to the assassination.

Under normal circumstances, evidence related to this element would be incorporated as background for the legal assumption and discussed in the next two elements, but as you will see, extraordinary issues with the quality and quantity of evidence for this Proposition entails giving it its own element; analyzing all the evidence *together* will reveal a pattern of *inauthenticity* and *inherent unreliability*. To this latter point, if the evidence is so unreliable it won't be admissible, we won't get to court, and the buck stops here.

Under this element, we seek to ask two questions:

1. Even *if* the evidence is authentic, does it necessarily prove the claim with which it is associated?
2. *Is* the evidence authentic?

Let's go to the first question. You should know that even authentic evidence does not necessarily achieve what its proponents claim that it does. Take these two examples of evidence provided as proof that Oswald was located on the floor of the depository at 12:30 p.m.:

1. A witness claimed to observe Oswald at the southeast corner of the sixth floor of the Depository at 12:30 p.m..
2. One or more fingerprints of Oswald were on the boxes in that area of the depository.

Looks pretty bad for Oswald, doesn't it? Well, not so fast. To understand why, it is helpful to first understand the difference between *direct* and *circumstantial* evidence.

The distinction is fairly simple: *direct* evidence supports the truth of an assertion *directly*, i.e., without an intervening inference. *Circumstantial* evidence, by contrast, requires one or more *intervening inference(s)* to support the truth of the assertion.

Below are two examples of direct evidence:

- Eyewitness Identifications
- Confessions

And here are examples of circumstantial evidence:

- Fingerprints
- Videotape
- Photographs
- Sound Recordings
- DNA evidence

So, for example, if a witness sees Oswald in the "sniper's nest" at 12:30 p.m., that is *direct* evidence Oswald was at the "sniper's nest" at 12:30 p.m., evidence which does not require a direct intervening inference from which to draw a conclusion (though, as we are about to see, it does require one or more intervening inferences related to the *authentication* of that direct evidence).

On the other hand, if Oswald's fingerprints were on the boxes in the "sniper's nest", that is *circumstantial* evidence he was at the "sniper's nest" at 12:30 p.m, evidence which *does* require an intervening inference. We have to make the inductive leap that the fact that a fingerprint *was* placed on a box could somehow logically be linked to the *time* it was placed on the box.

There are problems with both these types of evidence. For example, the direct evidence could be problematic if the witness had *poor vision*, or had excellent vision but was *located too far away* to make a proper identification, or if in fact at the police lineup the witness first identified *someone else* as being in the "sniper's nest" (or otherwise refused to make the identification), or if at the lineup Oswald had on a dirty T-shirt while the others in the lineup were in three-piece suits, or a witness provided an identification that would have been physically impossible given the geometric relationship of witness, witnessee, and surrounding reality in three-dimensional space (i.e. the witness reported a *standing* shooter when a very short opening in a window would only support a *sitting* shooter), or the witness had made *other* identifications that turned out later to be *erroneous*, or the witness was *bribed*, or was *threatened*, or was *unduly influenced* by the media, or was *induced* to make the claim by a group of detectives at the lineup, or had his testimony *misreported*.

Hmmmm . . . not as solid as we thought!! I guess now you know why a *proper* trial has a technique known as cross-examination, which allows the defense to probe these areas for any points of weakness.

Circumstantial evidence has its own problems. You will note that circumstantial evidence requires one or more intervening inferences: for example, to conclude that "Oswald's fingerprints on the boxes were evidence that Oswald was located at the 'sniper's nest' at 12:30 p.m.," your intervening inference would have to be that the *only* time those fingerprints could have been put on the boxes by Oswald was if *in fact* he was located at the nest at 12:30 p.m.

However, since Oswald worked at the Depository on a day-to-day basis, he could have handled those boxes at a different time, and, additionally, we cannot be absolutely *certain* that those fingerprints were Oswald's, we only *assume* that they were. For example, to believe that these fingerprints were Oswald's, we would have to reject the hypotheses that the fingerprint analysis was incorrect, and/or that the fingerprints were planted on the boxes at a later time by either Dallas detectives or the FBI (and this evidence would be less likely to support the element if the fingerprints of others were *also* on the boxes, which could potentially implicate those others as either accomplices or "the" assassin himself).

To reject the hypotheses that the analysis was incorrect and/or that the fingerprints were planted, the evidence would need to be properly *authenticated*, and that takes us to our second question, *is the evidence <u>authentic</u>?*

In this regard, *Federal Rule Of Evidence* 901 (a) provides as follows:

ARTICLE IX. AUTHENTICATION AND IDENTIFICATION

Rule 901. Authenticating or Identifying Evidence

(a) In General. To satisfy the requirement of authenticating or identifying an item of evidence, the proponent must produce evidence sufficient to support a finding that the item is what the proponent claims it is.

As the rule states, the proponent of a claim "must produce evidence sufficient to support a finding that the item is what the proponent claims it is." In other words, the evidence must be *genuine*.

If the prosecution says that a defendant used *this* knife to stab a victim, then the prosecution must produce *this* knife and not some other knife that *looks like* that knife, and be able to *prove* it. If the prosecution says that the defendant shot the victim with a .22 caliber pistol, then it had better not produce as evidence shotgun pellets. If the prosecution's proof that a defendant murdered a victim is blood on the clothes, the material on the clothes should be *blood*, not *paint*. If the prosecution says that it is Oswald's fingerprint on the box, it should be able to prove that it was Oswald's fingerprint, and not someone else's, and that even if it was Oswald's fingerprint, it was placed there by Oswald, not someone else, and if it was Oswald's fingerprint placed there by Oswald himself, it was placed there at 12:30 p.m.

There are two techniques used to authenticate evidence, *ready identification* and *chain of custody*. Ready identification is used when an item has a unique, one-of-a-kind characteristic, and chain of custody is used when an object does *not* have a uniquely identifying characteristic.

As Steven Emanuel and Joel Friedman explained, "[t]he chain of custody method of authentication requires that every 'link' in the chain of custody — every person who has handled or possessed the object since it was first recognized as being relevant to the case — must explain what he did with it." (*Emanuel On Evidence*, p. 465). This distinction was articulated by the Supreme Court of Montana in *State of Montana v. Sox*, 212 Mont. 488 at 491-2; 689 P.2d 252 (1984):

> **There are essentially two recognized methods of identifying physical evidence: ready identification and chain of custody.** The former method is used when the article has a unique characteristic that makes it readily identifiable. The exhibits in the instant case lend themselves to ready identifiability; the computer components had Canadian stock stickers attached to them and one component had even had its sticker realigned in a unique manner by Barnhart. The guitar too, was very unique and easily identifiable.
>
> In his book on evidentiary foundations, Imwinkelried assures us that when introducing a readily identifiable piece of evidence, "the foundation is complete so long as the witness testifies that he or she previously observed the characteristic and presently recalls the characteristic." E. Imwinkelried, *Evidentiary Foundations* (1980), at p. 81. Only when the evidence is so commonplace as to be non-unique or when the witness has failed to observe its uniqueness is it necessary to lay a chain of custody foundation.

The Alabama Supreme Court in 1991 explained the significance of the chain of custody, as well as the significance of the concept of "links "and "missing links" (*Ex parte Holton*, 590 So.2d 918, 920 (Ala. 1991); emphasis supplied):

> The chain of custody is composed of 'links'. A 'link' is anyone who handled the item. **The State must identify each link from the**

time the item was seized. In order to show a proper chain of custody, the record must show each link and also the following with regard to each link's possession of the item: (1) [the] receipt of the item; (2) [the] ultimate disposition of the item, i.e., transfer, destruction, or retention; and (3) [the] safeguarding and handling of the item between receipt and disposition.

If the State, or any other proponent of demonstrative evidence, fails to identify a link or fails to show for the record any one of the three criteria as to each link, the result is a 'missing' link, and the item is inadmissible. If, however, the State has shown each link and has shown all three criteria as to each link, but has done so with circumstantial evidence, as opposed to the direct testimony of the 'link', as to one or more [of the] criteria or as to one or more links, the result is a 'weak' link. When the link is 'weak', a question of credibility and weight is presented, not one of admissibility.

How are links authenticated? Through a series of technical requirements. These technical requirements for establishing a chain of custody are extremely rigorous. Consider this description of proper protocol for a drug prosecution ("Chapter 10. Authentication And Identification," "Testimony of Witness With Knowledge," 31 Fed. Prac. & Proc. Evid. § 7106(b)(1), 38-40; paragraph separations added by author; emphasis supplied):

> [I]n a drug prosecution a chain of custody for contraband seized from the defendant would typically be established in the following manner.
>
> The government might first call as a witness the arresting officer to testify that he found in defendant's possession a bag containing a white powder. This witness would testify that he kept the bag and its contents **in his possession** and secure until he placed it into an evidence container and **sealed that container in a way that would reveal if it had been opened.** The officer then might **testify that he gave the container to a police chemist.**
>
> The chemist then might be called as a witness to confirm that, when he received the container, **it had not been opened.** The chemist might further testify that he opened the container, removed the contents, and **conducted tests to establish the**

nature of those contents. Finally, the chemist would testify that he placed the contents back into the container, resealed it, brought it to court, and that **the container shows no indication that it subsequently had been opened.**

This foundation is sufficient to authenticate the bag and its contents because the perceptions of the two witnesses, combined with the circumstantial evidence that the container had not been disturbed except by the chemist, would be sufficient to sustain a finding that the exhibit was the same item and in the same condition as the item found in defendant's possession. Further, **the chemist now would be permitted to testify as to the results of his analysis of the evidence since the chain of custody tying the evidence to the defendant establishes the relevance of that testimony.**

The standards in a murder case with a death penalty as a consequence, needless to say, can be no less rigorous.

The bottom line: if the key evidence in The Case Against Oswald does not satisfy legal requirements that have been used to authenticate evidence, it is *at the very least* not admissible. And, in certain circumstances, a failure to meet these parameters may be seen as meta-evidence that the evidence has been *manufactured*, which would taint the credibility of all the other evidence in the case.

ELEMENT TWO

Lee Harvey Oswald, at the time of the assassination, was present at the window from which it was alleged that the shots were fired (the sixth floor of the southeast window of the Texas School Book Depository), and the weapon purported to be Oswald's Mannlicher-Carcano 6.5 mm Italian rifle was in Oswald's possession at the time it was fired.

If the shots were fired from the southeast window of the sixth floor of the Texas School Book Depository, and Oswald was not even at that window, then obviously he did not fire the shots. Moreover, even if he *was* at the window, if he was not holding the rifle, then obviously he did not fire the shots. In either of these situations the proposition would be positively disproven.

ELEMENT THREE

A rifleman of Lee Harvey Oswald's capabilities could plausibly have fired 3 separate shots using the Mannlicher-Carcano within the elapsed time of the shooting and with the requisite accuracy required.

The assassin, or assassins, had a challenging shot. For a period of time, there was an oak tree between the sixth floor window and the President's limousine, which was traveling at approximately eleven miles per hour. The final shot that hit the President was approximately 80 yards from the sixth-floor window, 20 yards shy of a football field away. In addition, the complete shot sequence from the first to the last shot took place anywhere from approximately 5.5 to 7 seconds, very close to the limits established by the Warren Commission regarding how fast the rifle could be fired.

That's not all: even if Oswald were the best shot in the world, the Mannlicher-Carcano had to be of a certain level of quality for the shot to be made. For example, the scope on the rifle should have been calibrated with its target (in other words, if you have a bull's-eye in the crosshairs, and instead hit the outer ring of a target, not to mention missing it entirely, you do not have a properly-sighted scope!). The same reasoning would be true for the bolt and firing pin and any other rifle component.

If Oswald cannot make the shot, he cannot be a gunman, lone or otherwise.

ELEMENT FOUR

Lee Harvey Oswald was not framed for the murder of President John F. Kennedy.

Issues with the evidence against Lee Harvey Oswald may lead to an inference, if not an outright deduction, that Oswald was framed for murder. If that is the case, then we will be led on a path to gather evidence outside the official case that can be used to confirm and/or further develop this hypothesis. If we take that route, we may find an extraordinary amount of evidence not considered by the Warren Commission which demonstrates that very point. The more evidence that is found, the lower the confidence level for this element, which could easily drop below the threshold requirement.

If this element is not established beyond a reasonable doubt, then there is a significant possibility, if not certainty, that Oswald was framed, and if that is the case, the only possible verdict that could be returned is "not guilty."

Conclusion

So much for the analysis of the necessity of the elements of *Propositions One* and *Two*.

We've come a long way. The essential background has been covered.

Let us now look at the evidence underlying the first element of *Proposition One*, and apply what we've learned.

Chapter 9: Proposition One, Element One: Exactly 3 Shots Fired

Initial Discussion

Let's analyze our first element:

> *Exactly three shots were fired from the sixth-floor southeast window of the Texas School Book Depository at Dealey Plaza on November 22, 1963 — no more, no less — and the three shells found on the floor of the Depository — in the possession of the Warren Commission — were fired from Lee Harvey Oswald's rifle, to the exclusion of all other weapons in the world.*

This element is a composite derived from three conclusions of the *Warren Report*, and a statement by FBI Firearms Identification Expert Robert Frazier in hearings before the Commission, first the conclusion 2 on p. 19 that three shots were fired,

2. The weight of the evidence indicates that there were three shots fired.

Next, conclusion 4 on p. 19 that Oswald fired the shots,

4. The shots which killed President Kennedy and wounded Governor Connally were fired by Lee Harvey Oswald. This con-

Next, a statement by FBI agent Robert Frazier in hearings before the Warren Commission that the three shells in the possession of the Commission were fired from Oswald's rifle and only Oswald's rifle (3 H 416):

Mr. FRAZIER. I am sorry—yes, 543, 544, and 545. These three cartridge cases were placed one at a time on the comparison microscope, and the surfaces having the breech-face marks or the bolt marks were compared with those on the test cartridge cases, Exhibit 557. As a result of comparing the pattern of microscopic markings on the test cartridge cases and those marks on Exhibits 543, 544, and 545, both of the face of the bolt and the firing pin, I concluded that these three had been fired in this particular weapon.

And finally, the conclusion 11 on p. 22 that *only* Oswald fired the shots:

11. On the basis of the evidence before the Commission it concludes that Oswald acted alone. Therefore, to determine the motives for the

The relationship of this last conclusion to the others is clear: if Oswald acted alone, then obviously no other shots were fired other than the three he was alleged to have fired.

These conclusions above were based on evidence reported by the Warren Commission. In subsequent sections of their report, they provided the following types of evidence:

1. **Photographs** of spent hulls and a live round (as above).
2. **Officer testimony** regarding the number of empty shells found (three).
3. **Earwitness testimony** regarding the number of shots fired (the majority of the witnesses interviewed by the Warren Commission reported hearing three shots).
4. **Forensic evidence** related to the wounds of JFK/Connally, as well as certain ballistic evidence and evidence of bullet strikes.

Naturally, we are going to take a much closer look at this evidence in this chapter, but for now let us assume that this is *all* the evidence (and therefore we met our requirement that the evidence be *comprehensive*), and that the Warren Commission is 100% *credible*. Let us also assume that we are confident that this evidence is *sufficient*, and since it all tells the same story, it obviously is *consistent*. Therefore, our four parameters based on these assumptions would be met.

If that is the case, what would our confidence level be regarding this element? Very high, as follows:

Minimum Confidence	Maximum Confidence
99	**100**

Take a good look at those numbers, the last time you're going to see numbers that high . . . from now on, they are headed inexorably South.

As you might have guessed by virtue of the fact that you have this book in your hand, at least one of the assumptions above is incorrect: we have not seen *all* the evidence, not by a long shot. There are numerous pieces of the puzzle which the Warren Commission did not bother to share with their American audience when they first published the Report. As the months and years passed, and as more and more information was revealed, ultimately this extremely high confidence level began to sink into the quicksand created by these new revelations. When we analyze the evidence originally hidden from our view, we see that there is definitely another (seamy) side to the story.

Consider the following screen captures from Commission Documents utilized by the Warren Commission but not released in the 27 Hearing and Exhibit Volumes. The following capture is from Page 1 of Commission Document 1, a Summary Report by the FBI provided to the Warren Commission of the evidence gathered, dated December 9, 1963, but only revealed to the public in May of 1966 (*Accessories After the Fact*, p. 148), over a year and a half after the publication of the Report on September 24, 1964: [1]

> As the motorcade was traveling through downtown Dallas on
>
> Elm Street about fifty yards west of the intersection with Houston
>
> Street (Exhibit 1), three shots rang out. Two bullets struck
>
> President Kennedy, and one wounded Governor Connally. The

At first glance, this paragraph seems to indicate that of the three shots fired, 2 separate shots hit President Kennedy, and another shot wounded Governor Connally: three shots, three separate hits. However, there is an ambiguity in the sentence "Two bullets struck President Kennedy, and one wounded Governor Connally." One possible interpretation of this sentence — in a departure from the plain meaning of the text — is that one of the bullets referenced as having struck President Kennedy could have passed through the President's body to strike Governor Connally. Under that interpretation, there would still be three separate hits, but by two shots, not three.

However, a complete refutation of this alternative interpretation was provided just seventeen pages later. According to Page 18 of Commission Document 1, the bullet that struck President Kennedy in the back — the only of the two bullets that could have passed through

---

[1] For more information on the release of these significant documents, and the difficulty of making them available to the public, see in general http://www.maryferrell.org/wiki/index.php/ Freeing_the_JFK_Files.

the body of President Kennedy to strike Governor Connally — did in fact *not* transit the President's body: [1]

> **Immediately after President Kennedy and Governor Connally were admitted to Parkland Memorial Hospital, a bullet was found on one of the stretchers. Medical examination of the President's body revealed that one of the bullets had entered just below his shoulder to the right of the spinal column at an angle of 45 to 60 degrees downward, that there was no point of exit, and that the bullet was not in the body.**

This statement, written before the autopsy report was delivered on December 23 (RH 457), was confirmed less than five weeks later in a Supplement to the December 9, 1963 FBI report. Because it was dated January 13, 1964, the Supplement post-dated the receipt of the autopsy report, and included the information contained within that autopsy report, confirming what had previously been "unofficial" reports: [2]

> **Medical examination of the President's body had revealed that the bullet which entered his back had penetrated to a distance of less than a finger length. (Exhibits 59 and 60)**

With the information provided by these latter two paragraphs, the shot sequence (read in conjunction with the Zapruder film which reveals three separate hits) is clearly established: Shot 1 strikes President Kennedy, entering his back, but only penetrating to a distance of less than a finger length; some time later, Shot 2 strikes Governor Connally (the bullet which struck President Kennedy in the back not exiting Kennedy's body), and still later, Shot 3 strikes President Kennedy in the head. Three separate shots, three separate hits.

---

[1] http://www.maryferrell.org/mffweb/archive/viewer/showDoc.do?docId=10402&relPageId=25 (retrieved August 19, 2011).
[2] "FBI Sup. Investigation of Assass. Pres. Kennedy dated 13 Jan 1964," http://www.maryferrell.org/mffweb/archive/viewer/showDoc.do?docId=10507&relPageId=8 (retrieved July 6, 2011).

This sequence of events was anticipated in a telephone conversation recorded at 1:40 pm between President Lyndon Johnson and FBI director J. Edgar Hoover on November 29, 1963: [1]

LBJ   How many...how many shots were fired?

JEH   Three.

LBJ   Any of them fired at me?

JEH   No. All three at the President...and we have them. Two of the shots fired at the President were splintered...but they had characteristics on them so that our ballistics experts were able to prove that they were fired by this gun ...the third shot which hit the President..he was hit by the first and the third ...second shot hit the Governor. The third shot is a complete bullet.. and that ruled out of the President's head...it tore a large part of the President's head off...and, in trying to massage his heart at the hospital ...on the way to the hospital...they apparently loosened that and it fell on to the stretcher. And we recovered that. And we have that. And we have the gun here also.

Over the next few weeks, media reports transmitted this information to the public at large. *The New York Times* started it off by indirectly confirming the three shots, three-hit scenario on December 18th, 1963, stating that the first bullet which hit President Kennedy did not pass through his body: [2]

First Wound Small

The findings of pathologists who conducted an autopsy on Mr. Kennedy's body at the Bethesda, Md., Naval Hospital have not been made public. However, a source familiar with the results gave the following account:

The first bullet made what was described as a small, neat wound in the back and penetrated two or three inches.

The source said this bullet had struck no vital organs and was not likely to have inflicted a fatal wound.

---

[1] "Telephone Conversation Between the President and J. Edgar Hoover (from Mr. Hoover), November 29, 1963, 1: 40 PM," http://www.historymatters.com/archive/jfk/lbjlib/phone_calls/Nov_1963/html/LBJ-Nov-1963_0239a.htm (retrieved June 30, 2011).

[2] "2d Shot Reported Fatal to Kennedy," *The New York Times*, December 18, 1963.

This finding was echoed by the *Times* the next day: [1]

Special to The New York Times
WASHINGTON, Dec. 18—
Officials declined all comment
today on reports of what pathol-
ogists found in an autopsy on
President Kennedy's body.

The reports gave detailed
support to the Federal Bureau
of Investigation's finding that
two bullets had hit Mr. Kennedy from the rear. The F.B.I.
came to this conclusion in its
report on the assassination.

The pathologists were said
to have found that a first bullet
hit the President in the back.
The bullet lodged in the body.
It assertedly did not hit any
vital organs.

Five days after this article appeared, both the FBI and the Warren
Commission received a copy of the official autopsy report on
December 23, 1963 (*Accessories After The Fact*, p. 148). On January 4,
1964, the *Journal of the American Medical Association* (possibly
utilizing this information) specifically verified the three shots, three-
hit scenario transmitted by Director Hoover to President Johnson: [2]

Kennedy Shot Twice in Back.—President Kennedy was shot twice from the rear by the assassin
who struck him down in Dallas. This unofficial
finding by a team of pathologists who performed
an autopsy on the President's body cleared up confusion over whether Kennedy was shot once or
twice and whether both bullets came from the
same direction.

The autopsy was performed at Bethesda Naval
Hospital on the night of Nov 22 after Kennedy's
body was brought back to Washington from Dallas.

The first bullet reportedly hit Kennedy in the
upper part of the right back shoulder. The bullet
did not go through his body and was recovered
during the autopsy.

The second bullet hit Texas Gov. John B. Connally who was riding in the President's car. The
third bullet hit Kennedy in the back of the right
side of the head. A small fragment of this bullet
also angled down and passed out through Kennedy's throat, it was reported.

---

[1] "Officials Silent on Kennedy Shots," *The New York Times*, December 19, 1963.

[2] "Washington News," *Journal of the American Medical Association*, January 4, 1964, Vol 187, No.
1, pp. A15-A17, http://jama.ama-assn.org.libproxy.lib.unc.edu/content/187/1/A15.full.pdf+html
(retrieved July 4, 2011).

As if to remove all possible doubt, *The New York Times* summarized and confirmed the foregoing (with far more than enough time to analyze the existing medical evidence), on January 19, 1964, nearly 2 *months* after the assassination! [1]

> *Did one bullet strike the President from the front indicating an accomplice?*
> The number of bullets reported, their direction and damage have been matters of wide dispute.
> Investigators are now satisfied that the first of three bullets hit the President in the back of his right shoulder, several inches below the collar line. That bullet lodged in his shoulder. The second bullet wounded Gov. John B. Connally, of Texas.

So, let's sum this all up. According to FBI (through reports directly to the President and to the Warren Commission), and media sources as reputable as *The New York Times* and the *Journal of the American Medical Association* (based on the medical evidence gathered from the autopsy report and other sources), Shot 1 hit President Kennedy, Shot 2 hit Governor Connally, and Shot 3 hit President Kennedy. Once again, three shots, three hits. All of this evidence entirely consistent with an edited version of our element, "Exactly three shots were fired from . . . Lee Harvey Oswald's rifle."

How surprising then, to come across this shocking headline on page 111 of the *Warren Report*:

THE SHOT THAT MISSED

Uh oh!! What have we here? According to the element, only *three* shots were fired. And the conclusions provided by the FBI and media *were* consistent with that element. So what is this? A shot that *missed*?

---

[1] "12 Perplexing Questions About Kennedy Assassination Examined," *The New York Times*, December 19, 1963.

If in fact there *was* a shot that missed, that is an *extra* shot. And since $3 + 1 = 4$, that means that *four* shots were fired, not *three*!

Also, what it means is that if we are 100% confident in the judgments of the FBI provided to the Warren Commission and to President Johnson, and 100% confident in the judgments of the Warren Commission as provided in their *Report vis a vis* this headline, then we can be 100% confident that the element "Exactly three shots were fired from . . . Lee Harvey Oswald's rifle." is *false*, resulting in this modified confidence level regarding the element:

Minimum Confidence	Maximum Confidence
0	**0**

If the above were truly the case, this would be a pretty short chapter. As it turns out, however, the Warren Report fudged on their headline just a few lines later, saying that it was only *probable* that there was a shot that missed (and therefore only *likely* that the element three bullets were fired was false, not *certain*). The Warren Report actually rejected the conclusions of the FBI based on their claimed analysis of the evidence, rejecting the "*three* shots, three hits" scenario in favor of a "*two* shots, three hits" scenario which has subsequently been referred to as the *single bullet theory*.

With only two shots doing all the damage (according to the official version), that meant that one of the shots missed purely from a logical perspective, though the Commission could not identify which shot. As the Commission summarized (WR 111): [1]

> From the initial findings that (*a*) one shot passed through the President's neck and then most probably passed through the Governor's body, (*b*) a subsequent shot penetrated the President's head, (*c*) no other shot struck any part of the automobile, and (*d*) three shots were fired, it follows that one shot probably missed the car and its occupants. The evidence is inconclusive as to whether it was the first, second, or third shot which missed.

Astute readers will note two transformations in the evidentiary findings here, with the FBI telling us that the President was shot in the *back* with a bullet that did *not* pass through his body, and the

---

[1] "Warren Commission Report, Current Section: The Shot That Missed," http://www.maryferrell. org /mffweb/archive/viewer/showDoc.do?absPageId=73535 (retrieved July 5, 2011).

Commission completely ignoring this information and manufacturing a new reality, "reporting" that the President was shot in the *neck* with a bullet that *did* pass through his body, one of the many seismic changes in the factual landscape necessitated by the political desire (as we will shortly see) to promulgate a *lone assassin* theory.

Unfortunately for the credibility of the Warren Commission, we can be almost certain that this reversal of judgment must be incorrect, based on the extraordinarily unlikely possibility that basic medical findings arrived at over a two-month period can plausibly be about-faced; in other words, that a team of medical professionals erroneously reported to the FBI that a bullet entered the *back* and did *not* transit the President's body when in fact it really entered the *neck* and *did* transit the President's body. A "mistake" — in this author's and his wife's and his father's humble opinion — which would be essentially *impossible* for a medical professional to make (the author's wife is a Physician's Assistant with over thirty years experience, the author's father is a retired podiatric surgeon with over forty-five years experience). Anyone who happens to disagree with this assessment is urged to consult with a forensic pathologist near them.

Based on this revised finding, we can be *absolutely certain* that our previous potential hypothesis that we could have 100% confidence in the judgments of both the FBI and the Warren Commission was *false,* since they have transmitted information which is demonstrably *incompatible.* Someone, somewhere, is either grossly incompetent or is not telling the truth, if not both.

Clearly, we have discovered even at this very early stage some confidence-rattling inconsistencies in what has been reported as "the" evidence, and it is in fact inconsistencies like these which have rendered the Kennedy case very much a live issue. Obviously, 4 bullets would demonstrate a conspiracy, and the failure of the Warren Commission to admit to evidence clearly pointing to more bullets than 3 results from flaws in their analysis and investigation, flaws which were recognized by the *House Select Committee On Assassinations* in their 1979 report (HSCA Report 97): [1]

---

[1] "House Select Committee on Assassinations Final Report, Current Section: C. The Committee Believes . . ., That President John F. Kennedy was Probably Assassinated as the Result of a ConspiracyReport," http://www.maryferrell.org/mffweb/archive/viewer/showDoc.do?docId=800&relPageId=127 (retrieved June 30, 2011).

(1) Since the Warren Commission's and FBI's investigation into the possibility of a conspiracy was seriously flawed, their failure to develop evidence of a conspiracy could not be given independent weight.

But why were these respective investigations flawed? Maybe because they were *designed* to be flawed!

According to a memo from acting Attorney General Nicholas Katzenbach to Press Secretary Bill Moyers on November 25, 1963, the whole notion of a conspiracy was to be quashed from the outset; that is to say, the lone assassin *hypothesis* was, at the very beginning of these "investigations," elevated to the status of a *conclusion* which no evidence found dare contradict ("Memo from Katzenbach to Moyers," November 25, 1963):[1]

November 25, 1963

MEMORANDUM FOR MR. MOYERS

      It is important that all of the facts surrounding President Kennedy's Assassination be made public in a way which will satisfy people in the United States and abroad that all the facts have been told and that a statement to this effect be made now.

      1. The public must be satisfied that Oswald was the assassin; that he did not have confederates who are still at large; and that the evidence was such that he would have been convicted at trial.

      2. Speculation about Oswald's motivation ought to be cut off, and we should have some basis for rebutting thought that this was a Communist conspiracy or (as the Iron Curtain press is saying) a right-wing conspiracy to blame it on the Communists. Unfortunately the facts on Oswald seem about too pat-- too obvious (Marxist, Cuba, Russian wife, etc.). The

Obviously, a memo like this turns an *investigation* (a search for truth with no pre-established conclusions) into an *inquisition* (transmitting only that information consistent with a pre-conceived conclusion which itself may be inconsistent with the facts).

---

[1] http://www.history-matters.com/archive/jfk/fbi/105-82555/124-10010-10135/html/124-10010-10135_0002a.htm (retrieved August 09, 2011).

But *why* an inquisition instead of an investigation? As acting Attorney General, why would Katzenbach *want* to cut off speculation about Oswald's motivation? Wouldn't Oswald's potential involvement in a conspiracy be something that the American people would want to know about, and the discovery of this involvement, if in fact it was the case, the *duty* of the American government to discover? Let's face it, if there *were* people involved in a conspiracy, then they would have been just as guilty of the crime of murder as Oswald was (if in fact he was), and to cut off speculation about a conspiracy would be to let the murderers of President Kennedy go free!

When you analyze it, you realize that Katzenbach *could not possibly know* on November 25, only three days after the assassination, when virtually no investigation to speak of had been completed, that a conspiracy was nonexistent! So, right out-of-the-box the searchers for truth were improperly put on a short leash by the people in charge (Katzenbach, most likely acting under orders from his boss, President Johnson), and the wheels of the great machinery of deception began their inexorable motion forward.

Given the serious gaps in the investigatory skills of the Warren Commission and the FBI noted by the *HSCA Report*, gaps motivated by the memo, memos like his memo, and the inevitable subterranean conversations much like his memo, assassination researchers over the last decades have stepped into the void and uncovered literally thousands of pages of evidence contradicting the primary conclusions of the Warren Commission. With reference to the element that only three shots were fired, the evidence to the contrary points to these following conclusions:

1. The evidence indicates that only two empty shells were discovered at the Texas School Book Depository, not three; with only two empty shells, Oswald could not have fired three shots, and/or if the shells in the possession of the Commission were not the same as those found on the floor of the Depository, any controversy ostensibly raised by the following points would be moot.
2. The available audio evidence (and analysis) provides no support for the conclusion that exactly 3 bullets were fired.
3. There was evidence of more bullets *found* than could be accounted for by only three separate shots.
4. There was evidence of more bullets *fired* than those ostensibly fired from the Texas School Book Depository.

5. There was evidence of *multiple* shots to the head of President Kennedy, not just one shot.

6. There was evidence of *multiple* shots to Governor Connally, not just one shot.

7. As the FBI reported, the President was shot in the back, not in the neck, with a bullet that did not pass through President Kennedy's body (and therefore there were at least four separate hits to President Kennedy and Governor Connally, with the extra shot making at least five bullets).

Let us cover these in order, and as we do so, discover their impact on the confidence level of our element.

Reason 1: The evidence indicates that only two empty shells were discovered at the Texas School Book Depository, not three; with only two empty shells, Oswald could not have fired three shots, and/or if the shells in the possession of the Commission were not the same as those found on the floor of the Depository, any controversy ostensibly raised by the following points would be moot.

One of the more intriguing observations noted by the Kennedy assassination research community over the years is that the primary assumption of the Warren Commission that *three* empty shells were found at the Texas School Book Depository turns out to have an overwhelming (and ultimately dispositive) amount of contradictory evidence. But more than that, when you follow the threads emanating from this evidence, you find that you will be lead to some well-hidden skeletons in the closet via a route of twist and turns the most hack Hollywood screenwriter would have been embarrassed to pen.

Unintentional twist and turns, of course, functionally identical to what is referred to in Hollywood as a *continuity error*. [1]

What is a continuity error? It is an error in a film whose fundamental flaw leads to the suspension of the suspension of disbelief we normally have when watching a movie. So if you ever "got into" a film, the continuity error takes you right out of it.

A very simple example of a continuity error is the following: man and woman are having dinner in restaurant. Alternating close-ups of both. Shot 1: Man *wearing* tie, asks woman a question. Shot 2: woman answers question. Shot 3: man *not wearing* tie, asks a follow-up question. Shot 4: woman answers second question. Shot 5: man *wearing* tie, appears satisfied with answer.

Can you *make up a story* to explain how the tie disappeared in the third shot? Sure you can! "Between the questions and the answers, the man with the tie took it off really fast, then he put it back on." And in the history of the cinema, many fans who could not stand the thought of their star directors making such elemental mistakes would invent such stories.

But at the end of the day, we all know that the story is false, just as ridiculous as the error, and the bottom line is that the continuity error

[1] F or examples, see http://en.wikipedia.org/wiki/Continuity_%28fiction%29#Continuity_errors (retrieved September 19, 2011).

is just what it appears to be: an indication that you are just watching a movie, and not a particularly well-made one at that.

As we go through the testimony, you will see more than one example of the Warren Commission version of the continuity error. And as you find them, you may find yourself asking the question "am I viewing *reality*, or am I viewing a *projection* of what is claimed to be reality?"

We can start with the witness reports, beginning with the testimony of Howard Brennan, who in another context was one of the Commission's star witnesses; it is worth noting that this star witness nonetheless provided a statement which contradicted one of the Commission's central propositions. According to Brennan, only *two* shots were fired, not *three* (3 H 154):[1]

> Mr. Brennan. I positively thought that the first shot was a backfire of a motorcycle. And then something made me think that someone was throwing firecrackers from the Texas Book Store, and a possibility it was the second shot. But I glanced up or looked up and I saw this man taking aim for his last shot. The first shot and last shot is my only positive recollection of two shots.

Confirmation of the Brennan statement comes from Bonnie Ray Williams, who was located directly below the sixth floor at the southeast corner of the Texas School Book Depository, and obviously was in a position to hear shots from the floor immediately above. The statement below is from Williams' affidavit of November 22 (Ce 2003; 24 H 229):[2]

> Who, after being by me duly sworn, on oath deposes and says: I went to work at 8 am this morning. I worked on the 6th floor today with Mr. Bill Danry, Charles and a Billy Lovelady. Charles was outside and couldn't get back in, so I guess he went home. We worked up until about 10 minutes to 12. Then we went downstairs. We rode the elevator to the 1st floor and got our lunches. I went back on the 5th floor with a fellow called Hank and Junior, I don't know his last name. Just after we got on the 5th floor we saw the President coming around the corner on Houston from Main Street. I heard 2 shots it sounded like they came from just above us. We ran to the west side of the building. We didn't see anybody. We looked down and

So, in that statement, Williams corroborated the report by Brennan. The FBI gave their report of their interview with him, which

---

[1] http://www.history-matters.com/archive/jfk/wc/wcvols/wh3/html/WC_Vol3_0081b.htm (retrieved December 15, 2011).

[2] http://www.history-matters.com/archive/jfk/wc/wcvols/wh24/html/WH_Vol24_0124a.htm (retrieved December 15, 2011).

confirmed the statement ("FBI Gemberling Report of 30 Nov 1963 re: Oswald," CD 5, p. 330): [1]

> in front of the Texas School Book Depository. While they were watching this car pass, WILLIAMS heard two shots which sounded like they came from right over his head. He stated he was not hanging out the window, but did glance up and saw no one. He

But, as we will see over and over in this book, early testimony confirming a conspiracy hypothesis is later replaced with testimony that confirms the lone assassin hypothesis, whether it is a back wound that becomes a neck wound, or a shot which lodges in the body that becomes a shot which passes through a body, or a shot at the base of the head which becomes a shot to the top of the head, or a shot from the front which becomes a shot from the back, etc. etc. This is no different: later testimony by Williams provides a shift from two shots to three shots (3 H 179): [2]

> Mr. McCLOY. How many shots did you hear fired?
> Mr. WILLIAMS. I heard three shots. But at first I told the FBI I only heard two—they took me down—because I was excited, and I couldn't remember too well. But later on, as everything began to die down, I got my memory even a little better than on the 22d, I remembered three shots, because there was a pause between the first two shots. There was two real quick. There was three shots.

Readers familiar with the case will notice a problem with the next to the last sentence in that paragraph of testimony, which we will cover after focusing on another paragraph providing more significant details regarding the shots (3 H 175): [3]

> Mr. BALL. Did you notice—where did you think the shots came from?
> Mr. WILLIAMS. Well, the first shot—I really did not pay any attention to it, because I did not know what was happening. The second shot, it sounded like it was right in the building, the second and third shot. And it sounded—it even shook the building, the side we were on. Cement fell on my head.

One detail immediately jumps out. Williams changed his story to say that three shots were fired, but he could only positively state that *two* of them were fired from the Depository — yet to confirm the

[1] http://www.maryferrell.org/mffweb/archive/viewer/showDoc.do?docId=10406&relPageId=335 (retrieved December 15, 2011).

[2] http://www.history-matters.com/archive/jfk/wc/wcvols/wh3/html/WC_Vol3_0094a.htm (retrieved December 15, 2011).

[3] http://www.history-matters.com/archive/jfk/wc/wcvols/wh3/html/WC_Vol3_0092a.htm (retrieved December 15, 2011).

element of the Warren Commission, *all* three shots had to be fired from the sixth floor of the Texas School Book Depository, where Oswald was said to have been located at the time of the shooting. Now, if you read this testimony closely, you can see that the testimony is highly unlikely to support that conclusion! Think about it: he didn't "pay any attention to" the first shot, but the second and third shots were so loud and so powerful that they "shook the building" to the extent that cement fell on Williams' head. Could a building-shaking, cement-crumbling, head-dusting shot be something that Williams would not pay "attention to," as he indicated in his testimony related to the first shot?

If the facts of the preceding do not smell like one or more continuity errors to you, another significant problem with the story should trigger the alarm. The story has to conform with the timing of the shots that the Warren Commission told us had to take place based on test firing with rifle. According to the Commission, 2.3 seconds had to elapse between shots (WR 97):[1]

> edge of each to determine the precise course of events.[265]   Tests of the assassin's rifle disclosed that at least 2.3 seconds were required between shots.[266]   In evaluating the films in the light of these timing guides,

If this test data is valid, we would expect the following pattern to be heard by Williams, with a 2.3 second interval designated by the ellipses:

BANG! . . . . BANG! . . . . BANG!

But the Williams testimony ("There was two real quick") indicates that the shots were more like the following pattern:

bang! . . . . BANG! . BANG!

The timing of the second and third shots is an important issue, and numerous witnesses heard the same pattern by Williams, indicating that the distance in time between shots was extremely brief, certainly much less than 2.3 seconds. So, if Williams actually *did* hear that pattern above his head, the shots in all likelihood *were not* — and

---

[1] http://www.history-matters.com/archive/jfk/wc/wr/html/WCReport_0061a.htm (retrieved December 15, 2011).

indeed, *could not have been* — fired from the Mannlicher-Carcano said to have been in the possession of Oswald.

Another continuity error? Most definitely!!

This testimony, by both Brennan and Williams, with its several inconsistencies, itself inconsistent with testimony by Harold Norman and James Jarman that they heard three shots, indicates that witness testimony cannot always be relied on (especially when witness testimony may have been mis-reported, as discussed in the *Appendix* [more on this later]). Luckily, there are other ways to discover the truth, which hopefully will take us out of the world of continuity errors and into the world of the reality we expect to find.

One way, and perhaps the best way, is to follow the receipt trail left by the shells which were discovered on the sixth floor. At every step of the way, for the most part, the passing of the shells was recorded on paper. When we look at that paper trail, we make some interesting discoveries that tell us, ultimately, everything we need to know.

Some foreshadowing of what is to come was indicated by CE 3145, which tells us that after the shells were discovered, Lieutenant J. C. ("Carl") Day, who had possession of the shells, was driven to City Hall by FBI Special Agent Bardwell Odum, *not* by a member of the Dallas Police Department (26 H 830): [1]

"could be done. Agent Odum, Dallas office of the F.B.I. drove Lieutenant Day to the City Hall. The rifle had no manufacturer's

When Day arrived at City Hall, he completed the earliest known document logging the discovery of this evidence (a Crime Scene Search [CSS] form from the Dallas Identification Bureau written by Lieutenant Day dated November 22, 1963, submitted between 1:30 pm and 2:15 pm CST, within two hours of the assassination). This document, which at first glance appears innocuous enough, turns out to be one of the most critical documents Kennedy assassination research has ever unearthed, a document whose first known appearance (to this author) was in the book *Searching The Shadows* by Steven Airhart, published in 1993 (this document can also be found in

---

[1] http://www.history-matters.com/archive/jfk/wc/wcvols/wh26/html/WH_Vol26_0433b.htm (retrieved December 15, 2011).

the *Dallas Municipal Archives*, Box 9, Folder 4, Item 31). [1] Like many of the documents in the Kennedy case, the primary significance of this document is really best seen in the context of other documents (which we are subsequently to examine), and when we do examine those documents, we find that this CSS form can truly be said to be the Rosetta Stone of the Kennedy assassination:

---

[1] "CSS Form (Crime Scene Section), by J. C. Day. Form listing evidence found on the sixth floor of the Texas School Book Depository, (Original), 11/22/63. 00002641," http://jfk.ci.dallas.tx.us/26/2641-001.gif (retrieved September 07, 2011). This higher-quality image comes from the book *Searching The Shadows*, p. 207.

The *first* important detail of the CSS form immediately jumps out at us: *two*, not *three* shells, were submitted to the Identification Bureau, the submitting officers being Lieutenant Day (of the Identification Bureau) and Dallas police photographer Robert Studebaker:

Did I say that the shells were submitted to the Identification Bureau? Well, the letterhead of the document so indicates, and that indeed was the procedural requirement, but take a closer look at the section titled "Signature of Person Receiving Specimen", which provides us a *second* key detail:

The signature reads as follows: "Charles T. Brown, Jr. Spec. Agent, FBI, Dallas". Well below that in a separate place at the bottom of the document, almost as an afterthought, is additional writing by Lieutenant Day: "Vince Drain also present — actually took possession of all evidence. Day".

Both Brown and Drain were associated with the Dallas FBI office, so what this means is that these empty shells were *not* turned over to the Identification Bureau as the letterhead would indicate, but rather, to the *FBI*. Odum of the FBI drove Day to the ID Bureau, Brown of the FBI took possession from Day at the ID Bureau, and so we have two mutually confirming key pieces of documentary evidence that tell us right at the beginning the FBI is heavily involved with the possession of the ballistic evidence.

Now, many readers will not find this odd, but it is. At this early stage of the game —"1:30 to 2:15" pm (Central Standard Time, or CST), according to the "Time" field at the top of the memo, the *third* key detail . . .

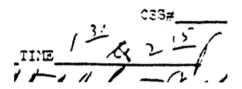

. . . the transfer of possession of ballistic evidence to the FBI would have been an extraordinary anomaly. Why? Because the Dallas Police Department *alone* had jurisdiction over the case, and the FBI had *none*, as shown by this exchange between FBI Director J. Edgar Hoover and Warren Commission Chairman Earl Warren on May 14, 1964 (5 H 115): [1]

> The CHAIRMAN. You have told us that you had no jurisdiction down there in Dallas over this crime.
> Mr. HOOVER. That is correct.
> The CHAIRMAN. Because there is no Federal crime committed. And I assume that that caused you some embarrassment and some confusion in doing your work?
> Mr. HOOVER. It most certainly did.

Dallas Police Chief Jesse Curry discussed this aspect of the case with the Commission on April 22 1964, relating a conversation between himself and Captain John Will Fritz of the Dallas Police Department (4 H 195): [2]

> Mr. CURRY. Now, subsequent to that, we felt this, that this was a murder that had been committed in the county, city and county of Dallas, and that we had prior, I mean we had jurisdiction over this. The FBI actually had no jurisdiction over it, the Secret Service actually had no jurisdiction over it. But in an effort to cooperate with these agencies we went all out to do whatever they wanted us to do that we could do to let them observe what was taking place, but actually we knew that this was a case that happened in Dallas, Tex., and would have to be tried in Dallas, Tex., and it was our responsibility to gather the evidence and present the evidence.
> We kept getting calls from the FBI. They wanted this evidence up in Washington, in the laboratory, and there was some discussion, Fritz told me, he says, "Well, I need the evidence here, I need to get some people to try to identify the gun, to try to identify this pistol and these things, and if it is in Washington how can I do it?"
> But we finally, the night, about midnight of Friday night, we agreed to let the FBI have all the evidence and they said they would bring it to their laboratory and they would have an agent stand by and when they were finished with it to return it to us.

---

[1] http://www.history-matters.com/archive/jfk/wc/wcvols/wh5/html/WC_Vol5_0063a.htm (retrieved December 15, 2011).

[2] http://www.history-matters.com/archive/jfk/wc/wcvols/wh4/html/WC_Vol4_0102a.htm (retrieved December 15, 2011).

And so the FBI was provided the evidence, apparently because this was a "special investigation" called for by President Johnson according to Director Hoover in that same testimony (5 H 98): [1]

Mr. RANKIN. You have provided many things to us in assisting the Commission in connection with this investigation and I assume, at least in a general way, you are familiar with the investigation of the assassination of President Kennedy, is that correct?

Mr. HOOVER. That is correct. When President Johnson returned to Washington he communicated with me within the first 24 hours, and asked the Bureau to pick up the investigation of the assassination because as you are aware, there is no Federal jurisdiction for such an investigation. It is not a Federal crime to kill or attack the President or the Vice President or any of the continuity of officers who would succeed to the Presidency.

However, the President has a right to request the Bureau to make special investigations, and in this instance he asked that this investigation be made. I immediately assigned a special force headed by the special agent in charge at Dallas, Tex., to initiate the investigation, and to get all details and facts concerning it, which we obtained, and then prepared a report which we submitted to the Attorney General for transmission to the President.

According to Hoover, though, this so-called "special investigation" was not requested by Johnson until *after* Johnson returned to Washington ("When President Johnson returned to Washington . . ."). This statement conforms with the facts, since Johnson would not have called for this special investigation any earlier. In the first place, Johnson had not been informed that President Kennedy had died until **1:10 p.m.** CST (RH 75), and until that time could not have been certain that he would be President. Then, Johnson remained at Parkland Hospital until **1:40 p.m.** CST, after which he departed for Air Force One at Love Field, where he was sworn in as President at **2:38 p.m** CST. After the swearing-in ceremony, he was flown to Andrews Air Force Base, located approximately 10 miles southeast of Washington DC (in Prince George's County, Maryland), where he arrived at approximately **5:00 p.m** CST. [2] He was then flown by helicopter to the White House, when he touched down at **5:26 pm** CST (RH 144). In this whirlwind of a day, Johnson was obviously too preoccupied to call Hoover, and so when Hoover tells us that Johnson contacted him *after* **5:26 p.m.** CST, we can believe him.

---

[1] http://www.history-matters.com/archive/jfk/wc/wcvols/wh5/html/WC_Vol5_0054b.htm (retrieved December 15, 2011).

[2] Times not from *Reclaiming History* are from http://en.wikipedia.org/wiki/First_inauguration _of_Lyndon_B._Johnson (retrieved September 07, 2011).

And there's the rub: the FBI had no jurisdiction over the case, and the normal Dallas police procedure would have been to turn over the evidence to personnel at the Crime Scene Search Section of the Dallas Identification Bureau (for example, an FBI agent at Parkland Memorial Hospital refused to accept a bullet found on a stretcher by a Parkland employee; see discussion at RH 84, Paragraph 2 re: CE 399).

But here this procedure was violated. An order essentially re-designating jurisdiction had supposedly been given, but that order could not have been given *any earlier* than 5:26 p.m, or more likely, 6:00 pm CST. And yet, when we look at the time that the shells were handed over to Brown of the FBI, we can see that the time of the handoff was much earlier, at the outside around *2:15 p.m.* CST:[1]

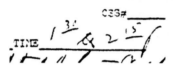

This means that approximately 5 *hours* before the earliest time Johnson could have given the order to Hoover that the FBI should take command of the investigation, the FBI had *already moved in* to take possession of the evidence!

The question now is, *who* gave that order? We know it wasn't *Johnson*, and from a legal perspective it couldn't have been *Hoover*, the head of the FBI reporting to Johnson (and to whom Brown ultimately reported), because Hoover tells us in his testimony that he didn't give any such order until after "President Johnson returned to Washington," which was at 5:26 pm CST.

So if Johnson didn't give the order, and Hoover didn't give it, *who did*? Who, only one hour after the death of the President, would have had the authority to take an action of this nature on their own, absent specific orders, and in violation of the code within which State and Federal criminal investigations operated, and more importantly, who could have *anticipated* this direction, given that it was not decided much later by those in charge? It is critical to note that this handoff had to consist of *coordinated edicts*, one by the head of the Dallas Police Department, and one by the head of the Federal Bureau of investigation — this could only be a *bilateral*, not a *unilateral* decision — and we know by the April 22 testimony of Curry that this was an agreement not easily arrived at, an agreement that took literally hours

---

[1] That this time is accurate is confirmed by 26 H 830, quoting a January 08, 1964 letter by Day which states that Lieutenant Day returned to Elm Street at "about 2:45 pm."

to achieve. So, well before this agreement was in fact achieved, who could have convinced Day and Studebaker to hand over the Evidence of the Century to those outside the scope of legitimate authority when no such edicts were given and the President's death was announced just an *hour* earlier?

Now *that's* a continuity error!

Maybe we can't see the rat yet, but we sure can smell it, and by the smell we can be fairly sure it's a big one. Let's carry on with the story and see where the scent takes us.

After Brown (and supposedly Drain) had received the envelope with the 2 spent hulls and the live round, those items were sent to Special Agent (SA) J. Doyle Williams of the Dallas FBI Office, who made a photograph of this evidence (and whose initials appear on the identification card on the table) (*Bloody Treason*, p. 111): [1]

A cover sheet prepared for the photograph tells us that what we are seeing is no optical illusion: there are only "two 6.5" hulls in the very first dated and identified photograph taken of the empty shells, as stated in the 3rd line of the description in this photograph (*Bloody Treason*, p. 110): [2]

---

[1] This photo is located in box 173 b of the FBI Dallas Field Office File 89-43, RG 65, JFK Collection, National Archives, RIF 124-10063-10042.

[2] See also FBI File 89-43-1A [28], Evidence Envelope dated November 22, 1963, National Archives; Crime Scene Search Form, November 22, 1963, box 9, folder 4, items 31 and 32.

File No. _____ 89- 43-1A²⁸

Date Received _____ 11-22-63

From _____
                    (NAME OF CONTRIBUTOR)

_____
                    (ADDRESS OF CONTRIBUTOR)

_____
                    (CITY AND STATE)

By _____
                    (NAME OF SPECIAL AGENT)

To Be Returned   Yes ☐
                        No ☑

Description:

[handwritten] 2 negatives + 4 prints of each) two "6.5 bullet hulls + 1 "live" round of 6.5 ammunit.. from rifle found on 6th Floor of Texas Book Depository, Dallas on 11-22-63.

Photographer Williams dictated a memorandum on November 23 detailing the photographic session of November 22, which was released by the government many months after the Warren Commission report was issued (CD 5, p. 169): [1]

_____

[1] http://www.maryferrell.org/mffweb/archive/viewer/showDoc.do?docId=10406&relPageId=175 (retrieved December 15, 2011).

FEDERAL BUREAU of INVESTIGATION

Date __11/23/63__

On November 22, 1963, SA J. DOYLE WILLIAMS photographed a 6.5 caliber 1940 model rifle made in Italy, Serial Number C2766, mounting a 4 x 18 coated scope. The scope was manufactured by Ordinance Optics, Incorporated, Hollywood, California.

The rifle was in possession of the Dallas Police Department Crime Laboratory.

A Speedgraphic camera, 4 x 5, was used with camera settings at F32 at 100th of a second. Each photograph was identified with a description of the weapon together with the initials JDW, Federal Bureau of Investigation Dallas.

Two photographs were also made on November 22, 1963, of two 6.5 ammunition hulls obtained from the Dallas Police Department Crime Laboratory. Also photographed along with the two above items was one "live" round of 6.5 ammunition obtained from Captain WILL FRITZ of the Dallas Police Department.

Each photograph of the above items was identified in the photograph with the initials JDW and the date November 22, 1963, Federal Bureau of Investigation.

A speedgraphic 4 x 5, camera was used with a lense setting of F32 at 100th of a second.

The above film were developed in the Federal Bureau of Investigation Office on November 23, 1963, by Investigative Clerk JOE PEARCE and are being retained in custody of the Dallas Federal Bureau of Investigation Office.

_169_

on __11/22/63__ at __Dallas, Texas__ _____ File # __DL 89-43__

by Special Agent ____J. DOYLE WILLIAMS/ejg____ Date dictated __11/23/63__

The photograph by Williams, along with the cover sheet description and his memorandum above, indicates clearly that on November 22 the Dallas FBI had assumed possession of the two empty shells and the live round, possession that was lengthy enough in time to allow for an extensive photographic session, and these documents taken together confirm the 2:15 pm receipt by Brown of the evidence as indicated by the November 22 CSS Form.

Even though the preceding documents and the November 22 CSS Form prove an early afternoon receipt by the FBI, that's not the official story. So what *is* the official story? It's this:

> The evidence was in the possession of the Dallas Police Department (*not* the FBI) until 11:45 p.m. CST, when it was to be sent to Washington with Vincent Drain.

This story is immediately suspect because Drain's own affidavit regarding the chain of possession (in Warren Commission Document 5, pp. 159-161) [1] *nowhere mentions* that after he assumed custody of the evidence he delivered the evidence to J. Doyle Williams to be photographed, proving that the Williams photo was taken *before* Drain collected the evidence in a box at 11:45 p.m. CST, and that therefore the FBI had possession *well before* 11:45 pm (i.e. 2:15 pm). Drain was on an extremely tight timeline, and certainly would not have dallied in Dallas for a Williams photo session, as proven by a statement he made in a taped interview (*No More Silence*, p. 249; emphasis supplied):

> By the time we got it all boxed up, it was near midnight. **Meanwhile Washington was calling down about every fifteen minutes wanting to know where the material was.** All of a sudden I learned that neither American nor Braniff had any flights to Washington out of Dallas after midnight. **We were told that the FBI in Washington wanted the material by morning if we had to walk it up there.** That's being facetious, but . . .
>
> Fortunately, the commanding general over at Carswell in Fort Worth happened to be a good friend of mine and was head of SAC (Strategic Air Command) at the time. So I called him and was told that **the President had asked him to give us all the help that we needed. Another agent took me to Fort Worth where they had a C-135 tanker plane and crew ready.**

---

[1] http://www.maryferrell.org/mffweb/archive/viewer/showDoc.do?docId=10406&relPageId=165 (retrieved December 15, 2011).

Definitely a sense of urgency up there in Washington. No time for more photos, Drain, get a move on! Quite the coincidence too, that the person selected to carry this critical evidence *just happened* to have a good friend with the Strategic Air Command (the commander of the Carswell Air Force base) ready to pitch in with a tanker plane to transport these *select* future exhibits (such as two empty cartridge cases, the live round, metal fragments, a shirt, a blanket, and a paper bag), a friend who also *just happened* to have been contacted by President Johnson *before* Drain made his request. It's a small world after all!

Drain arrived at Andrews Air Force base in the C-135 tanker plane at 6:30 AM EST (CD 5, p. 160) [1] on November 23. After Drain left Andrews Air Force Base and delivered the evidence to the Washington FBI laboratory (accompanied by armed guard), the evidence was inventoried in a letter prepared on November 23. Here is the relevant section of the screen capture of the inventory listing the evidence received by Drain (CE 2003, p. 132: 24 H 262): [2]

Evidence received from **Special Agent Vincent E. Drain of the Dallas Office** of the FBI on 11/23/63:

Q6 6.5 millimeter Mannlicher-Carcano cartridge case from building
Q7 6.5 millimeter Mannlicher-Carcano cartridge case from building
Q8 6.5 millimeter Mannlicher-Carcano cartridge from rifle

You will note once again that only *two* shells, not *three*, were sent to the FBI. Take this as another note: FBI laboratory identification numbers Q6 and Q7 refer to the 2 empty shells (Q8 refers to a live round that was said to have been found in a rifle alleged to be Oswald's). Remember those "Q" numbers, you will be glad you did!!

This vital evidence, delivered into the hands of the FBI on November 22, left Washington approximately 18 hours later, around midnight of November 23, returning to the Dallas Police Department Sunday morning, November 24 (*No More Silence*, p. 250), when Oswald was still alive and a forthcoming trial was very much alive as a possibility. A receipt for these items as being delivered into the

---

[1] http://www.maryferrell.org/mffweb/archive/viewer/showDoc.do?docId=10406&relPageId=166 (retrieved December 15, 2011).
[2] "Warren Commission Hearings, Volume XXIV, Current Section: CE 2003 - Dallas Police Department file on investigation of the assassination of the President (CD 81b, all pages)," http://www.maryferrell.org/mffweb/archive/viewer/showDoc.do?docId=1140&relPageId=280 (retrieved June 30, 2011).

custody of chief of police Jesse Curry was ostensibly prepared at 3:40 p.m., November 24, 1963 (CD 5, p. 161).[1]

But this material was only to remain briefly in Dallas. It was returned *yet again* to the custody of Vince Drain of the FBI at 2:00 pm on November 26 (two days after Oswald had been murdered), as noted by Lieutenant Day in his testimony (4 H 273):[2]

> Mr. BELIN. I am going to now hand you what has been marked as 738 and ask you to state if you know what this is.
> Mr. DAY. Yes, sir. This is a photograph of most of the evidence that was returned to the FBI the second time on November 26, 1963. It was released to Agent Vince Drain at 2 p.m., November 26.

There is important documentary evidence indicating the transmission of the evidence the second time to the FBI, on November 26 (after Oswald had been killed, when there was now no forthcoming trial). Observing CE 738 ("Photograph of property released by the Dallas Police Department to the FBI on November 26, 1963," 17 H 512),[3] we can see that four days after the assassination, there were still only *two* bullets:

Screen capture of CE 738 showing only two shells.	*A clearer picture of the two shells, which appeared on p. 88 of Dallas Police Chief Jesse Curry's book **JFK Assassination File**.*

Now, remember that the FBI had identified these shells as "Q6" and "Q7" before returning them to Dallas. But which is which? Is Q6 the one on the left, or the one on the right? Apparently when the

---

[1] http://www.maryferrell.org/mffweb/archive/viewer/showDoc.do?docId=10406&relPageId=167 (retrieved December 15, 2011).

[2] http://www.history-matters.com/archive/jfk/wc/wcvols/wh4/html/WC_Vol4_0141a.htm (retrieved December 15, 2011).

[3] http://www.history-matters.com/archive/jfk/wc/wcvols/wh17/html/WH_Vol17_0269b.htm (retrieved December 15, 2011).

shells were returned to Dallas from the Washington FBI office, they were sent back not in *separate* envelopes, but both together in *one* envelope, with no identifying information affixed. We can only infer this, because the Dallas Police Department property clerk's invoice listing a description of items that were sent back to the FBI (dated November 26, 1963), and clearly showing in the last row that only "2" (not "3") spent hulls were found under the window of the sixth floor of the Texas School Book Depository (CE 2003 at 24 H 252 and 332), has no "Q" number designations (see bottom row): [1]

Let's zoom in on that:

Sloppy, sloppy! The significance of the missing "Q" nomenclature, which at this juncture would appear to be simply an arcane detail, will become readily apparent.

In any event, to get back to the main point, things aren't looking up for the claim that *3*, not *2* hulls were found on the sixth floor.

---

[1] http://www.history-matters.com/archive/jfk/wc/wcvols/wh24/html/WH_Vol24_0175b.htm (retrieved July 11, 2011).

Indeed, all the evidence we have looked at so far is telling the same story, but unfortunately for the Warren Commission and the lone assassin hypothesis, the story it is telling — 2 — does not match the story they have told — 3.

We are in debt to researchers Josiah Thompson, Steven Airheart, John Armstrong, and Noel Tywman for shining the spotlight on this issue and uncovering the key documents we have just seen. [1] Of the books by these researchers, Twyman paid the most attention to this issue, publishing the documents he discovered in his excellent book *Bloody Treason*.

Unfortunately for Mr. Twyman, his years-long detective work was met with scorn by ace prosecutor Vincent Bugliosi, who devoted a few pages to an analysis of the issue in his magnum opus on the Kennedy assassination, *Reclaiming History*, and sought to explain this most anomalous of anomalies, 2 vs. 3.

"Very easy to understand, no problem at all," the ace prosecutor informs us (Bugliosi is the Warren Commission's *apologist emeritus*, the type of guy who will tell you that there is a very simple explanation for why an actor's tie would appear in one shot and then immediately disappear in another, only to immediately appear again). Here is the resolution Bugliosi most graciously provided for his readers (*Reclaiming History*, Endnotes, p. 419):

> Unbeknownst to his readers, all Twyman had managed to prove was something that has been a well-known and established *fact* for years: that on the night of November 22 the Dallas police turned over to the FBI only two of the three cartridge cases they had recovered from the sixth floor, along with the live round found in the rifle's firing chamber. The third shell (along with Oswald's wallet, identification, and notebook) was retained by Captain Fritz (who, let's not forget, was in charge of the investigation at this point) "to be used," Fritz said, "for comparison tests" since his office was trying to determine where the cartridges had been bought. Fritz kept the shell in his desk drawer until the early morning hours of November 27, when it was turned over to FBI agent James P. Hosty Jr. (7 H 404, WC affidavit of John Will Fritz; CE 2003, 24 H 347)[*]

Okay, let's get this one straight: yes, it is true that all the documents necessary for establishing a chain of custody for this vital

---

[1] In addition, excellent analysis of this issue was provided by Michael Weisberg in his article "Three Cartridge Cases: Chain Of Possession," *The Third Decade*, Volume 6, Issue 4, http://www.maryferrell.org/mffweb/archive/viewer/showDoc.do?absPageId=521580, and Jerry Rose in his article "Shell Games, part 1," *The Third Decade*, Volume 4, Issue 5, http://www.maryferrell.org/mffweb/archive/viewer/showDoc.do?absPageId=521352.

evidence demonstrate conclusively that only 2/3 of this evidence actually existed on November 22, 1963, but according to Mr. Bugliosi, we are to ignore these documents, and instead rely on the following story: that in the most significant murder investigation in history, in what would have been the trial of the century in the United States of America, Police Captain John Will Fritz egregiously deviated from the protocol of his own office by not having the evidence he supposedly received logged in the same manner as all the other evidence in the case, as found in over 32 detailed pages found in Commission Exhibit 2003 (24 H 330), down to the most insignificant items, such as film exposure instructions [24 H 334], an address label advertisement [24 H 334], a stack of envelopes [24 H 331] and foreign coins in a Kodak film bag [24 H 340]), but, rather, without bothering to inform anyone in writing, squirreled away an empty shell that supposedly contained a bullet that could have killed the President of the United States — one of the most key pieces of evidence in this most significant of murder cases — *in his desk drawer*!!

The reader should note that Bugliosi delivers this news with a metaphorical straight face; the withering tone that would be present were he on the side of the defense is entirely absent here. An "explanation" entirely improbable from the outset; no wonder Bugliosi buried this analysis in an endnote contained on a CD to his book, which, were it attached to the book proper, would be found somewhere around page 2077.

It is perhaps not a coincidence that this extra bullet turned up only after Oswald died, when no pesky defense attorneys could throw the spotlight on highly suspect lapses in the chain of custody via dissection of the evidentiary remains.

The significance of this issue cannot be overstated; if in fact Captain Fritz had *not* stored the bullet in his desk drawer, and if in fact no bullet had been found, then there would not only be a conspiracy to kill President Kennedy, but also an "after-the-fact" conspiracy to cover up evidence of the initial conspiracy; indeed, not just a *cover-up* of evidence, but even worse, a *manufacturing* of evidence, framing an innocent man to prevent an investigation that could reveal the existence of the guilty.

Unfortunately for the plausibility of this story of Captain Fritz, it doesn't quite resonate with the facts. The first problem is the CSS Form of November 22, which we saw was timestamped between 1:30 and 2:15 p.m:

You will note the names of the three officers who submitted the evidence of the two spent hulls to the Dallas Police Identification Bureau, which turned out to be, surprisingly enough, "Lt. JC Day," "R.L. Studebaker," and *Captain Fritz*"!

So, according to this document, less than two hours after the assassination, Day, Studebaker, and Fritz had brought back only *two* spent hulls, which we know from the same document were *immediately* turned over to Brown of the FBI. Therefore,

There was no third shell for Fritz to confiscate!

An additional problem for the story, if one is needed (and one isn't), is the date of the Property Invoice Receipt logged by the Warren Commission. Let's take a closer look at that receipt:

And now, its date:

When we put 2 + 2 together, the meaning is quite clear: Captain Fritz claimed that he had possession of an empty shell from November

22 through November 27. However, as of November 26, 1963, neither he, nor any of his peers, followed the protocol of his office in logging that evidence, as this Property Clerk's Invoice makes all too clear. From an official perspective, as of November 26, 1963, *this shell did not exist*. And since these official protocols are designed precisely to ensure the integrity of evidence labeled as such, and to discourage the planting of false evidence, this was a most egregious failure of protocol indeed.

Little help comes from a final piece of documentation, Warren Commission Exhibit 2003, which is officially identified as the "Dallas Police Department file on investigation of the assassination of the President." Among the many documents contained in that exhibit is the following evidence sheet. Notice the number of rounds that were supposedly turned over to the Warren Commission (CE 2003: 24 H 260): [1]

```
1  .3⁸ Cal pistol, 2" barrel, S&W, Rev.        W. M. McDonald, MPD, took it from Oswald
   sandblast finish, brown wooden handles      at 231 W. Jefferson, gave it to Sgt. Jerry
   ser.# 510210. Rel. to FBI agent 11-22-63    Hill who gave it to Det. Baker.
   and again 11-26-63
Bullet fragments taken from body of
Governor Connally                              Mrs. Audrey Bell, Operating room nurse,to
                                               Bob Nolan, D.P.S., to Capt. Fritz, to Crime
Live round 6.5                                 lab, to FBI.
                                             ( Recovered by Dept. Sheriff Luke Mooney at
6.5 spent rounds (3)                         ( 411 Eln, 6th floor, southeast window.
                                             (
1  Man's brown sport shirt "Taken from
   Lee Harvey Oswald
```

This document is already implausible because, according to the official story, only *two* bullets were handed over on November 22nd and November 26th, but this document says "3." Thus, this evidence plainly contradicts the official story, and if that story is true, this document cannot possibly be legitimate. We can prove this by zooming in on the relevant portion of the screen capture, where we notice something strange:

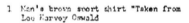

Somehow, this 3 doesn't look quite right. It almost has a *hand-drawn* quality, particularly at the bottom. We can confirm our intuitive perception by comparing this "3" (labeled as "C" below) with 2 other 3s

[1] "Warren Commission Hearings, Volume XXIV, Current Section: CE 2003 - Dallas Police Department file on investigation of the assassination of the President (CD 81b, all pages)," http://www.maryferrell.org/mffweb/archive/viewer/showDoc.do?docId=1140&relPageId=278 (retrieved June 30, 2011).

that appear on the page, one in the phrase "231 W. Jefferson," ("A") and another in the phrase ".38 Slug" ("B"). When we do that, we can see a marked difference between these 3 examples:

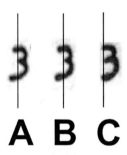

Letter	Phrase Appeared In
A	231 W. Jefferson
B	.38 Slug
C	6.5 Spent Rounds (3)

Notice the distinct difference between the first two 3s, A and B, and the last 3, C, with its hand-drawn quality. In particular, notice how the base and top of the 3 in A and B goes well past the vertical line drawn through the middle of the number, whereas it just barely goes past those areas in the C version. Also, notice the empty space in the bottom area of the number, which is quite prominent in the hand drawn version, and compressed in the other two.

Though these discrepancies clearly indicate something anomalous about this number, absolute proof that a change was made was provided in Gary Shaw's 1976 book *Cover-Up*, on p. 159. Mr. Shaw had discovered the original version of this document in Dallas Police Department records, and it failed to resemble the Warren Commission version of the document in at least one very key area:

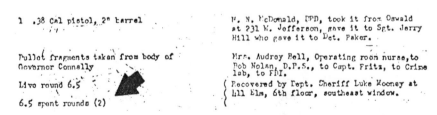

Let's zoom in again on the relevant portion of the screen capture:

6.5 spent rounds (2)

When you compare the two images side-by-side, the discrepancy (and modification of the number) is absolutely confirmed:

6.5 spent rounds (2)	6.5 spent rounds (3)
The line on the original Oswald evidence sheet as it appears on the record from the Dallas Police Department.	*The line as it appears in Warren Commission Exhibit 2003.*

At this stage of the game, the *only* documentary evidence we have seen that 3 shells were found turns out, on closer examination, to be an apparent *forgery*. So, what are we to make of all the evidence (which we formerly thought of as legitimate) that three shells were found: for example, the photograph CE 510 (17 H 221), which shows 3 shells on the sixth floor of the Texas School Book Depository, and the testimony of Luke Mooney (3 H 286), Fritz, and Day, among others, that three shells were found? Is this evidence and testimony as solid as we would like it to be? Not necessarily. Take a look at CE 510, which shows three shells:

Does this photograph represent the shells in their actual position? Not according to Luke Mooney's testimony (3 H 286): [1]

> Mr. BALL. Well, we will label these cartridges, the empty shells as "A", "B", and "C."
>
> Now, I didn't quite understand—did you say it was your memory that "A" and "B" were not that close together?
>
> Mr. MOONEY. Just from my memory, it seems that this cartridge ought to have been over this way a little further.
>
> Mr. BALL. You mean the "B" cartridge should be closer to the "C?"
>
> Mr. MOONEY. Closer to the "C"; yes, sir.

That is a slight problem, which is slightly amplified by a second problem: there is no date which *appears in the photograph*, nor any identifying information regarding the photographer which *appears in the photograph*. Given this missing information, the exhibit could have been a "re-creation" (read: *re-invention*) of the way the shells were *supposed to* have been located on the floor, a photograph that could have been taken anywhere from 2 to 8 days, or even more, after November 22 — and that would be *more than* a slight problem, because the photograph would not be authentic from the standpoint of *Federal Rule Of Evidence* 901 (a), which you will recall provides as follows:

ARTICLE IX. AUTHENTICATION AND IDENTIFICATION

Rule 901. Authenticating or Identifying Evidence

(a) In General. To satisfy the requirement of authenticating or identifying an item of evidence, the proponent must produce evidence sufficient to support a finding that the item is what the proponent claims it is.

If the photograph was a "re-invention", then it would not be considered *real* evidence, but *demonstrative* evidence, evidence of a lower quality because it would not be the thing itself but rather something which purported to resemble the thing itself (like diagrams, models, simulations, etc.). However, the claim by the officers was that this *was* real evidence, but if in fact it was *only* demonstrative evidence, then to that extent the photograph would be *inauthentic*.

If you were a judge, how would *you* rule on the admissibility of a photograph officers claimed was *real* when you found out later it was only *demonstrative*?

---

[1] https://www.maryferrell.org/mffweb/archive/viewer/showDoc.do?docId=39&relPageId=294 (retrieved March 30, 2012).

Now, you might think it implausible that *any* of the photographs exhibited before the Warren Commission would be re-creations, but if there is nothing else we learn from the Kennedy case, we at least will learn this: "implausible" is sometimes just a synonym for "certain," as proven by this *evidence* of one such reconstruction (4 H 269): [1]

> Mr. BELIN. I am going to hand you what has been marked as Commission Exhibit 733 and ask you to state if you know what this is.
> Mr. DAY. This is the southeast corner of the sixth floor at the window where the shooting apparently occurred. The boxes in front of the window, to the best of our knowledge, in the position they were in when we arrived there on November 22, 1963.
> Mr. BELIN. So 733 represents a reconstruction in that sense, is that correct?
> Mr. DAY. Yes, sir.
> Mr. BELIN. What about Exhibit——
> Mr. DAY. This, by the way, was taken on November 25, 1963.

So, we know from this testimony that *not every* photograph exhibited by the Warren Commission as a record of the scene on November 22 was *taken* on November 22 (not to mention that not every photograph exhibited by the Warren Commission was of the genuine reality)! Now, considering the man-hours and set-up time involved, do we really believe that only *one* photograph was taken on November 25, or even some later date? Isn't it entirely fair to speculate that *other* photographs were taken on November 25 (or later), not just one, and that perhaps *some, most,* or *all* of these November 25 (or later) photos were "reconstructions" as well? If that was the case, and CE 510 was one of those photos, then all that is needed is for someone to testify that CE 510 was *actually* taken on November 22, and who would be able to prove them wrong?

Lacking the authenticating information in the photograph itself by which the legitimacy of the photograph could be substantiated, and considering the testimony of Mooney that the shells were in a slightly different position from what he *claimed* he observed, the validity of this photograph must be seen as suspect, especially in light of the evidence we have just seen (and are about to see).

OK, if identifying information is lacking in the photo, what about the testimony of Mooney and others that they did *in fact* find *three* shells on the scene? That is *direct*, not *circumstantial* evidence. Well, one simple explanation — apart from the obvious possibility that they

---

[1] http://www.history-matters.com/archive/jfk/wc/wcvols/wh4/html/WC_Vol4_0139a.htm (retrieved December 15, 2011).

are mistaken, and two additional possibilities we will discuss later — is that *they weren't telling the truth.*

To those who may find this difficult to believe, we can take the word of Vincent Bugliosi that "**police are human beings like everyone else, and a few have been known, in their effort to be looked upon as heroes, not only to magnify what they did or saw, but actually to make false claims** . . ." (RH 889; emphasis supplied). Earlier in his book, Bugliosi also advises us (in the context of how defendants seek to establish their innocence) that "**many times . . . evidence is fabricated**" (RH 827; emphasis supplied), but of course it can work the other way as well, and is more likely to, since the police have custody over the evidence, and as a prosecutor with decades of experience, and one who knows that police are capable of making false claims, Bugliosi should know all about that.

We can also add to Bugliosi's rationale for why police would make false claims that perhaps they were *under pressure* to make these claims. With the media broadcasting the "Oswald as lone assassin" story 24/7 month after month after November 22, the pressure on the officers to give the "correct" testimony must have been intense, not to mention the fact that in some of these cases, their jobs might have been on the line.

So, if the photographs and testimony are potentially suspect, is there any other way to verify the existence (or lack thereof) of the third shell? Yes, by using a key technique in police investigation used to document the chain of custody. Using this technique, one can literally follow the virtual ownership of a piece of evidence throughout its lifespan.

This technique is the *marking of items of evidence at the scene of the crime — and at the time of discovery — by those persons who have uncovered that evidence.* For example, at the time and place a bullet is found, the initials and/or name of the finder need to be scratched into the metal using a tool designed for the purpose, which at the time of the Kennedy assassination was a **diamond point pencil**. In fact, the very *existence* of such a specialized tool should tell you something about the ubiquity of a standard process for identifying evidence throughout the criminal justice system in United States of America in the 1960s (and today, it might be added), and that in turn should tell you something about the *importance* of this process. In the case of the Kennedy assassination, which up to that time was certainly the most important criminal prosecution of the 20th century in the United States, we can be sure that everyone handling the evidence, especially before Oswald was murdered and a trial was imminent, was well aware that they needed to get all their SOP ducks in a row, and any *variations* from this practice would be very telling indeed.

To illustrate how this technique works using a very simple example, let's assume that a bullet was found at the scene of the crime, and the first person to find the bullet was Andy. Subsequently, Andy passed it off to Brian, and then Brian later passed it off to Charlie. At each transition point, the respective parties were to carve their initials on the bullet with the diamond point pencil, Andy using "A," Brian using "B," and Charlie using "C." If that were the case, and the protocol were followed, the bullet would look something like the following:

Later, at the trial, Andy, Brian, and Charlie would be brought in to testify that the initials on the bullet were theirs and theirs alone (bringing along any ancillary materials such as receipts, etc., which described in detail the item in question). And in this "happy path" scenario, the chain of custody for this particular bullet would be established.

Naturally, this could be extended to any number of parties: if we suppose that two additional parties, David and Edward, were also transferred the bullet later in time, then we would expect to see this:

And that's the happy path for parties A through E. But not all paths are happy, and that's when the brains of the citizens in the jury box need to go on red alert. Imagine that Andy, Brian, Charlie, David, and Edward were the key personnel in the chain of custody sequence. If so, we know what the bullet is supposed to look like. But, suppose instead the bullet offered into evidence at trial revealed only *these* initials:

That would be a major problem indeed! According to the evidence of the bullet, *evidence that trumps any testimony to the contrary*, the only people who handled *this* bullet were Brian and Edward. And, if Andy, Charlie, and David actually *did* mark a bullet, then we can be sure that the bullet that they marked was *not this one*! That would mean that there were *two* bullets, one which was actually present at the scene of the crime, the other surreptitiously later introduced into evidence!

This is such a serious problem that even if we had what some might refer to as a "minor" gap in the chain of custody, that so-called *minor* gap would actually be a *major* gap:

The reason that one letter lost is a major gap is that the person who *first* found the bullet was Andy. Andy marked his bullet. Yet Andy's initial is not on this bullet, is it? This means that this bullet was *not* the one found by Andy. So, even though there is a legitimate chain of custody following, that chain of custody is *irrelevant*, because we know that this bullet could *not* have been the bullet found by Andy — the bullet at the scene of the crime, and the only one that counts.

The problem would be even worse if we then went to David, and asked him if he carved his initials in the bullet, and he told us "No." That would be a second problem, a case of *false identification* to go along with our previous case of *missing identification*. Where false identification was concerned, the initials would be forged, not the bullet, but the end result would be the same.

If we have either (or both) of these types of mal-identification, false or missing, this bullet would therefore not be admissible into evidence, and any case relying on this bullet would be finished. A continuity error, a literal one, that could not be overcome. And for want of this nail, the kingdom would be lost — the nail in the coffin, so to speak.

Now that we have the basic concept in mind, let's track the chain of custody for the Kennedy shells and live round. When we look at the testimony related to the *live round* alleged to have been found on the sixth floor, we can see that *the procedure was followed* as established. The first person considered to have possession was Lieutenant Day, who in testimony before the Warren Commission on April 22 stated that he marked the live round at the scene of the crime, just like it was supposed to be (4 H 258):[1]

> Mr. DAY. Captain Fritz was present. After we got the photographs I asked him if he was ready for me to pick it up, and he said, yes. I picked the gun up by the wooden stock. I noted that the stock was too rough apparently to take fingerprints, so I picked it up, and Captain Fritz opened the bolt as I held the gun. A live round fell to the floor.
> Mr. BELIN. Did you initial that live round at all?
> Mr. DAY. Yes, sir; my name is on it.
> Mr. BELIN. When did you place your name on this live round, if you remember?
> Mr. DAY. How?
> Mr. BELIN. When?
> Mr. DAY. At the time, that was marked at the scene.

Now let's find out if that same procedure was followed with the *empty* shells discovered.

Warning: you are about to enter THE CONFUSION ZONE, a world of flip-flops, memory lapses, misidentifications, shifts, contradictions, and ambiguity. If your brain is in fifth gear, time to shift down to first. Slow down . . . study well. You shall be rewarded!

---

[1] http://www.history-matters.com/archive/jfk/wc/wcvols/wh4/html/WC_Vol4_0133b.htm (retrieved August 19, 2011).

David Belin, Assistant Counsel of the Warren Commission, had interviewed Day in Dallas just two weeks prior to his April 22 testimony (4 H 254), and in that interview Day told Belin that he had marked *all* the empty shells *at the scene*, in the same manner as he had marked the live round, following the standard operating procedure.

Day's April 22 testimony, however, revoked that claim, with the astonishing new information that his name was *not* scratched on the third empty shell! (4 H 254): [1]

> Mr. BELIN. Is there any other testimony you have with regard to the chain of possession of this shell from the time it was first found until the time it got back to your office?
> Mr. DAY. No, sir; I told you in our conversation in Dallas that I marked those at the scene. After reviewing my records, I didn't think I was on all three of those hulls that you have, indicating I did not mark them at the scene, then I remembered putting them in the envelope, and Sims taking them.
> It was further confirmed today when I noticed that the third hull, which I did not give you, or come to me through you, does not have my mark on it.

In case this testimony left any doubt that the shells were not marked at the scene as required, Day reiterated the point (4 H 255): [2]

> Mr. DAY. I remember you asking me if I marked them.
> Mr. BELIN. Yes.
> Mr. DAY. I remember I told you I did.
> Mr. BELIN. All right.
> Mr. DAY. I got to reviewing this, and I got to wondering about whether I did mark those at the scene.
> Mr. BELIN. Your testimony now is that you did not mark any of the hulls at the scene?
> Mr. DAY. Those three; no, sir.

So what happened? How was it that only *two* hulls were marked by Day, and how were any marked *at all*, if they weren't marked at the scene?

Well, as the story went, Day claims to have put the three hulls in an envelope, and then he turned them over to Richard Sims, a homicide detective with the Dallas Police Department (DPD), without marking them at the time (4 H 253): [3]

[1] http://www.history-matters.com/archive/jfk/wc/wcvols/wh4/html/WC_Vol4_0131b.htm (retrieved August 19, 2011).
[2] http://www.history-matters.com/archive/jfk/wc/wcvols/wh4/html/WC_Vol4_0132a.htm (retrieved August 19, 2011).
[3] http://www.history-matters.com/archive/jfk/wc/wcvols/wh4/html/WC_Vol4_0131a.htm (retrieved August 19, 2011).

Mr. BELIN. All right. You have mentioned these three hulls. Did you put any initials on those at all, any means of identification?

Mr. DAY. At that time they were placed in an envelope and the envelope marked. The three hulls were not marked at that time. Mr. Sims took possession of them.

Mr. BELIN. Well, did you at any time put any mark on the shells?

Mr. DAY. Yes, sir.

Of course, we know Day did *not* turn

3 hulls over to *Sims* of the DPD,

because the CSS form of November 22 clearly indicates that

2 hulls were turned over to *Brown* of the FBI.

Therefore, there should be a "B" on this bullet, and not an "S", which is our clue to be on the lookout for future examples of BS.

We are already in major trouble with this testimony, but the trouble has only just begun . . .

So, when did Day supposedly mark the hulls? As the story goes, when two of them had been returned to Day at 10 pm — but then Day dropped another bombshell (4 H 254): [1]

Mr. BELIN. Now, at what time did you put any initials, if you did put any such initials, on the hull itself?

Mr. DAY. At about 10 o'clock when I noticed it back in the identification bureau in this envelope.

Mr. BELIN. Had the envelope been opened yet or not?

Mr. DAY. Yes, sir; it had been opened.

Mr. BELIN. Had the shells been out of your possession then?

Mr. DAY. Mr. Sims had the shells from the time they were moved from the building or he took them from me at that time, and the shells I did not see again until around 10 o'clock.

Mr. BELIN. Who gave them to you at 10 o'clock?

Mr. DAY. They were in this group of evidence being collected to turn over to the FBI. I don't know who brought them back.

Mr. BELIN. Was the envelope sealed?

Mr. DAY. No, sir.

Mr. BELIN. Had it been sealed when you gave it to Mr. Sims?

Mr. DAY. No, sir; no.

So, in this version of the shell game, 2 of the shells *were* marked, but only after they had been transported in an *unsealed* envelope, an envelope that was opened *before* Day had a chance to mark the shells

---

[1] http://www.history-matters.com/archive/jfk/wc/wcvols/wh4/html/WC_Vol4_0131b.htm (retrieved August 19, 2011).

(and, in a total departure from the chain of custody concept, giving someone else the opportunity to substitute different shells into the envelope)!

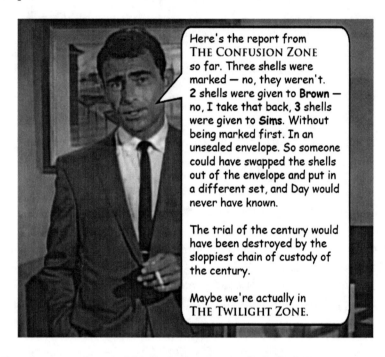

Here's the report from THE CONFUSION ZONE so far. Three shells were marked — no, they weren't. 2 shells were given to **Brown** — no, I take that back, 3 shells were given to **Sims**. Without being marked first. In an unsealed envelope. So someone could have swapped the shells out of the envelope and put in a different set, and Day would never have known.

The trial of the century would have been destroyed by the sloppiest chain of custody of the century.

Maybe we're actually in THE TWILIGHT ZONE.

For those readers rubbing their eyes in disbelief, Day reiterated his testimony (4 H 256): [1]

Mr. BELIN. Now, I believe you originally stated that you had all three of these cartridge hulls put in Exhibit 717, is that correct?
Mr. DAY. Yes, sir.
Mr. BELIN. And then you turned it over to Detective Sims?
Mr. DAY. Yes, sir.
Mr. BELIN. Was the envelope sealed when you turned it over to Detective Sims?
Mr. DAY. No, sir; I don't think so.
Mr. BELIN. Did you seal it?
Mr. DAY. No, sir.
Mr. BELIN. When you got the envelope back later that night was the envelope sealed?
Mr. DAY. I don't think so.
Mr. BELIN. To the best of your knowledge, had it been sealed and reopened or was it just unsealed?
Mr. DAY. To the best of my knowledge it was not sealed. It is possible I could be wrong on that, but I don't think it was sealed.

---

[1] http://www.history-matters.com/archive/jfk/wc/wcvols/wh4/html/WC_Vol4_0132b.htm (retrieved August 19, 2011).

The envelope not only was not *sealed*, its contents were just barely identified adequately . . . perhaps (4 H 253): [1]

Mr. DAY. This is the envelope the shells were placed in.
Mr. BELIN. How many shells were placed in that envelope?
Mr. DAY. Three.
Mr. BELIN. It says here that, it is written on here, "Two of the three spent hulls under window on sixth floor."
Mr. DAY. Yes, sir.
Mr. BELIN. Did you put all three there?
Mr. DAY. Three were in there when they were turned over to Detective Sims at that time. The only writing on it was, "Lieut. J. C. Day." Down here at the bottom.
Mr. BELIN. I see.
Mr. DAY. "Dallas Police Department," and the date.

But were they identified *at the time of delivery* to Sims? No, there was no writing on the envelope identifying the contents when it was supposedly given to Sims to be transferred to the Identification Bureau! (4 H 254): [2]

Mr. BELIN. In other words, you didn't put the writing in that says, "Two of the three spent hulls."
Mr. DAY. Not then. About 10 o'clock in the evening this envelope came back to me with two hulls in it. I say it came to me, it was in a group of stuff, a group of evidence, we were getting ready to release to the FBI. I don't know who brought them back. Vince Drain, FBI, was present with the stuff. the first I noticed it. At that time there were two hulls inside.
    I was advised the homicide division was retaining the third for their use. At that time I marked the two hulls inside of this, still inside this envelope.

So, in this version of the story, *three* shells were earlier in the afternoon sent to the Identification Bureau of the homicide division in an **unmarked** and **unsealed** envelope, the homicide division retained one, and then returned *two* for subsequent delivery to the FBI (Drain making his first appearance at 10:00 pm), which Day proceeded to mark, along with the envelope said to have conveyed them.

Now, *which* shells were delivered to Drain in the envelope? The shells identified as Commission Exhibits **545** and **544**. Here is the

---

[1] http://www.history-matters.com/archive/jfk/wc/wcvols/wh4/html/WC_Vol4_0131a.htm (retrieved December 15, 2011).

[2] http://www.history-matters.com/archive/jfk/wc/wcvols/wh4/html/WC_Vol4_0131b.htm (retrieved August 19, 2011).

testimony related to CE **545**, the first shell identified as being in the envelope: [1]

> Mr. BELIN. Handing you what has been marked "Exhibit 545," I will ask you to state if you know what this is.
> Mr. DAY. This is one of the hulls in the envelope which I opened at 10 o'clock. It has my name written on the end of it.
> Mr. BELIN. When you say, on the end of it, where on the end of it?
> Mr. DAY. On the small end where the slug would go.
> Mr. BELIN. And it has "Day" on it?
> Mr. DAY. Scratched on there; yes, sir.
> Mr. BELIN. With what instrument did you scratch it on?
> Mr. DAY. A diamond point pencil.
> Mr. BELIN. Did anyone else scratch any initials on it that you know of?
> Mr. DAY. I didn't see them.   I didn't examine it too close at that time.

Notice here that Day, whose memory up to this point has been something short of razor-sharp, remembers clearly making the mark, using a diamond point pencil.

The next testimony refers to CE **544**, the other shell that was in the envelope: [2]

> Mr. BELIN. Now, handing you what has been marked as Commission Exhibit 544, I will ask you to state if you know what this is.
> Mr. DAY. This is the second hull that was in the envelope when I marked the two hulls that night on November 22.
> Mr. BELIN. I have now marked this envelope, which was formerly a part of Commission Exhibits 543 and 544 with a separate Commission Exhibit No. 717, and I believe you testify now that Commission Exhibit 544 was the other shell that was in the envelope which has now been marked as Commission Exhibit No. 717.
> Mr. DAY. Yes.
> Mr. BELIN. Does that cartridge case, Exhibit 544, have your name on it again?
> Mr. DAY. It has my name on the small end where the slug would go into the shell.

And now the final testimony, related to last empty shell, Exhibit **543**, the shell which was unmarked — well, at least by Day (4 H 255): [3]

[1] http://www.history-matters.com/archive/jfk/wc/wcvols/wh4/html/WC_Vol4_0131b.htm (retrieved August 19, 2011).

[2] http://www.history-matters.com/archive/jfk/wc/wcvols/wh4/html/WC_Vol4_0132a.htm (retrieved August 19, 2011).

[3] http://www.history-matters.com/archive/jfk/wc/wcvols/wh4/html/WC_Vol4_0132a.htm (retrieved August 19, 2011).

Mr. BELIN. Now, I am going to ask you to state if you know what Commission Exhibit 543 is?

Mr. DAY. That is a hull that does not have my marking on it.

Mr. BELIN. Do you know whether or not this was one of the hulls that was found at the School Book Depository Building?

Mr. DAY. I think it is.

Mr. BELIN. What makes you think it is?

Mr. DAY. It has the initials "G. D." on it, which is George Doughty, the captain that I worked under.

Mr. BELIN. Was he there at the scene?

Mr. DAY. No, sir; this hull came up, this hull that is not marked came up, later. I didn't send that.

Mr. BELIN. This was——

Mr. DAY. That was retained. That is the hull that was retained by homicide division when the other two were originally sent in with the gun.

Mr. BELIN. You are referring now to Commission Exhibit 543 as being the one that was retained in your possession for a while?

Mr. DAY. It is the one that I did not see again.

So, the verdict is in: CE 543 did *not* have Day's mark on it. In other words, a vital link in the chain of custody had been severed, and *precisely on the shell which all the documentary evidence we have seen so far indicates never existed before November 27.*

However, the shell *was* stated to have the initials "GD" on it, and the stipulated reason these initials were on the shell is that it was *not* sent to Washington like the other two. This provides a coherent story for the identification which is missing ("Day") but which ought to be present.

To help you keep track of just what is going on, the story just told can be summarized with the following model derived from Day's April 22 testimony:

	SENT TO FRITZ	SENT TO WASHINGTON	
	CE 543	**CE 544**	**CE 545**
Shells Received 11/22 @ 10 PM: 2	GD	DAY	DAY

Here is how to read this model (designed to give you a bird's-eye view of testimony at-a-glance):

From left to right, you see that on November 22 at 10 p.m., 2 shells were received by Day. One shell, identified as CE 543, with the initials "GD", had been sent to Fritz earlier. The two other shells CE 544 and 545, both with the initials "Day" that were scratched on the shells at 10 p.m., were subsequently sent to Washington.

Unfortunately, this explanation, perhaps thought to be by its creators rather innocuous on the surface, and a credible explanation for a key gap in the chain of custody, turns out to be an absolute disaster for the prosecution, for the following six reasons:

1. Notwithstanding the explanation, Day's name *still* was supposed to be scratched on 3 shells, not 2. This testimony, if true, simply verifies what all the other evidence has been telling us, that only 2 shells were discovered.
2. Evidence was handled *inconsistently*; the live round was marked on the scene, the other shells were not, indicating a key deviation from protocol.
3. Day not only reverses his testimony (shells *were* marked at the scene . . . no, they actually *weren't*), but he reverses it in *the wrong direction*; it not only indicates that his testimony inherently lacks credibility, but by testifying that the shells were not marked on the scene, he provides testimony to not only his poor memory but also to his failure to follow protocol.
4. The marks Day reportedly put on the shells were put on shells which were in an *unsealed* (and *unmarked*) envelope; considering Day's exceptionally poor memory, he could not possibly be reliably considered to have identified these shells; since the envelope was not sealed or marked (two other egregious protocol violations), other shells could have been placed in the envelope without Day's knowledge, and so "identifying" them later would have been pointless.
5. Day's testimony that 3 shells were turned over to *Sims* of the DPD is contradicted by the CSS form that proves that 2 shells were turned over to *Brown* of the FBI.
6. **Most importantly, this testimony *proves* that the Fritz story is, without question, completely false. *Indeed, this testimony is a <u>hydrogen bomb</u> that completely obliterates the validity of the chain of custody that connects shells that were found on the***

sixth floor with shells that were fired from Oswald's rifle.

How does it do that?

Because the story, if true, is *impossible*!

We can discover why this is so when we understand the FBI prefix designations given to evidence as it was logged. Remember those "Q" numbers? Well, you should realize that "Q" wasn't the only FBI prefix, there was also a "C" prefix, which indicated that the item qualified was an evidentiary exhibit (the "Q" prefix indicated that this evidentiary item was first sent to the FBI lab, where it was given an FBI laboratory examination number).

As you continue your journey through THE CONFUSION ZONE, we enter a shifting universe where "C" numbers become "Q" numbers, and "Q" numbers become associated with "CE" numbers. Relax . . . a table will be coming up shortly that will summarize all of this for you. The reason for this work will soon become clear . . .

So, we are going to be mapping "Q" numbers to "C" numbers, and ultimately those numbers to the most important "CE" (Commission

Exhibit) numbers. That will help us track what went where and when, which is something we have to do to unravel this mess.

In general, whenever you find yourself lost in a maze, it is helpful to retrace your steps and work backwards so you can find your way out:

We are able to retrace the steps and unravel the thread thanks to page 71 of Commission Document 735, which contained a listing of the personal effects of Lee Harvey Oswald and his wife Marina, as well as articles of an "evidentiary hearing nature."

This valuable document, a second Rosetta Stone in the Kennedy assassination, will allow us to ultimately create a table linking all of these "C," "Q," and "CE" designations.

Let us start by going from "C" to "Q". The listing in CD 735 maps the "C" designation to the "Q" designation for C6 and C7 as follows (CD 735, p. 73): [1]

---

[1] http://www.maryferrell.org/mffweb/archive/viewer/showDoc.do?docId=11133&relPageId=80 (retrieved August 19, 2011).

C6	**6.5 mm. Mannlicher-Carcano cartridge case from building (Q6).** ·
C7	**6.5 mm. Mannlicher-Carcano cartridge case from building (Q7).**

So, **C6** = **Q6**, and **C7** = **Q7**. C38 was similarly mapped two pages later (CD 735, p. 73):[1]

C38	**6.5 Mannlicher-Carcano cartridge case from Depository (Q48).**

Likewise, **C38** = **Q48**.

Now that the "C" and "Q" designations of the empty shells have been identified with each other, we need to identify the "C" and "Q" designations of these shells with the Warren Commission exhibit "CE" numbers.

When we examine key Warren Commission testimony, a third Rosetta Stone, we learn that **Q6 is identical to CE 543** (3 H 508):[2]

> Mr. EISENBERG. Now, could you get to that photograph you just mentioned, Q–6?
> Mr. NICOL. I photographed the Q–6 in three different positions, which I designated as 1, 2, and 3.
> Mr. DULLES. Have we identified Q–6 before on the record?
> Mr. EISENBERG. Yes. Q–6, I think it is stated on the record, is the equivalent of our Commission Exhibit 543.

Elsewhere we learn that **C7/Q7 is identical to CE 544**, as shown in CE 562 (3 H 425; 17 H 252):[3]

> Mr. EISENBERG. I think you have identified the next picture I am holding as having been taken by you?
> Mr. FRAZIER. Yes, sir; it was. That is a 70-diameter magnification photograph of Exhibit 544 on the right, and the test from the rifle on the left.
> Mr. EISENBERG. And this bears the numbers C–14 and C–7, and is a firing-pin photograph?
> Mr. FRAZIER. Yes, sir.

---

[1] http://www.maryferrell.org/mffweb/archive/viewer/showDoc.do?docId=11133&relPageId=82 (retrieved August 19, 2011).

[2] http://www.history-matters.com/archive/jfk/wc/wcvols/wh3/html/WC_Vol3_0258b.htm (retrieved August 19, 2011).

[3] http://www.history-matters.com/archive/jfk/wc/wcvols/wh3/html/WC_Vol3_0217a.htm (retrieved August 19, 2011).

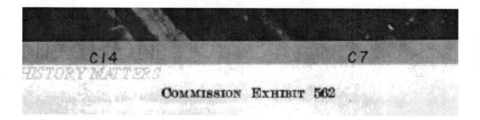

COMMISSION EXHIBIT 562

And, finally, **Q48 is identical to CE 545** (3 H 505): [1]

> Mr. NICOL. I took photographs of the specimen which I referred to, or was referred to, as Q-48, which would be this.
> Mr. EISENBERG. Yes.   That is Commission Exhibit 545.

When we put this information together, we derive the following evidence index table which tells us, for example, that **CE 543** is also referred to in other (FBI) contexts by the designation **C6** as well as **Q6**:

HERE IS THE ULTIMATE PAYOFF FOR OUR HARD WORK:

	is also this "C" number ...	...and also this "Q" number.
CE 543	C6	Q6
CE 544	C7	Q7
CE 545	C38	Q48

Because we have this table, if I ask you the question "**CE 545** was given what 'Q' number by the FBI?" you will have no trouble in answering . . . **Q48**!

So, now that we understand which designations match up with which, let's take another look at our model of the testimony given by Day on April 22, 1964, but this time with the "Q" numbers from the table above referenced to the "CE" numbers:

---

[1] http://www.history-matters.com/archive/jfk/wc/wcvols/wh3/html/WC_Vol3_0257a.htm (retrieved August 19, 2011).

	Q6	Q7	Q48
	SENT TO FRITZ	**SENT TO WASHINGTON**	
	CE 543	**CE 544**	**CE 545**
Shells Received 11/22 @ 10 PM: [2]	GD	DAY	DAY

With this revised version of our model, it should now be no problem to answer the question, "in terms of Q numbers, which shells delivered at 10 PM were to be sent to *Washington*?" And, since the model above says that **Q7** = **CE 544** and **Q48** = **CE 545**, we have our answer:

The shells sent to Washington — CE 544 and CE 545 — should respectively have been identified (per the 11/23/63 FBI Evidence Received letter) as Q7 and Q48.

But your memory should be telling you a different story, and when we take a second look at the 11/23/63 FBI Evidence Received letter, we are absolutely astonished to verify that in fact this was *not* the case (CE 2003, p. 132: 24 H 262): [1]

Evidence received from Special Agent Vincent E. Drain of the Dallas Office of the FBI on 11/23/63:

Q6   6.5 millimeter Mannlicher-Carcano cartridge case from building
Q7   6.5 millimeter Mannlicher-Carcano cartridge case from building
Q8   6.5 millimeter Mannlicher-Carcano cartridge from rifle

Instead of "Q7" and "Q48," we see instead "Q6" and "Q7." Oops!

At first, one might think there was a typographical error by the agents in Washington (even though the sequential nature of the numbers [6 to 7 to 8] would belie that possibility), but, in fact, the highest "Q" number listed in that first receipt of evidence by the FBI was **Q15** (CE 2003, p. 132: 24 H 262) [2],

---

[1] "Warren Commission Hearings, Volume XXIV, Current Section: CE 2003 - Dallas Police Department file on investigation of the assassination of the President (CD 81b, all pages)," http://www.maryferrell.org/mffweb/archive/viewer/showDoc.do?docId=1140&relPageId=280 (retrieved June 30, 2011).

[2] "Warren Commission Hearings, Volume XXIV, Current Section: CE 2003 - Dallas Police Department file on investigation of the assassination of the President (CD 81b, all pages)," http://www.maryferrell.org/mffweb/archive/viewer/showDoc.do?docId=1140&relPageId=280 (retrieved June 30, 2011).

Evidence obtained by FBI Laboratory personnel during examination of the
    President's limousine:

Q14 Three metal fragments recovered from rear floor board carpet
Q15 Scraping from inside surface of windshield

Also Submitted: Photograph of rifle, K1
                 Finger and palm prints of Lee Harvey Oswald

Results of examinations:

and therefore on that day (November 23), from the FBI's
perspective, *Q48 did not exist at all, and therefore could not possibly
have been sent to Washington*!

Further verification that the FBI correctly reported the receipt of
"Q" numbers Q6 and Q7 is provided by CE 717, the envelope used to
transmit the evidence to the FBI: note on the right-hand side the "Q"
numbers "**Q6, Q7**" (CE 717: 17 H 501): [1]

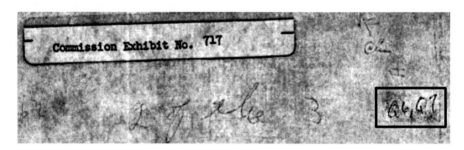

Ouch!

This is what we call a major, major, MAJOR problem for the Fritz
story. Here's why: when we view the model of Day's testimony, we see
that *one, and only one shell*, should have been in Fritz' drawer, and that
shell would have been **CE 543**:

	SENT TO FRITZ	SENT TO WASHINGTON	
	CE 543	**CE 544**	**CE 545**
Shells Received 11/22 @ 10 PM: [2]	GD	DAY	DAY

[1] http://www.history-matters.com/archive/jfk/wc/wcvols/wh17/html/WH_Vol17_0264a.htm
(retrieved August 16, 2011).

Remember, there are only *three* shells according to the official story, and if CE 544 and 545 have been sent to Washington, the only one left that could be conceivably found in Fritz' desk drawer *has to have been* CE 543.

Now let's look at the Model with the "Q" numbers referenced again (to better able you to see the problem, I will highlight the area on which you should focus):

		Q6	**Q7**	**Q48**
		SENT TO FRITZ	SENT TO WASHINGTON	
	Shells Received 11/22 @ 10 PM: [2]	**CE 543**	**CE 544**	**CE 545**
		GD	DAY	DAY

Note that as we saw earlier, CE 543 is identified as "Q6," and surprise of surprises, the FBI has told us in more than one way (the property inventory record as well as the notations on CE 717) that shell Q6 (along with Q7) was actually in . . . *Washington!*

And so now we have direct from the FBI itself *absolutely positive* confirmation that the story that Fritz is telling *cannot possibly* be true:

CE 543, a/k/a Q6, could not possibly have been in Fritz' drawer in *Dallas, Texas* when CE 2003 (the 11/23/63 FBI Evidence receipt) and CE 717 (the transmittal envelope) *prove* it was in *Washington, DC!*

Besides conclusively destroying the story told by Fritz, this testimony by Day coupled with the evidentiary record also destroys the legitimacy of the marks supposedly representing the actual chain of custody.

This is because we know that the shells that were sent to DC according to the FBI evidence receipt and the transmittal envelope — CE 543 [Q6] and CE 544 [Q7] — had *contrary* marks, one by "GD," the other by "Day," when in fact according to the official story as told on April 22 by Day, both should have had the *same* mark, "Day" (Day marked only the shells that were to be sent to Washington, as you will remember, but **Q6**, which *was* in Washington, did *not* have **Day's** mark, it had "**GD"s!**)

This would indicate that at least one shell was sent to DC without the necessary mark required to establish a chain of custody (again, according to the story, because it was sent to **Washington, Q6** should have had the mark **"Day"** and not **"GD"**), and therefore Q6 *had to have* been surreptitiously introduced into the evidentiary mix!

Furthermore, if in fact there *was* a shell in the desk drawer of Fritz, that would be an extra "Q" number, since the others had been accounted for, and so we can be absolutely sure that that bullet was *not* fired from the rifle owned by Lee Harvey Oswald, since the evidence shows that, at maximum, only *three* bullets were fired in that rifle, and if there *was* an extra bullet, then it was not fired in that rifle on that day, as its marks would indicate, but rather, was *planted* there!

Wow.

This, folks, we can term with no fear of contradiction, is an evidentiary *debacle*.

Needless to say, if this story with its multiplicity of continuity errors were left to stand on its own, the credibility of the Warren Commission could have easily been destroyed with the application of a small dose of elementary deductive logic. However, it appears that some sharp-eyed attorneys in Washington noted that this story would essentially destroy The Case Against Lee Harvey Oswald, so it seems they decided to dispatch a Hollywood script doctor to do reconstructive surgery on the narrative.

When the old story fails, it's time to roll out a new one! And now, consequently, we are about to see a completely different version of events designed to rehabilitate the prior analysis.

Unfortunately for them, the story-masters were only digging themselves into an ever greater ditch, a ditch that the wise Kennedy assassination student would be careful to examine closely. As Bugliosi noted (*Reclaiming History*, pp. 899-900):

accurate memories of an event or statement tend to fade with time. So **how do we deal with the many Warren Commission witnesses . . . whose memory supposedly got better with time?** Assuming their first statement was intended to be a complete one, and there is no question that the witnesses said what they are reported to have said, **we must, almost by definition, reject *sensational* additions to their original story.**

**Are these "additions" by witnesses in the Kennedy
case always flat-out lies on their part? In many cases, yes,
just as some of their original statements are often
completely fabricated** in the hope of getting five minutes of
fame or attention. But many times, witnesses are not
knowingly telling a falsehood. As time goes by, they naturally
forget some of what they saw or heard, and these new voids in
their memory are frequently filled in with details derived from
the power of suggestion or their own imagination, or from
knowledge of later events that make the details more likely or
even inevitable, or from the recollections of others that
witnesses unconsciously embrace as their own — that is, the
witness ends up saying he saw something that he himself never
saw. . . .

[T]he addition of new elements to their stories,
particularly important details that would never have been
omitted by them in the original telling if they were true,
has to be taken, as they say in Latin, *cum grano salis* (with
a grain of salt). . . .

No hard and fast rules can be employed, without exception,
to determine the credibility of the various witnesses . . . other
than the dictates of **logic** and common sense.

Witnesses sometimes are *coached* to change their testimony;
however, there is such a thing as a *bad* coach, you know, the kind who
calls for a "Hail Mary" pass on the one-yard line. This makes it easy to
tell when coaching has occurred, and this final paragraph gives us the
way to tell the true from the false, particularly when the revisions are
spun purely from thin air. *Logic*, as Bugliosi noted, is absolutely key in
this regard. Vincent Bugliosi noted, "[t]**he problem with fabricated
stories is that inconsistencies frequently occur.** As opposed to the
truth, which is compatible with its environment, **falsehoods, as
Daniel Webster said, not only disagree with truths, but usually
quarrel among themselves.**" (RH 882; emphasis supplied).

Logic is the spotlight that makes these inconsistencies visible for
all the world to see. No better example of that can be given than the
following.

The rehabilitation effort began very quietly with an affidavit by
Day given on May 7, just over a month after his Warren Commission
testimony.

Here is the pertinent part of that affidavit, which introduces only one subtle change, anticipating more significant changes which will come in a later affidavit (7 H 401-402; pages consolidated by author): [1]

When testifying before the President's Commission, I stated I did not remember who returned the two spent 6.5 hulls and envelope to my possession on the night of November 22, 1963. Since returning to Dallas Detective C. N. Dhority has called my attention to the fact he brought the three hulls in the envelope to me and asked me to check them again for fingerprints even though I had checked them when they were picked up on the sixth floor of the Texas School Book Depository about 1:20 p.m. November 22, 1963 by Detective R. M. Sims and myself and placed in a manila envelope. Since talking to Dhority I remember now that he was the one who returned the shells to me about 10:00 p.m. and stated that his office wanted to retain one. He left me two shells and the envelope that Detective Sims and I had previously marked. It was then that I scratched my name on the two shells that were released at 11:45 p.m. to Agent Vince Drain along with the rifle and other evidence.

This version has only one small change from the previous story. In the previous story, only *two* hulls were returned to Day at 10 p.m., but in this new version, *three* hulls were returned. Just a small change, which results in the following revision of the model, a change from "2" to "3":

Shells Received 11/22 @ 10 PM: 3	SENT TO FRITZ	SENT TO WASHINGTON	
	CE 543	CE 544	CE 545
	GD	DAY	DAY

But this subtle shift was only a precursor to that yet to come.

A far more interesting set of changes, one to be reflected in a later affidavit, was handwritten on the version that is archived at the Dallas Municipal Archives website: [2]

[1] http://www.history-matters.com/archive/jfk/wc/wcvols/wh7/html/WC_Vol7_0205a.htm (retrieved August 19, 2011).
[2] "Affidavit In Any Fact-typed, by J. C. Day. Statement by J. C. Day concerning the confusion regarding the number of spent hulls found at the Texas School Book Depository immediately after the assassination, (Carbon Copy Signed and Annotated), 05/07/64," http://jfk.ci.dallas.tx.us/26/2634-001.gif (retrieved August 24, 2011).

AFFIDAVIT IN ANY FACT

THE STATE OF TEXAS
COUNTY OF DALLAS

BEFORE ME, ... Mary McLean

a Notary Public in and for said County, State of Texas, on this day personally appeared ....

....

Who, after being by me duly sworn, on oath deposes and says: when testif.in before the Presidnt's Commission, I stated i did not remember who returned the two spent 6.5 hulls and envelope to my possession on the night of November .., 1963. Since returning to Dallas Detective C. "C. Dhority has called my attention to the fact he brought the three hulls in the envelope to me and asked me to check them again for fingerprints ever though I had checked them when they were picked up on the sixth floor of the Texas School Book Depository about 1:2. pm November .., 1963 by Detective C. .. .im and myself and placed in a manila envelope. Sinse talking to Dhority I remember now that he was the one who returned the hulls to me about 10:0 am and stated that his office wanted to retain one. He left me two shells and the envelope that Detective Lim and I had previously marked. It was then that I scratched my name on the two shells that were released at 11:45 pm to Agent Vince Drain along with the rifle and other evidence.

SUBSCRIBED AND SWORN TO BEFORE ME THIS.....7.....DAY OF ....May.........A.D. 19.....

Now, the handwriting at the bottom of the May 7 affidavit reveals some profound differences in the model. According to the original model, "Day" appeared only *once* on each of two shells, and "GD" appeared only *once* on one shell. But these changes anticipate a different, forthcoming affidavit, with writing on *one more shell each* by both Day and "GD." From the top to the bottom, the handwriting reads as follows:

Comm 545	Third one — does not have GD. Day
Comm 544	one of the 2 has Day & GD
C 543	secd of first two has Day — GD
	this is the one that has bent [place] & one causing confusion

We will go in depth regarding these changes more in a moment, especially the point about the "bent [place]", but now let's look at the revised affidavit which officially incorporated the notations of this handwriting, delivered over a month later on June 23, 1964 (don't be intimidated by all these words, I will highlight the important lines in the next screen capture) (7 H 402):[1]

> The following affidavit is made to clear up confusion regarding the three spent 6.5 hulls, commission numbers 543, 544, and 545, found by the 6th floor window of the Texas School Book Depository on November 22, 1963. The hulls were picked up by Detective R. M. Sims and Lieutenant J. C. Day and placed in an envelope. Detective R. L. Studebaker was also present. The envelope was marked and dated by Sims and Day. Detective Sims took the hulls after they were checked for fingerprints by Day. The third hull, commision number 545, was later released directly to the FBI by the Dallas Police Department Homicide Division. At 10:00 P.M. November 22, 1963, Detective C. N. Dhority brought the three hulls in the marked envelope back to Lieutenant Day in the Identification Bureau office to recheck for prints. Dhority retained one hull, commission number 545 and left the other two, commission numbers 543, 544 along with the envelope with me to be sent to the FBI. Vince Drain, FBI agent, took custody at 11:45 A.M. the same day. When I appeared before the commission April 22, 1964, I could not find my name on one of the hulls, identified as commission number 543, and thought this was the hull that had been retained by Dhority. On June 8, 1964, the three hulls, commission numbers 543, 544, and 545, were back in Dallas and were examined by Captain G. M. Doughty and myself at the local FBI office. Close examination with a magnifying glass under a good light disclosed that my name "Day" was on all three hulls, at the small end. Also GD for Captain George Doughty was on two of them. Commission numbers 543 and 544 were the first two sent to Washington on November 22, 1963. They have Doughty's initials where he marked the hulls as they were released to Vince Drain at 11:45 P.M. on November 22, 1963 by Doughty and Day. The third hull, commission number 545, does not have Doughty's mark, but is plainly marked "Day". In Washington, I had numbers 543 and 545 switched because I didn't find my name on number 543. I can identify commission numbers 543, 544, and 545 from my name on them, as the three hulls found on the sixth floor of the Texas School Book Depository on November 22, 1963. As to the time I scratched my name on the hulls, I do not remember whether it was at the window when picked up or at 10:00 P.M. November 22, 1963, when they were returned to me by Dhority in the marked envelope. It had to be one or the other, because this is the only time I had all three hulls in my possession. Both Detective R. L. Studebaker and Detective R. M. Sims, who were present at the window when the hulls were picked up, state I marked them as they were found under the window.
> Signed this 23d day of June 1964.
>
> (S)   J. C. Day,
>   J. C. DAY.

At a heavy cost to the credibility of J. C. Day, but a necessary expense for the Warren Commission, this affidavit seeks to salvage the

[1] http://www.history-matters.com/archive/jfk/wc/wcvols/wh7/html/WC_Vol7_0205b.htm (retrieved August 19, 2011).

legitimacy of the chain of custody by revising the initial story in its most fundamental aspects. Alas for the authors of this new version of events, who probably thought that this would address the issues raised in the previous affidavit, it only served to seal an already well-nailed coffin.

Let us zoom in on and highlight the most relevant portion of this testimony:

> myself at the local FBI office. Close examination with a magnifying glass under a good light disclosed that my name "Day" was on all three hulls, at the small end. Also GD for Captain George Doughty was on two of them. Commission numbers 543 and 544 were the first two sent to Washington on November 22, 1963. They have Doughty's initials where he marked the hulls as they were released to Vince Drain at 11:45 P.M. on November 22, 1963 by Doughty and Day. The third hull, commission number 545, does not have Doughty's mark, but is plainly marked "Day". In Washington, I had numbers 543 and 545 switched because I didn't find my name on number 543. I can identify com-

In this testimony, we come across no less than *four* reversals in the story:

1. Day's name was not on *two* hulls, but *three*;
2. Doughty's initials were not on *one* hull, but *two*;
3. Doughty's initials were now said to have been placed on the *two* shells because they were going to be sent to **Washington**, but in the old version those initials were to be placed just on the *one* shell said to have remained in **Dallas**;
4. Shells CE **543** and 545 were sent to Washington, not shells CE **544** and 545;

Quite the makeover, *n'est-ce pas?*

More than a mere touch-up job, this is a complete overhaul of the prior testimony, necessitated by the apocalyptic effect the previous testimony had on the chain of custody sequence. This testimony, when consolidated, results in the new, supposedly final model of what transpired in Dallas on November 22 at the Dallas Police Department with reference to the empty shells:

Q6	Q7	Q48
SENT TO WASHINGTON		SENT TO FRITZ
CE 543	**CE 544**	**CE 545**
GD	GD	DAY
DAY	DAY	

Shells Received 11/22 @ 10 PM: 3

The dramatic differences between the "before" model and the "after" model can be revealed when we compare them side-by-side:

		Q6	Q7	Q48
Before *(April 22 Testimony)*	Shells Received 11/22 @ 10 PM: 2	SENT TO FRITZ	SENT TO WASHINGTON	
		CE 543	**CE 544**	**CE 545**
		GD	DAY	DAY
After *(June 23 Affidavit)*	Shells Received 11/22 @ 10 PM: 3	SENT TO WASHINGTON		SENT TO FRITZ
		CE 543	**CE 544**	**CE 545**
		GD	GD	DAY
		DAY	DAY	

Well, the most complimentary thing that can be said about this June 23 model and its myriad changes is that at least, on the surface, it solves the problem of why the FBI reported that Q6 (CE543) and Q7 (CE 544) were sent to Washington. And, if one does not examine the story too closely, that is just what it does. However, conversely, when one *does* examine the story too closely, it does not.

Here is the gotcha with this new version:

It cannot *possibly* be true!

How do we know this?

For this reason: the legitimacy of the "I confused the shells" story depends on the plausibility of the notion that Day *could have* confused CE 543 with CE 545 on April 22. The record shows, however, that Day did *not* confuse the shells; to the contrary, he *correctly* identified them. And since they were *correctly* identified, he obviously *did not* have them confused.

The reason we can be absolutely sure that the cells were identified correctly was due to the fact that *there is no possibility* those shells could have been confused. To be more specific, it is *logically impossible* to have confused those shells. And because you *can't* confuse what's *impossible* to confuse, the "confusion" was therefore nonexistent.

To illustrate the point, let's consider the following imaginary dialogue between Belin and Day, referring to the following exhibits, three geometrical figures with identifying marks:

Exhibit 100	Exhibit 101	Exhibit 102
(circle) GD	(square) DAY	(triangle) DAY

Mr. BELIN: I am going to ask you to state if you know what Exhibit 100 is.

Mr. DAY: That is a circle.

Mr. BELIN: And are the initials "GD" on it?

Mr. DAY: Yes.

Mr. BELIN: And why were they placed on it?

Mr. DAY: *Because* it is a circle, and because it is neither a square nor a triangle.

Mr. BELIN: And is your name on it?

Mr. DAY: Well, I don't see it there, and I can't imagine why I *would* see it there, because I was *not* to put my name on the circle. I was *only* to put my name on the square and the triangle.

Mr. BELIN: All right, now can you tell me what Exhibit 101 is?

Mr. DAY: That is a square.

Mr. BELIN: And is your name on it?

Mr. DAY: Yes, it is, just like it was supposed to be.

Mr. BELIN: Finally, Mr. Day, can you please tell me what Exhibit 102 is?

Mr. DAY: That is a triangle.

Mr. BELIN: And is that your name on it?

Mr. DAY: Plain as day! I scratched it on there myself with a diamond point pencil.

Mr. BELIN: Very good, Mr. Day. You are dismissed.

Now, imagine, a month after this testimony has been given, the following affidavit is received by the Warren Commission:

> The following affidavit is made to clear up confusion regarding the testimony I gave regarding the three geometrical figures. When I appeared before the Commission, I could not find my name on one of the figures, the circle identified as Exhibit 100. Close examination with a magnifying glass under a good light disclosed that my name "Day" actually *was* on Exhibit 100, even though under my original testimony my name was not supposed to be there in the first place. In that testimony, I had Exhibits 100 (the circle), and 102 (the triangle) switched because I didn't find my name on Exhibit 100, even though my testimony, again, was that the geometrical shape I did *not* write my name on was a *circle*. Now that I know my name is actually on Exhibit 100, I realize the confusion I created. Therefore, I now modify my testimony to say that Exhibit 100, a circle, is actually Exhibit 102, a triangle, and that Exhibit 102, a triangle, is actually Exhibit 100, a circle. I sincerely hope this clears up the confusion.

Absurd? Absolutely! But no more or less absurd than the June 23, 1964 affidavit signed by Day appearing on page 402 of the 7th volume of the Warren Commission exhibits.

The example above simplifies the issue to make it more clear, but *the point it makes pertains to any exhibits which are self-identifying due to their unique properties*. A *circle*, which has an *infinite* number of sides, the *most* number of sides possible for a geometrical figure, could never be confused with a *triangle*, which has *three* sides, the *least* number of sides possible for a polygon. Furthermore, if someone *wants* to tell you that a circle is a triangle, and that a triangle is a circle, pull out the straitjacket — or the lie detector.

So, the question now is, do either CE 543 and CD 545 have any unique properties like our geometrical figures that render them also self-identifying, and therefore *impossible* to confuse?

As it turns out, they *both* do.

Let's first take a look at CE 543. When we examine the testimony given by Day on April 22, 1964, we find that CE 543 can be completely separated from the other two cartridge cases through the unique combination of three properties:

1) that case, if it had a marking by Day at all, had a marking by Day **so small/faint/nondescript that it could not be seen** without a magnifying glass and a good light, AND
2) "**GD**" was scratched on the case, AND
3) the case was **dented** on the end.

These properties have been taken directly from the testimony. The text below we saw earlier, and provides us with our first two unique identifying factors, 1) the practically invisible marking by Day ("that is a hull that does not have my marking on it") and 2) the "GD" initials ("it has the initials 'G.D.' on it"):

Mr. BELIN. Now, I am going to ask you to state if you know what Commission Exhibit 543 is?
Mr. DAY. That is a hull that does not have my marking on it. ⟵ **PROPERTY 1**
Mr. BELIN. Do you know whether or not this was one of the hulls that was found at the School Book Depository Building?
Mr. DAY. I think it is.
Mr. BELIN. What makes you think it is? ⟵ **PROPERTY 2**
Mr. DAY. It has the initials "G. D." on it, which is George Doughty, the captain that I worked under.

And here is testimony related to point 3, the cartridge being bent on the end. This discovery was provided not by Day, but by counsel David Belin ("it appears to be flattened out here"), removing Day's ability to perceive correctly as a source of error:

Mr. BELIN. You are referring now to Commission Exhibit 543 as being the one that was retained in your possession for a while?
Mr. DAY. It is the one that I did not see again. ⟵ **PROPERTY 3**
Mr. BELIN. It appears to be flattened out here. Do you know or have you any independent recollection as to whether or not it was flattened out at the small end when you saw it?
Mr. DAY. No, sir; I don't.

Further confirmation that there was a dent on the mouth of the CE 543 cartridge case (and that counsel Belin was observing reality correctly) was provided by the *House Select Committee On Assassinations* nearly a decade and a half later, which attempted to explain the origin of the malformation (7 HSCA 371):[1]

---

[1] "HSCA Report, Volume VII, Current Section: Kennedy Shooting" http://www.maryferrell.org/ mffweb/archive/viewer/showDoc.do?docId=82&relPageId=381 (retrieved June 30, 2011).

(156)   It is the opinion of the panel that the dent on the mouth of the CE 543 cartridge case was produced when the cartridge case was ejected from the rifle. This condition was duplicated during test-firing of the CE 139 rifle by the panel. (See fig. 2.) The dent had nothing to do with loading the bullet during the manufacturing process, nor is it the type of deformation expected if the case were stepped on.

This testimony is mutually confirming, but even so we still we might want to see photographic evidence of the dent referred to. What is the nature of the dent, and how significant is it?

In this regard, we are in debt to Josiah Thompson, who went to the National Archives and took an extremely clear photograph of CE 543, and the dent Belin mentioned (*Six Seconds In Dallas*, p. 144; arrow superimposed by author):

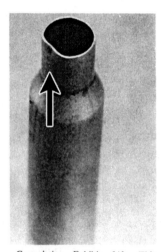

Commission Exhibit 543: This dented cartridge case found on the sixth floor of the Depository could not (in this condition) have held a projectile on November 22.

Lieutenant Day, with his twenty-three years experience (4 H 249), and who supposedly fingerprinted this cartridge at least once, perhaps twice, didn't remember noticing this? Well, others did: three separate sources identifying a dent clearly present.

Needless to say, this dent is a key identifying detail, one which neither of the other hulls possessed (according to all available evidence), thus enabling discrimination from the other two cartridge cases.

Now, when we put all these three properties together:

1) The marking by Day **so small/faint/nondescript that it cannot be seen** without a magnifying glass and a good light, WITH

2) The initials "**GD**" scratched on the case, WITH

3) The case being **dented** on the end,

we can see there is *no other* empty cartridge case which has this *unique* combination of properties, and that *only* CE **543** possesses them.

In this manner, and for these combined three reasons, CE 543 is just as different from the other two as a circle is different from a square and a triangle.

Likewise, CE **545** also has a unique property: for all of the differences indicated between the April 22 testimony and the July 23 affidavit, there is area on which those two disparate testimonies agree: *it is the <u>only</u> one of the three empty cartridge cases which did <u>not</u> have the initials "GD" inscribed,* as we can see when we take a look at our models side-by-side again, focusing on the CE 545 column:

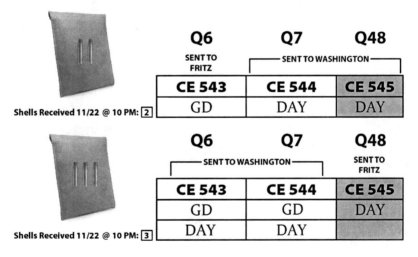

So, CE 545, for a different reason, is likewise unique. Two cartridges, as different as night and day — or as GD and Day. Consequently, we realize that there is no misidentification possible here either.

Now that we know that, let us summarize everything we have learned in a table (even though Day did not say that he confused **544** with 543, I'm including it also in the table so that you can see he did not confuse 543 with 544 either):

	543	545	544
"Day" invisible?	YES	NO	NO
Has "GD"?	YES	NO	YES
Has dent?	YES	NO	NO

As you can see, from an identification perspective, shells 543 and 545 are as different as "YES" is from "NO" . . .

Accordingly, when we re-examine the disastrous (for The Case Against Oswald) April 22 Belin/Day exchanges related to CE 543, the first describing Properties 1 (**invisible Day**) and 2 (**GD**),

> Mr. BELIN. Now, I am going to ask you to state if you know what Commission Exhibit 543 is?
> Mr. DAY. That is a hull that does not have my marking on it. ⟵ **PROPERTY 1**
> Mr. BELIN. Do you know whether or not this was one of the hulls that was found at the School Book Depository Building?
> Mr. DAY. I think it is.
> Mr. BELIN. What makes you think it is? **PROPERTY 2**
> Mr. DAY. It has the initials "G. D." on it, which is George Doughty, the captain that I worked under.

and the second describing Property 3 (**flattened/dented**),

> Mr. BELIN. You are referring now to Commission Exhibit 543 as being the one that was retained in your possession for a while?
> Mr. DAY. It is the one that I did not see again.   **PROPERTY 3**
> Mr. BELIN. It appears to be flattened out here. Do you know or have you any independent recollection as to whether or not it was flattened out at the small end when you saw it?
> Mr. DAY. No, sir; I don't.

we see that there is *no way* CE 543 could have been, in those exchanges, confused with CE 545:

> **CE 543 was the *only* shell with *all* 3 properties identified in the testimony above (and therefore the shell identified as CE 543 *had* to be CE 543), AND CE 545 did not have "G.D." inscribed on it (and therefore the shell identified as CE 543 *could not* be CD 545)!**

Either of those two reasons alone would have sufficed to demonstrate that confusion was impossible, but when seen together, mutually confirm what logic invariably dictates.

So, the desperate attempt to manufacture a new reality was fatally flawed, and now here comes the repercussion:

This attempt not only failed to establish the legitimacy of a shell that desperately needed it, but it had the unintended consequence of utterly destroying the chain of custody said to have tied the bullets supposedly found on the sixth floor of the Texas School Book Depository with the bullets fired from the Mannlicher-Carcano (also said to have been found on the sixth floor, and said to be Oswald's) — not only for one shell, *but all of them*!

We discover this when we see that the attempted revised model implicit in the June 23 affidavit

	Q6	Q7	Q48
	SENT TO WASHINGTON		SENT TO FRITZ
	CE 543	**CE 544**	**CE 545**
	GD	GD	DAY
Shells Received 11/22 @ 10 PM: 3	DAY	DAY	

is incorrect from the "Sent to Washington" perspective, and actually must be adjusted in relation to the impossibility factor which tells us that the April 22 Day testimony — and not the June 23 Day affidavit — was that which was to be utilized to decide which shell was sent to Fritz, and which shells were sent to Washington.

When we overlay with a gray highlight in the table below the shells which Washington claimed to have received *from* Dallas (24 H 262) comparing to that underneath which was claimed to have been sent *to* Washington by Dallas according to the April 22 testimony (4 H 255), the problem (with the adjustment made) is dramatically apparent:

REPORTED AS SENT TO WASHINGTON

	Q6	Q7	Q48
	SENT TO FRITZ	SENT TO WASHINGTON	
	CE 543	**CE 544**	**CE 545**
	GD	GD	DAY
Shells Received 11/22 @ 10 PM: 3	DAY	DAY	

And now, at long last, we can see the implications inherent in the *only model derivable from all the evidence*. So here they are:

1) Shells Q6 (CE 543) and Q7 (CE 544) were the ones reported by the FBI as sent to Washington. Therefore, Shell Q6 (CE 543) *said to have* been located in Dallas (in the custody of Fritz) on November 23 (according to Day's April 22 testimony), *could not have*. Since that shell was *not* in the possession of Fritz in Dallas on November 23, it had to have originated elsewhere, and therefore must have been *planted*, and pretty quickly too, *within five days* after the assassination (a third shell was sent to the FBI on November 27 from Dallas). Needless to say, in either event, the inscriptions "GD" and "Day," if present on Q6, had to have been inscribed later, and these forgeries, instead of proving Oswald's *guilt*, would instead prove that *none of the evidence against him could be trusted*, by proving a conspiracy to protect the identity of the true assassin(s) of the President.

2) Shell Q48 (CE 545), said to have been sent to *Washington* on November 23 according to Day's April 22 testimony, was *not*. Indeed, because the highest Q number was Q15, it *could not have*. Q6 (CE 543) and Q7 (CE 544), according to the FBI, were the *only* shells sent to Washington. With *no plausible origination point*, whether Washington or Dallas, this shell's pedigree is completely unknown, and most likely was also *planted*.

3) Shell Q7 (CE 544), which formerly had retained a formally untainted status, now has its chain of custody compromised as well. The FBI record shows that it was (reportedly) sent to Washington, and the testimony by Day on April 22 and June 23 confirms this, but it contains *two* marks, one by "G.D" and one by "Day"; according to both the April 22 and June 23 testimony, it should contain only *one* mark, "Day," if you believe the April 22 testimony, or "G.D.", if you believe the June 23 affidavit. Because logic dictates that only the April 22 testimony can be true, however, this means that if the mark "G.D," was actually present on this shell, it was *forged*. At any rate, for the foregoing reason, and also because it has marks by *both* where it should only have marks by *one*, the chain of custody for this shell is *also illegitimate*.

Now, that is something!

Remember, we started this section of the chapter simply trying to show that only one of the three cartridge cases claimed to have been found in the Texas School Book Depository (and linked with Oswald's rifle) had an illegitimate origin, but surprise of surprises, we now find that *all* of the empty cartridge cases have a broken chain of title, and for that reason, cannot be used as evidence in this case! For The Case Against Oswald, that's cataclysmic, because of all the evidence, more than any other, this is the evidence that MUST be valid for the case to proceed.

Suddenly, with a *POOF!*, the Case Against Oswald has vanished in a puff of smoke!

Faced with this dismal reality, what argument can the defenders of the Warren Commission possibly make in response?

Well, one avenue would be to attempt to discredit the testimony of J.C. Day, who (for these keepers of the "Oswald alone did it" flame) provided information about as appetizing as an anthrax cocktail. Discredit Day, and you provide some hope, however small, of salvaging a completely sunken prosecution.

This avenue of attack would proceed by attempting to show that Day was either mistaken, or lying, when he stated that "G.D" was on the shell. Given the record-setting number of flip-flops, memory lapses, misidentifications, protocol violations, and narrative shifts found in the Day testimony, this would be trivially easy to do. (Both politics and Kennedy assassination research make strange bedfellows!)

As luck would have it, these newly-inducted members of the Oswald Defense team have an additional piece of documentary evidence on their side, a letter drafted to David Belin by Day the day after the testimony was given, which indicates that indeed, the marks on at least one of the shells, insofar as "GD" is concerned, are not necessarily legitimate: [1]

---

[1] http://jfk.ci.dallas.tx.us/25/2595-001.gif (retrieved August 30, 2011).

April 23, 1964

Mr. David W. Belin
President's Commission on Assassination
200 Maryland Avenue NE
Washington 2, D.C.

Sir:

In regard to the third hull which I stated has GD for
George Doughty scratched on it, Captain Doughty does
not remember handling this.

Please check again to see if possibly it can be VD or
VED for Vince Drain.

Very truly yours,

J. C. Day
Lieutenant of Police
Identification Bureau

JCD:mel

The new line of argument would go something like this: "Oh, Day was just mistaken, the initials that he claimed to be Doughty's were actually someone else's, like Vince Drain's." This line of argument would conveniently forget that there is a story behind those GD initials, so if those in fact were not the initials of Doughty, the story would obviously have been illegitimate.

This potential argument was not substantiated by testimony in any event, because just two months after this letter was written, Day claimed that *Doughty was present with him when he was verifying the initials*, and Doughty must have suddenly had a memory/vision recall that completely foreclosed this new hypothesis as a possibility (7 H 402): [1]

by Dhority. On June 8, 1964, the three hulls, commission numbers 543, 544, and 545, were back in Dallas and were examined by Captain G. M. Doughty and myself at the local FBI office. Close examination with a magnifying glass under a good light disclosed that my name "Day" was on all three hulls, at the small end. Also GD for Captain George Doughty was on two of them. Commission

---

[1] http://www.history-matters.com/archive/jfk/wc/wcvols/wh7/html/WC_Vol7_0205b.htm
(retrieved August 19, 2011).

So, this latter testimony eliminates as a source of error a confusion of letters: with Doughty present, and his ostensible affirmation of the identification of initials using a magnifying glass under a good light, we can eliminate the possibility of any other individual's initials being on the bullet (again, based on *this* testimony).

Still, the letter does give room for doubt regarding the legitimacy of initials that actually were there, given the discrepancy between that letter and the testimony. Since the Warren Commission would have been well aware of a letter received by Assistant Counsel David Belin (if it was sent), you would think that the Commission would have called Captain George Doughty as a witness to testify to the authenticity of his initials, or at the very least, provide an affidavit regarding the same. In fact, regardless of whether or not they received the letter, to legitimate the lineage of the initials they would have *had* to have done one or the other.

They didn't!

That's right . . . search the over 20,000 pages of hearings and exhibits of the Warren Commission for *an affidavit or testimony by Doughty that the initials on the shell were his*, and you will come up short, as proven by the upcoming screen capture of the index to the Warren Commission hearings. Note that George Doughty, unlike Kenneth Dowe whose name is immediately below his, has no "Testimony" referenced (15 H 764). [1] That's because *there isn't any*:

Doughty, George, vol. IV, 255; vol.
VII, 80, 132, 174, 402
Dowe, Kenneth Lawry:
Testimony, vol. XV, 430–438
Referred to, vol. XV, 264, 491

The only relevant references to Doughty — by Day, of all people — are the ones you have seen reproduced in this book.

In addition, you can search the index provided by the *House Select Committee On Assassinations* in its report of March 29, 1979, starting on page 573 of the *Final Report*, and you will find no reference to any testimony or affidavit by Doughty (HSCA Report 573): [2]

---

[1] http://www.history-matters.com/archive/jfk/wc/wcvols/wh15/html/WC_Vol15_0387b.htm (retrieved December 15, 2011).

[2] http://www.history-matters.com/archive/jfk/hsca/report/html/HSCA_Report_0302a.htm (retrieved December 15, 2011).

The author attempted to verify this omission by indexing not only the final HSCA report but also all of its appendices using *Adobe Acrobat Professional 10*, and found *not even one reference to Doughty*.

This is an ominous sign for the legitimacy of the "G.D." story; when Doughty is not called as a witness, nor asked to submit an affidavit of confirmation, especially in light of a letter to the Assistant Counsel of the Warren Commission that the testimony provided was most likely incorrect, one can be forgiven for assuming that the reason Doughty was not given the opportunity to verify this story was because, in fact, he *would not* verify the story. This would provide a very telling indication that the "evidence" that was offered by Day (in the form of testimony and an affidavit) did not rise to the level of proof, and therefore failed to establish the fact in dispute. Bugliosi elucidated this distinction for the non-lawyers among us (RH 827; emphasis supplied):

> [E]vidence is not synonymous with proof. Evidence is that which is offered (legitimate or not, whether it is believed or not) to prove a fact in dispute. Proof, on the other hand, occurs when the trier of fact is satisfied that the fact in dispute has been established by the evidence. In other words, **if the evidence offered proves the fact for which it is offered, it is proof. If it doesn't prove the fact, it isn't.**

This insight into the *binary* nature of American jurisprudence by the famed prosecutor provides the foundation for concluding that The Case Against Lee Harvey Oswald has *a key deductive flaw*. It brings us about full circle to the essential point we discussed earlier in this book: in the United States of America, a defendant is innocent until proven guilty. In addition, and as a corollary to this (with reference to the Bugliosi point above), no proposition or element is proven without evidence that actually "proves the fact for which it is offered," as Bugliosi termed it. So, not only is the confidence level for the guilt of a defendant **zero** before evidence is offered, likewise is the confidence level for a fact in dispute (either proposition or element) also **zero** before evidence is offered. And, if the evidence offered is *insufficient* to prove the fact, then the confidence level for that fact, from the legal perspective, *remains* **zero**.

When we look at the testimony of Day, we see the inescapable problem for those who maintain the conclusion that "Lee Harvey Oswald was the sole assassin of John Fitzgerald Kennedy":

Empty shells were found on the sixth floor of the Texas School Book Depository. Shells exhibited by the Warren Commission were tied to Oswald's rifle. *But were the shells found on the sixth floor the same shells exhibited by the Warren Commission?* That's the million-dollar question.

Now, the *one and only* person who can actually tie the cartridge cases discovered on the floor of the Texas School Book Depository with the cartridge cases exhibited by the Warren Commission (the ones fired from Oswald's rifle) is *Day*, the person whose name was on the shells, the person who by taking possession of those shells was the one who was supposed to mark them at the scene.

And yet, we have seen that Day's testimony *not only fails to prove the fact for which it is offered, it actually proves the <u>contrary</u>*! Since this testimony does in fact prove the contrary, the only avenue left open for the sponsors of the "Oswald as lone assassin" conclusion is to completely discredit the testimony of Day, to essentially throw it out as worthless. If they do that, however, that leads to the following inevitable conclusion:

There is *no testimony on the record* that can verify that the shells which were discovered on the floor of the Texas School Book Depository were the shells exhibited by the Warren Commission, the ones which evidence shows was fired from Oswald's rifle!

And that would lead us to our final deductive syllogism which would prove, inevitably, the main thesis of this book, that there is no legitimate case against Lee Harvey Oswald. This is because a case can be no stronger than the weakest link supporting it.

Imagine a case, a heavy one, suspended thirty feet above the ground by a chain. Now, cut one of the links out. Note that the case comes crashing to the ground:

If the confidence level for any element of the case is **zero**, that is, in effect, like removing one of the links of the chain.

And we can see, deductively, that *in fact* one of the key links in the chain has been completely removed, leading to the inevitable crash. There are two syllogisms which demonstrate this, the conclusion of the first syllogism being used as a premise of the second.

The first syllogism is as follows:

IF it is in fact true that the confidence level for a proposition or element or sub-element of a case starts at zero until proven, AND

IF it is in fact true that an essential sub-element of The Case Against Oswald is that the Texas School Book Depository shells be identical with those exhibited by the Warren Commission, AND

IF it is in fact true that Day's is the only testimony capable of linking the Texas School Book Depository shells to the shells possessed and exhibited by the Warren Commission, AND

IF it is in fact true that the "Q" numbers map onto the Commission Exhibit numbers of the shells as the Warren testimony indicated, AND

IF it is in fact true that as a consequence of this mapping, Day's testimony not only fails to prove the fact for which it is offered, but actually proves the opposite, AND

IF it is in fact true that the only way to escape Day's testimony is to *invalidate* it, AND

IF it is in fact true that invalidated testimony has no legal force and effect, as if it had not even existed,

THEN the confidence level for the sub-element that ties the Texas School Book Depository shells to the bullets exhibited by the Warren Commission remains at ZERO.

The second syllogism is related to the entire case:

IF it is in fact true that the confidence level for the sub-element that ties the Texas School Book Depository shells to the bullets exhibited by the Warren Commission is zero, AND
IF it is in fact true that if the confidence level for *any* essential element or sub-element in The Case Against Oswald is zero, the entire case *in effect* has a confidence level of zero,

THEN the confidence level for The Case Against Oswald as a whole is ZERO.

Who would've thought? All this from a group of marks carved or not carved on empty shells with or without a diamond point pencil.

The logic here is inexorable. If the premises of these two syllogisms are true, then the conclusions of these two syllogisms *must* be true.

Is there any way out at all for the lone assassin theorists? Well, since the logic is sound, the only way out is to dispute the truth of these premises. For example, these theorists may claim that the confidence level for an unproven allegation is not necessarily zero, but could be some higher number. And, in fact, that may be true outside of the courtroom, but from the perspective of the courtroom, that is how the system functions. It's a very *binary* system. As Bugliosi noted, *you either prove it or you don't.* Proof counts as 1, and failure to prove counts as 0. 1 = guilty and 0 = innocent, there is no middle ground.

Still, one can possibly understand the reluctance by some to overturn The Case Against Oswald on what others might (incorrectly) term a "technicality." Regarding this reluctance, there are four points that can be made.

In the first place, the testimony of Day, when it is analyzed, shows that the shells on the floor of the Depository cannot be shown to be the same shells in the possession of the Warren Commission (the ones fired from Oswald's rifle). Consequently, we are forced to consider the exceptionally strong possibilities that:

A. There were at least *two* sets of shells, and
B. The shells on the floor of the Depository were *not* fired from Oswald's rifle (severing the connection between Oswald and the assassination bullets), and
C. At least one set was — and perhaps *both* sets of shells were — planted.

The A, B, and C of it is that this is no "technicality" we are talking about; rather, we are talking about *framing an innocent man*, and if the "technicalities" (i.e. the rules for the admissibility of evidence and the protocols designed to satisfy them) expose a conspiracy, reveal obstruction of justice, save an innocent man from the electric chair, and free us up to pursue the actual murderers of a President of the United States, I say, "*Technicalities*? Bring 'em on!"

As to the second point, one would hope that observing the Constitution of the United States, and the laws of due process contained within it, would not give any American pause, nor be seen as a mere "technicality."

It also should be noted as a third point that the "technicality" would only arise if Day's testimony was *invalidated*; if it was not invalidated, Oswald's innocence would be demonstrated simply by accepting Day's testimony as legitimate evidence.

Finally, it really doesn't matter whether or not someone agrees with the rules of the game or not, and what pejorative names they give or don't give the rules . . . the rules are the rules . . . "three strikes, yer out!"

So much for the legalities of the significance of the chain of custody of the empty shells. A key point, an essential point, and perhaps the most dispositive point of all, because it not only demonstrates Oswald's formal *innocence*, it leads us to an important re-visitation regarding (what we originally saw in this chapter) other's *guilt*.

Remember the CSS form that showed that the empty shells were turned over to the FBI before any order to do so had been given? There was something fishy about that, but we weren't exactly sure what. And, remember the fast exodus of the evidence from Dallas by a person who just happened to have a friend in the Strategic Air Command, evidence designated for return to sender less than 18 hours after it was received? Something fishy about that too, it seemed, but again, we lacked the information that would allow us to place it into context.

However, in light of the deductive proof so graciously provided by Mr. Day, we can gain a new perspective on these ominous events. Day's testimony (coupled with the available documentary evidence) shows beyond any shadow of a doubt that *at least one* bullet has been planted, and since the chain of custody for all three bullets has been obliterated, *all* of them could have been. So, because we have this evidence, an idea that formerly some would have seen as "paranoid" can now be re-framed as a possible hypothesis whose primary virtue is that it explains some highly suspect events:

The empty shells which were sent *to* Washington were not the empty shells that returned *from* Washington!

In short, the hypothesis is that the trip to Washington on the C-135 was a one-way ticket with a two-fold purpose for the empty shells in Dallas, in a classic case of *evidence-laundering*. And the purpose of this evidence-laundering? Well, the most likely possibility is that the shells that were originally found were not fired from a Mannlicher-Carcano, and certainly not Oswald's Mannlicher-Carcano, a weapon defective in more ways than one, and a weapon no professional assassin would dare utilize. So, those shells (the real evidence that could be traced to the real perpetrators) had to go, and shells that were fired from Oswald's rifle in a "dry run" had to be swapped in.

Thus, the ultimate purpose: to pin the blame on Oswald so that the real assassins (and more importantly, those who directed the activity of the assassins) could go free.

And if this evidence laundering did in fact occur, it occurred *within twenty-four hours* of the assassination, which would itself indicate a very high degree of pre-planning and premeditated coordination between certain individuals in the DPD and the FBI *well in advance of the assassination!*

It goes without saying that if this hypothesis turned out to be true, one or more key officers of the Federal Bureau of Investigation (and other bodies as well, such as the DPD) would have committed, among numerous other crimes, TREASON against the United States of America.

Even in light of the evidence we have just seen, this possibility that the shells were intentionally switched in a premeditated manner is just going to be too much for people to cope with, or even believe, but it is a hypothesis that has more than deductive logic on its side: there is actually photographic evidence of the same. For comparison purposes, let's first take a look at a photo of one of the empty cartridge cases and the live round. CE 543 is all the way on the left, in this photograph from the National Archives, reproduced in the book *Hear No Evil* (*Hear No Evil*, p. 132):

But now let us compare the 2 empty hulls on the right in the above photograph to the 2 empty hulls on the left (placed by J. Doyle Williams in an upside-down position) in the below photograph taken on November 22 by the FBI (close-up and cropped by author), and see if you can notice any difference in coloration:

There certainly is, not only between the shells in the two photographs, but even between the 2 empty hulls on the left in the FBI photograph (with a more black hue) with the live round on the right (which has the silver tone characteristic of brass in black-and-white we would expect to see). If we were to go simply by appearances alone, we might postulate that the shells on the left were constituted from a different metal than the bullet on the right.

One could speculate that the difference in coloration in the second photo was produced by heat from firing, but why wasn't that difference produced in the first photograph?

An interesting observation, which could easily be seen as visual evidence of a bait and switch operation. Unfortunately, this observation, which is inductive in character, is not as strong as the deductive verification to which we were exposed over the last sixty or so pages. It is vulnerable to rival hypotheses, for example, that the photo has been retouched or poorly reproduced, or, if not, that perhaps the lighting on the shells on the left was different from the lighting on the bullets on the right, thus leading to what would be an apparent difference in coloration, but not one which existed in reality. And the reply to this would be, perhaps this latter point is so, but given that what we see in this photograph confirms what deductive analysis reveals to be true, we can use the deductive analysis as corroboration for what our initial visual perception tells us.

In light of this, it might have been useful to inquire of the first two people known to have possession after Day, FBI agents Brown and Williams, just what they knew on the subject, but there is no testimony on record from them regarding their role in the chain of custody. That's not surprising, because their testimony would directly contradict Day's testimony that he passed the bullets along to Sims of the Dallas Police Department, and not to Brown (and thereafter Williams). Consequently, as far as chain of custody testimony goes, Brown and Williams are the "invisible men," as shown from an analysis of the page references in the screen captures below from the Warren Commission index (Williams, 15 H 800; Brown, 15 H 757): [1]

---

[1] http://www.history-matters.com/archive/jfk/wc/wcvols/wh15/html/WC_Vol15_0405b.htm; http://www.history-matters.com/archive/jfk/wc/wcvols/wh15/html/WC_Vol15_0384a.htm (retrieved December 16, 2011).

Williams, Doyle, vol. V, 132, 144	Brown, Charles T., vol. I, 142–143, 165, 409; vol. X, 358, 361, 376–377, 379–380; vol. XV, 619
These scant two references to J. Doyle Williams referred to his acting as a stand-in in Connally's car in the assassination reenactments, not to his photograph of the empty shells and the live round (which does not appear in Warren Commission records).	*These references to Charles T. Brown involve, et. al., interviews with Oswald's mother and witnesses on a rifle range, not to his receipt of the empty shells and the live round. Vincent Drain, who assumed custody of the shells at 11:45 pm, nowhere mentions being in the presence of Brown at 2:15 pm (or any time) in his affidavit at CD 5, pp. 159-161.*

There is one thing we do know, though. As the possessors of the two empty shells on November 22, as proven by the CSS form and the Williams photograph and memo, the initials of Brown and Williams had to have been on at least *two* of the shells, a *requirement* to establish the chain of custody. And, according to the testimony of Day, they were *not*!

So, if Brown and Williams received the shells as the documents indicated, and scratched their initials on the shells as protocol dictated, and the shells exhibited by the Warren Commission did *not* have those initials, then we can be 100% confident that the shells that were exhibited in the Williams photograph (the ones that were found in the Texas School Book Depository), were *not* the shells in the possession of the Warren Commission, which means that these exhibited shells fired from Oswald's rifle were *not* fired on November 22, and therefore were *not* the ones used in the assassination!!

At some point you ask yourself, "how much more evidence do you need?", and yet it is amazing just how much more evidence there is that confirms what we desperately do not want to believe to be true. Apart from the numerous primary documents indicating only two shells were found, the Day and Doughty issues leading to a deductive proof of a violation of the chain of custody, the issues with Brown and Williams (and the failure to gather their testimony) leading to a second deductive proof of a violation of the chain of custody (as indicated by the absence of their initials), there is even *more* evidence of an inductive character that at least one bullet was planted, and most likely the others as well.

This relates to a series of ballistic marks created by the Mannlicher-Carcano that were, and were not, found on shells CE 543, 544, 545, and the live round, CE 141. Information regarding these marks can be found from three primary sources, a letter sent from J. Edgar Hoover to J. Lee Rankin, General Counsel of the Warren Commission, on June 02, 1964 (CE 2968; 26 H 449), Paragraphs 133 and 151 of the *House Select Committee On Assassinations Report of the Firearms Panel* (March 1979) (7 HSCA 368, 371), and information provided by an analysis of the cartridge cases for *Life* magazine by Josiah Thompson appearing in the book *Six Seconds In Dallas*, p. 145, published in 1967.

Now, because the material in the primary sources is difficult to understand in its raw form, I am about to present a table summarizing the points delineated in those materials. Readers who want to see the raw data can go to the website supporting this book, and download the "Appendices" document. Here is the URL:

http://www.krusch.com/jfk

The information in the appendix is difficult to understand, as noted, so here is a summary (NOTE: a legend beneath the table defines the initials present in the "Type" and "Source" rows):

	A	B	C	D	E	F
TYPE:	MFM	BM	SH	MB	DL	CM
SOURCE:	FBI	FBI	HSCA	FBI	HSCA	FBI/*JT
CE 543 (C6/Q6)	1		3	3	1	
CE 544 (C7/Q7)		1				1
CE 545 (C38/Q48)	1					1
CE 141 (C8/Q8)	2					1*

TYPE	SOURCE
A = MFM (Magazine Follower Mark)	FBI = Hoover Letter
B = BM (Bolt mark)	HSCA = Firearms Panel Report
C = SH (Striations on head)	JT = Josiah Thompson
D = MB (Marks on Base)	
E = DL (Dented lip)	
F = CM (Chambering Mark)	

You are going to find this table confusing, but no need to worry, you will be able to see instantly, and visually, the problem.

To understand the table, let's start with a column-centric view, and look at column A, which tells us that CE 543 had one magazine follower mark (the magazine follower is a spring-tensioned lever whose function is to push cartridges up the clip), CE 545 also had one magazine follower mark, and CE 141 had two magazine follower marks.

When we take a row-centric view, we learn that CE 543 not only has one magazine follower mark, it also had three striations on the head, three marks on the base, and a dented lip.

You don't need to understand what the marks indicate, all you need to understand is the differences in how the marks appear on the shells. Once you understand the table, you can concentrate on your visual impressions to draw some conclusions about what you are seeing, and the first thing you notice is that the marks on the empty shells and live round are *all over the map*. Is there any consistency at all? No, and some of the inconsistencies are quite telling.

For example, take a look at column B. Only *one* of the shells, **CE 544** has a mark from the bolt of Oswald's rifle. But wasn't he supposed to have made *three* shots? If so, why a mark from the bolt on CE 544 only? And take a look at column A; why does only **CE 544** lack the magazine follower mark?

	A	**B**	**C**	**D**	**E**	**F**
TYPE:	MFM	BM	SH	MB	DL	CM
SOURCE:	FBI	FBI	HSCA	FBI	HSCA	FBI/*JT
CE 543 (C6/Q6)	1		3	3	1	
CE 544 (C7/Q7)		1				1
CE 545 (C38/Q48)	1					1
CE 141 (C8/Q8)	2					1*

Most importantly, take a look at columns C through F: here we can see quite clearly that CE 543 can be differentiated from the other exhibits along not just one, but *four* parameters:

- The number of striations on the head (543 has 3, the others none);
- The number of marks on the base (543 has 3, the others none);

- A dented lip (543 has 1, the others none);
- Chambering marks (543 has none, the others each have one);

	A	B	C	D	E	F
TYPE:	MFM	BM	SH	MB	DL	CM
SOURCE:	FBI	FBI	HSCA	FBI	HSCA	FBI/*JT
CE 543 (C6/Q6)	1		3	3	1	
CE 544 (C7/Q7)		1				1
CE 545 (C38/Q48)	1					1
CE 141 (C8/Q8)	2					1*

There is something very different about this shell, and considering that it was the one that was supposedly handed off to Fritz (which the deductive proof demonstrates was impossible), that means something.

So, when we consider the issue of the mark on the bolt which is not present on CE 543 and CE 545, as well as the oddities associated with CE 543, including a dented lip, we see that only one of the empty shells, CE 544, has the marks that we would expect to find, which would be a possible indication that at least 2 of the bullets had an origin that requires additional explaining.

This table *by itself*, not even considering the chain of custody issues, throws doubt on the legitimacy of CE 543 and 545.

Okay, we've seen a lot of evidence so far — evidence not only of Oswald's innocence, but of others' guilt — and their guilt can be shown, in part, by the ridiculous story they have concocted and are asking us to believe.

So, before we move to this next phase related to the guilt of others, let's add up everything we've seen, categorizing the evidence by topic . . . fasten your seatbelts!

TESTIMONY/TESTIMONY CONTRADICTION
- In his initial testimony, Day said he placed his initials on 2 hulls: in subsequent testimony, he stated that he placed his initials on 3 hulls.
- In his initial testimony, Day said Doughty's initials were on 1 hull; in subsequent testimony, he contradicted himself and said that Doughty's initials were on 2 hulls.
- In his initial testimony, Day said that Doughty's initials were to be placed just on the 1 shell said to have remained

in *Dallas*; in his subsequent testimony, Day contradicted himself and said that Doughty's initials were placed on 2 shells because they were going to be sent to *Washington*.

- In his initial testimony, Day said that shells CE **543** and 545 were sent to Washington; in his subsequent testimony, Day contradicted himself and said that the shells sent to Washington were CE **544** and 545.
- In his initial testimony, Day said that 2 shells were delivered to him at 10:00 p.m.; in his subsequent testimony, he contradicted himself and said instead that 3 shells were sent to him at 10:00 p.m..
- In an initial statement to Belin, Day said that he marked *all* the shells at the scene; in his subsequent testimony, he contradicted himself and said that he did *not mark any* shells at the scene; and in a later affidavit, he said he was sure it was one or the other.

DOCUMENT/DOCUMENT CONTRADICTION

- A line on the original Oswald evidence sheet as it appears on the record from the Dallas Police Department says that 2 shells were submitted to the Warren Commission; that same document, classified elsewhere as CE 2003, shows instead that 3 shells were submitted, with a numeral that appears handwritten.

TESTIMONY/DOCUMENT CONTRADICTION

- **Sims** of the DPD testified that he received the shells from Day, and Day confirmed that story; the CSS form, however, clearly shows that Day submitted the shells to **Brown** of the FBI.
- As a supposed recipient of the shells, Sims testified that his initials should have been on either the shells *or* the envelope in which they had been supposedly placed, when protocol demanded that his initials or name be on *both*; the evidence, however, shows that his initials or name were on *neither*.
- Day testified that Doughty's initials were on a shell; a letter prepared by Day after his testimony was given states that Doughty did not remember handling that shell.

- Several officers testified to seeing 3 shells on the floor of the depository; an FBI photograph, however, only shows 2 shells.
- Several officers testified to seeing 3 shells on the floor of the depository; the CSS form, however, shows only 2 shells.
- Several officers testified to seeing 3 shells on the floor of the depository; the DPD evidence sheet shows only 2 shells.
- Several officers testified to seeing 3 shells on the floor of the depository; a photographic cover page, however, shows that only 2 shells were recovered.
- Several officers testified to seeing 3 shells on the floor of the depository; a DPD photograph shows only 2 shells recovered.
- Several officers testified to seeing 3 shells on the floor of the depository; however, a memorandum by Williams stated that he only photographed 2 shells.
- Day of the DPD and Drain of the FBI testified that the handoff of the shells to the FBI took place **after 10:00 p.m.** on November 22; however, the CSS form shows that the handoff actually occurred at **2:15 p.m.**, to Brown of the FBI, not Drain.

IDENTIFIER/DOCUMENT CONTRADICTION
- One shell was given a "Q" number that had not been issued on the day the shell supposedly received that number.

PROTOCOL/BEHAVIOR CONTRADICTION
- Protocol is to place evidence in an envelope that clearly identifies the contents; Day placed the shells in an **unmarked** envelope, with neither the quantity nor the nature of the contents identified.
- Protocol is to place evidence in an envelope that is sealed, preventing tampering; Day placed the shells in an **unsealed** envelope before marking them, so that someone else could have opened the envelope and substituted different shells, and Day would have had no way of knowing that. Thus, any marks placed after the envelope had been opened would be *invalidated.*

- The envelope *was*, in fact, opened by Williams of the FBI prior to being returned to Day, for the purpose of making a photograph.
- Protocol is to mark all evidence at the scene; in his initial testimony, Day indicated that he only scratched his initials on 2 shells, but he should have scratched his initials on all 3 shells.
- Protocol is to mark evidence if you have possession of it; even though **Brown** of the FBI was given custody of the shells, neither his initials nor name appear on the shells.
- Protocol is to mark evidence if you have possession of it; even though **Williams** of the FBI was given custody of the shells, neither his initials nor name appear on the shells.
- Fritz claimed that he retained possession of the third shell, but there is no documentary proof on the record that he did retain possession, which would make it the single piece of evidence in the case without documentary proof of receipt.
- Protocol was for the **DPD** to have *exclusive* control of the evidence; the shells were handed off to the **FBI** several hours before the official authorization to transfer control. Given the jurisdictional issues, this handoff would have required coordination between two separate agencies, a coordination which was at the time nonexistent.
- Protocol is to have each person who marked evidence *testify* that it is his or her mark; Day submitted an affidavit stating that Doughty identified Doughty's initials on shells, but this was not only hearsay, it was directly contradicted by a letter that Day had written, and the ultimate way to settle the inconsistency, to ask Doughty to testify, never took place.

TESTIMONY/IDENTIFIER CONTRADICTION
- A deductive analysis shows that the story provided by Day was logically impossible.
- Markings on the shells demonstrate that the testimony provided by Day was false.

EVIDENCE/EVIDENCE CONTRADICTION
- Inconsistent ballistic marks on the shells.
- Inconsistent coloration in photographs.

SUPPRESSED EVIDENCE

- Though his initials or name should have been on 2 of the shells, **Williams** was not called by the Commission to testify to explain why they were not.
- Though his initials or name should have been on 2 of the shells, **Brown** was not called by the Commission to testify to explain why they were not.
- Though his initials or name should have been on one or more of the shells, **Doughty** was not called by the Commission to identify them.
- An FBI photo showing only 2 shells was not listed as a Warren Commission exhibit.
- An FBI photo cover page describing only 2 shells was not listed as a Warren Commission exhibit.
- A CSS form which contradicted sworn testimony was not listed as a Warren Commission exhibit.
- Though there were myriad, numerous contradictions in his story, Day was not confronted with those contradictions directly; instead, he was allowed to submit an affidavit which did not address the issues and only provided hearsay evidence which was itself contradicted by documentation and a deductive analysis.

MYSTERIOUS

- Evidence was sent to Washington *twice.*

Good night!!!

And now, in a surprise appearance, coming back from the dead to accept his Oscar for the Most Incoherent, Most Unbelievable, Most Sinister Chain Of Custody Fact-Pattern in the History of American Jurisprudence, is none other than the one and only . . . J.C. a/k/a/ "Carl" Day:

Thank you for that warm round of applause! I am so touched by this award that I simply have to acknowledge all the people who put me here, and I have so many of these "thank-yous" that they could not fit in this tiny speech balloon . . . rather than leave anyone out, my remarks follow . . .

"Humble fellow that I am, I have to admit that an award like this has to be shared with all the people responsible. So, first and foremost, I not only want to thank all the "little people" behind the scenes who made my work possible (who wish to remain anonymous), I would like to give a special "thanks, boys, I couldn't have done it without you!" to the following:

Sims, Mooney, and Fritz, who in coordinating their story with me helped me pass the all-critical Asch threshold of 3;

David Belin, who could have batted his eyes 1000 times at my testimony, but instead barely raised an eyebrow;

Brown and Williams, who could have ratted me out, but didn't, or if they did try to rat me out, were shut down by the FBI supervisors, or if they went to the media, were ignored;

Chief "Justice" Earl Warren, who as the highest official of the highest judicial body in the land, and as chairman of the Warren Commission, could have insisted that Lee Harvey Oswald have posthumous counsel, but didn't, which assured that there were no adversarial eyes or voices that could have seen at the time what we were doing and would have been subsequently screaming from every rooftop in the land;

The Warren Commission, who could have asked Brown, Williams, and Doughty to testify, and if they had, would have instantly revealed the impossibility of my story;

And last but not least, individuals of the present day who are well aware of the millions of Americans in Wonderland who are absolutely clueless about what actually transpired on November 22, and do their essential part to make sure that the foundations of *The Oswald Wall* remain ever-buttressed.

And so, I have to give a very, very special thanks to the following people who have been busy manning the fog machines which provide the smoke screen on which the Wall is projected, and who have spooled up the projectors with their specially created film:

Vincent Bugliosi, for *Reclaiming History*, a masterpiece of sophistry and illusion;

Stephen King, for *11/22/63*, whose work of fiction injected the Trojan horse that "Oswald did it" into the minds of millions of Americans;

numerous professors in history departments across America whose job it is to put their stamp of approval on the "official" version of history, certifying it as authentic, so that alternative narratives of history are consequently seen as *inauthentic*;

the editors of the Lee Harvey Oswald article in *Wikipedia*, who, using the official version of history as their cover, disclaim any responsibility to investigate the truth and rely instead on this "official" view, allowing them to steadfastly remove any counter-evidence to the main thesis of their article that Oswald was the lone assassin, deleting external references to contrary websites, contrary evidence, books on the topic, etc.;

internet "trolls" like Paul May and Francois Carlier . . .

who not only pollute Internet forums devoted to the JFK assassination with multiple-megabytes of irrelevant data, and who not only refuse to take *The JFK Challenge*, but who also post phony reviews on *Amazon.Com* in their never-ending quest to ensure that people will never be exposed to the facts;

John McAdams of Marquette University, who more than any other single individual has made sure that public perceptions of what occurred are seen through his distorted lens, producing the illusion that those who find evidence of conspiracy into the assassination of President Kennedy are "crazy," and finally,

the editors of the search algorithm at *Google*, who make sure that the vast majority of searches related to the Kennedy assassination are pointed at McAdams' website.

Thank you, thank you all . . . I think you really like me!"

And a big "thank YOU" to you too, Carl, for sharing your responsibility for that award with such generosity!!!

Yes, it is no exaggeration to say that we have a massive black hole for the legitimacy of CE 543, and therefore the element that exactly 3 bullets were fired by Lee Harvey Oswald from the sixth floor of the Texas School Book Depository, not to mention a massive black hole for any elements in *Proposition Two* related to the authenticity of the shells in the possession of the Warren Commission.

The probability that at the very least CE 543 would be seen as inadmissible evidence perhaps led to the backpedaling in the paragraph below authored by the Warren Commission, where they themselves indicated a shaky confidence in their own element: "Did we say *three* shots? Well, it *might've* been *two*. Who's counting?" (WR 110): [1]

> The physical and other evidence examined by the Commission compels the conclusion that at least two shots were fired. As discussed previously, the nearly whole bullet discovered at Parkland Hospital and the two larger fragments found in the Presidential automobile, which were identified as coming from the assassination rifle, came from at least two separate bullets and possibly from three.[336] The most convincing evidence relating to the number of shots was provided by the presence on the sixth floor of three spent cartridges which were demonstrated to have been fired by the same rifle that fired the bullets which caused the wounds. It is possible that the assassin carried an empty shell in the rifle and fired only two shots, with the witnesses hearing multiple noises made by the same shot. Soon after the three

Now, who would have thought that Neil Simon would take a break from writing *The Odd Couple* to moonlight for the Warren Commission? "It is possible that the assassin carried an empty shell in the rifle . . .". An idea inherently ludicrous, if true, it would make a mockery of all the evidence the Warren Commission claimed to exist that three shots were heard, creating the Warren Commission version of the famous Zen koan: "if an empty shell is fired, does it make a sound?" How could *three* shots be heard when *two* shots were fired? Echoes? No, echoes come in pairs, so observers would have heard *four* shots, not *three*. Furthermore, as we will see in subsequent chapters, the amount of damage that was done in the Presidential limousine and on the surrounding environment could not possibly be explained by two bullets. And what thoughts could possibly have gone through Oswald's mind as he was loading that *empty shell* (or blank) in the rifle? Would that really be the act of a man with an intent to kill the President?

When the Warren Commission postulates the humorous scenario that Oswald would bring an empty shell to the assassination, we feel safe in speculating that they were more than a little spooked by the evidence (which you have seen in this chapter) that only two

---

[1] "Warren Report, p. 110" http://www.history-matters.com/archive/jfk/wc/wr/html/WCReport_0067b.htm (retrieved August 15, 2011).

cartridges were found, and that they could not be sure that a congressional investigation or wayward reporter would not stumble on the truth, and so decided to plant the ideological seeds necessary to justify a future reversal.

The existence of so much evidence of malfeasance by various parties (possibly inspiring the Warren Commission to plant the seeds for a reversal of one of their most primary elements) leads us to some important questions related to the many individuals who are seemingly involved in a conspiracy to obstruct justice. Here is the question of the day:

> **"Yes, the evidence clearly shows that at least one individual was reporting false information, but you have dozens involved in the Kennedy case, many telling the same story, which, when demonstrated false, reveals coordinated lying or coordinated memory failures or coordinated errors of perception or coordinated misanalysis. Just what is going on?"**

Related to this question, the author is able to conceive of four possible hypotheses that could possibly provide an answer. Here they are:

1. **The *Simple Error* Hypothesis**
   Under this hypothesis, the anomalies in the evidence could be explained by simple mistakes, failures of perception, etc.. For example, only 2 shells were on the ground, but the witnesses mistakenly thought they saw 3.

   This one can easily be rejected. Too many people reported seeing the *same* mistaken phenomenon to conclude that what they were reporting was a "mistake." Also, we have photographs that show 3 shells on the ground, so those photographs were either forged or legitimate, but could in no way be seen as "mistaken." So this one is out.

2. **The *False Reporting* Hypothesis**
   Before we can get to any hypothesis that relates to individuals lying, we first need to be sure that the testimony of these individuals was *reported correctly*. Apparent synchronization of erroneous claims might have been

achieved simply by reporting testimony *falsely*. In that case, what appeared to be the actions of *numerous* individuals may have been the actions of only *one*!

This is an extremely important topic, and if the allegation is true, has an extraordinary impact on all of the testimony reported in the case, affecting not only this issue but all others. Because of this, I have prepared a separate appendix that lists numerous examples of the Warren Commission (and witnesses before the Commission) falsely reporting reality, and is too large to include here because it will disrupt the main line of argument. The interested reader is urged to visit my website and download the appendix, which can be found in the "Appendices" document at the following URL:

http://www.krusch.com/jfk

If you like, you can download the document now, read it, and then return to this book, or just continue.

3.   **The *Double Coverage Fallback Plan* Hypothesis**
Based on the material in the Appendix described above, it is clear that we cannot necessarily rely on the Warren Commission's reporting of reality, but let's assume for the moment that we could, and also that the photographic evidence is valid. Is there any other way to explain how 2 shells were *reported* found in the receipt documents when the testimony and photographs claim that 3 shells were found?

Yes, surprisingly enough, there is. We can call this the *double coverage fallback plan* hypothesis. Under this hypothesis, we would assume that the plot to assassinate the President and to pin the blame on Oswald had been long in the planning, but the perpetrators of the plan at the time of planning could not be sure that everything would go as expected. Accordingly, all contingencies had to be prepared for, and therefore the evidentiary foundation had to support *multiple* conclusions.

So, under this plan, here is what could have transpired. 3 shells were planted on the scene since the lone assassin scenario was the desired option (note: this does not mean that 3 bullets were *fired* from that location, only that the evidence would be found there). Thus, there would be witnesses around to support *seeing* 3 shells, and any photographs that were taken of the scene would *record* 3 shells. However, until Oswald was apprehended and killed, the lone assassin scenario would be too dangerous to support, with at least one *very key* individual alive who would be able to *contradict* that scenario!

So, until Oswald was killed, the conspiracy option had to be left open, and what better way to do that than to palm one of the three shells, and put on the record documentary evidence that only 2 bullets were fired, thus proving that there was a conspiracy, so Oswald could be let off the hook. At the same time, the conspiracy could then be blamed on someone else like Cuba, justifying an invasion of Cuba if necessary, with a ready supply of Cuban patsies available if that option had to be chosen.

Once Oswald was killed, though, there was no need to postulate any conspiracy hypothesis in the media, and the documentary evidence that only 2 bullets were fired could be easily buried . . . just like, in fact, it was.

Admittedly, this is an extremely intriguing hypothesis, and it has one primary virtue, which is that it reduces the number of conspirators down to a very small number: the only ones who had to be a part of the plan were the ones who actually handled the evidence, Day, Fritz, and one or more key personnel at the FBI. Everyone else could be completely in the dark! It also accounts for all the inconsistencies that we've seen without having to suspect other possibly innocent individuals of participating in an after-the-fact conspiracy to cover up what really happened.

About this hypothesis, two points could be noted: needless to say, even though it states that 3 shells actually *were* present, it does not in any way, shape, or form provide support for the proposition that there was a "lone" assassin — to the contrary, it positively *contradicts* it, so you're not going to find the Bugliosis of the world rallying around this one. Also, as intriguing as it is, the only support for it is the evidence that we have seen, which may or may not be enough to sustain it given all the other alternative hypotheses we have to explore.

And there is at least one more of these, so let's give this one the final examination.

4. **The *Coordinated Lying* Hypothesis**
   As far as I can tell, this is the hypothesis which has the most evidence behind it, so let me return to the original question which inspired this lengthy exploration of the possibilities, "Is there any way to show that commission witnesses had been coordinating their misstatements?"

   With the evidence I have provided for the *false reporting* hypothesis, we now know that misstatements can be coordinated even if the person themselves did not make the statement, via the blue pencil technique. And, misstatements could obviously also be coordinated wherever there have been *rehearsals* designed to create this coordination.

   Consequently, we can discover the presence of re-authoring or rehearsals by inference: synchronized testimony, whether through editorial control or rehearsal, is easy to show precisely where there are identical misstatements — we can immediately infer the presence of synchronized testimony when two people make exactly the same mistake concurrent in time. If A states that "29 + 29 = 100," and B somewhat later states that "29 + 29 = 100," we know that the probability that two individuals would make a mistake that improbable on their own would be extremely unlikely. The odds are, conversely, extremely high that if the blue pencil wasn't used (and it most certainly could have been, as the Appendix demonstrated), the individuals in question pow-wowed beforehand and coordinated their statements, which sadly enough for them and their stories, are easily proven false, proving not only that each lied, but also that both agreed to tell the same lie . . .

Returning to the empty shells issue, let's look at a very simple example of coordinated testimony between Captain Fritz, Detective Sims, and Lieutenant Day. We will start with Fritz, and an affidavit he prepared attempting to confirm the testimony by Day. The credibility of Fritz is already under fire because he made a statement contradicted by multiple witnesses in the Craig matter (discussed in the Appendix), and unfortunately for the validity of this affidavit, Day's testimony reveals that the shells statement by Fritz must likewise be in error and also deficient in several respects. For example, in the following affidavit, Fritz states that *Sims* "brought the three empty hulls to my office." (7 H 404)

> fell after being ejected from the rifle. After the pictures were made, Detective R. M. Sims of the Homicide Bureau, who was assisting in the search of the building, brought the three empty hulls to my office. These were delivered to me in my office at the police headquarters. I kept the hulls in an envelope in my possession and later turned them over to C. N. Dhority of the Homicide Bureau and instructed him to take them to Lt. Day of the Identification Bureau. I told Detective Dhority that after these hulls were checked for prints to leave two of them to be delivered to the FBI and to bring one of them to my office to be used for comparison tests here in the office, as we were trying to find where the cartridges had been bought. When Detective Dhority returned from the Identification Bureau, he returned the one empty hull which I kept in my possession. Several days later, I believe on the night of November 27, Vince Drain of the FBI called me at home about one o'clock in the morning and said that the Commission wanted the other empty hull and a notebook that belonged to Oswald. I came to the office and delivered these things to the FBI. We have Mr. James P. Hosty's receipt for these items in our report.

Yet as we have already seen, the CSS form told us that it was *Brown*, not *Sims*, who received the empty shells from Day:

SIGNATURE OF PERSON
RECEIVING SPECIMEN *Charles T. Brown, Jr.*

SPECIMEN RELEASED TO *Lt. Day, FBI, Dallas*

And, according to that form, it was *two* shells delivered to Brown, not *three*. Nor is there any testimony or document on record that Brown in turn delivered even these two shells to Sims.

An additional problem for the story that Sims received the shells is that if Sims had actually taken possession of them, he should have marked them (being the next recipient in the chain of custody). But if you will recall the testimony of Day, he nowhere indicates that Sims' initials are on the shells, and, in fact, Sims himself would not state positively for the record that he initialed the shells, in yet another suspicious memory lapse all too reminiscent of the Day testimony; I mean, if *you* were an experienced officer and were initialing empty shells that could have been used to murder your President, isn't that something *you* would remember? Not Sims! (7 H 186): [1]

---

[1] http://www.history-matters.com/archive/jfk/wc/wcvols/wh7/html/WC_Vol7_0097b.htm (retrieved December 15, 2011).

Mr. Belin. Do you remember whether or not you ever initialed the hulls?
Mr. Sims. I don't know if I initialed the hulls or not.
Mr. Belin. If you would have initialed the hulls, what initials would you have used?
Mr. Sims. As a rule, RMS.
Mr. Belin. RMS?
Mr. Sims. Yes, sir; but I believe I initialed the hulls or the envelope that I put them in.

We can be forgiven for seeing waffling like this as a pathetic attempt to avoid a charge of perjury. As you will recall, RMS was *not seen* on the shells (according to the testimony of Day, who had the benefit of a magnifying glass and a good light), and we can also see (upon review) that Sims' name was *not* on the envelope (CE 717 at 17 H 501), as the testimony of Day likewise indicated (4 H 253):[1]

Mr. Day. Three were in there when they were turned over to Detective Sims at that time. The only writing on it was, "Lieut. J. C. Day." Down here at the bottom.
Mr. Belin. I see.
Mr. Day. "Dallas Police Department," and the date.

So Sims' professed "belief" (if in fact he *did* believe it) is as irrelevant as it is inaccurate.

So, here we have similar testimony by Day, Sims, and Fritz, *none* of it *corroborated* by hard documentary evidence, and *all* of it *contradicted* by that same evidence. Because they are all trying to tell the *same* story, a story not only *not backed up* by the necessary documents but *contradicted* by those documents, that's a textbook example of synchronized misstatements. And a dozen or 100 or 1000 synchronized misstatements will not only never add up to the truth, but they have a paradoxical effect in the *other* direction: the more there are, the greater the proof that "the fix was in."

There are other problems with the statement of Fritz: for example, we know from Day's testimony that the envelope ostensibly delivered to Fritz (and ostensibly by Sims) was *unmarked* and *unsealed*, a key fact Fritz neglects to mention. Also, according to Day's testimony of April 22, the envelope contained hulls that were not marked by Day at the scene, and so even if Sims actually *had* delivered an envelope to Fritz, we can't be sure that that envelope contained the shells that were found at the Texas School Book Depository — *can* we? And even if this most likely imaginary envelope did contain *three* shells, we

---

[1] http://www.history-matters.com/archive/jfk/wc/wcvols/wh4/html/WC_Vol4_0131a.htm (retrieved December 15, 2011).

know from the analysis of Day's testimony that it is absolutely certain that at least one of them was not fired from Lee Harvey Oswald's rifle.

Apart from these issues, there is an additional misstatement by Fritz, which alone throws the entire affidavit into doubt. Re-read these three sentences from the Fritz statement (7 H 404):

> possession. Several days later, I believe on the night of November 27, Vince Drain of the FBI called me at home about one o'clock in the morning and said that the Commission wanted the other empty hull and a notebook that belonged to Oswald. I came to the office and delivered these things to the FBI. We have Mr. James P. Hosty's receipt for these items in our report.

Unfortunately for Captain Fritz's story that he delivered the third hull on the night of November 27 to the FBI because "the Commission wanted the other empty hull," that was *impossible*. The Executive Order forming the Warren Commission was issued *two days later*, November 29, as the following screen captures from the Warren Report reveal (WR 471):[1]

APPENDIX I

IMMEDIATE RELEASE   NOVEMBER 30, 1963

Office of the White House Press Secretary

- -

THE WHITE HOUSE

EXECUTIVE ORDER
NO.11130
- - - -

APPOINTING A COMMISSION TO REPORT UPON THE
ASSASSINATION OF PRESIDENT JOHN F. KENNEDY

While the date of the press release was November 30, the actual date of appointment was November 29, as we can see from the bottom line:

All Executive departments and agencies are directed to furnish the Commission with such facilities, services and cooperation as it may request from time to time.

LYNDON B. JOHNSON

THE WHITE HOUSE,

November 29, 1963.

---

1 http://www.history-matters.com/archive/jfk/wc/wr/html/WCReport_0248a.htm (retrieved August 15, 2011).

Proof that the shell was turned over on November 27, and not a later date, such as November 30, was the following receipt prepared by James Hosty (CE 2003: 24 H 347):[1]

Received from Capt. Will Fritz at approximately 1:00 a.m. on 11/27/63:

Billfold and 16 cards and pictures taken from Lee Harvey Oswald on 11/22/63.

One notebook recovered from room of Lee Harvey Oswald at 1026 No. Beckley on 11/22/63. with names and addresses.

One 6.5 mm rifle hull recovered at Texas School Book Depository, 411 Elm Street, Dallas, Texas, on 11/22/63.

James P. Hosty, Jr.
Special Agent, FBI.

So, why is Fritz providing sworn testimony that the Commission requested the shell when the Commission *hadn't even been formed*? The charitable interpretation is that he was mistaken. But, taking into account the context of coordinated disinformation just revealed, we can be forgiven for disregarding this charitable interpretation.

The astute reader will have noticed that we have moved into some very interesting territory here. This chapter was supposedly designed to discuss evidence justifying or not justifying an element of the First Proposition of The Case Against Oswald, but now we see that the evidence that was supposed to convict Oswald has instead backfired into meta-evidence that that evidence *itself* is irredeemably tainted, which will have a major impact on our base legal assumption:

All the evidence in The Case Against Lee Harvey Oswald stipulated as admissible is *authentic*. The admissible evidentiary record is comprehensive, *credible*, sufficient, and consistent to the extent that it precludes reasonable doubt regarding both of the following propositions regarding the assassination of President John F. Kennedy:

---

[1] "Warren Commission Hearings, Volume XXIV, Current Section: CE 2003 - Dallas Police Department file on investigation of the assassination of the President (CD 81b, all pages)," http://www.maryferrell.org/mffweb/archive/viewer/showDoc.do?docId=1140&relPageId=365 (retrieved June 30, 2011).

Is the evidence in this case *authentic*, and if it is, is it *credible*? If it is not authentic in even one area, and/or could be shown to lack credibility in predictable key areas (revealing a pattern of dissimulation), it not only would fail to justify the guilt of Oswald, but in a boomerang effect, would now operate to demonstrate the guilt of his accusers!

So, as we proceed through the subsequent chapters, we are now occupying new ground: simultaneously evaluating the impact the evidence that we view with reference not just to the guilt of *Oswald*, but also to the guilt of his *accusers*, in criminal charges related to, at minimum, obstruction of justice, accessories after the fact to murder, and treason.

That is a totally different ballgame, one that the mind naturally resists, and, indeed, ought to resist. When we are talking about numerous people involved in the spreading of coordinated disinformation, in what may or may not have been a conspiracy to cover up the identity of the true assassins of the President using tools that would be the 1964 equivalent of what *Industrial Light and Magic* does for cinema today, we have to first cross a threshold to evaluate this evidence. The spread of coordinated disinformation is a serious charge, and leads us to one final remaining question related to that threshold, a question many readers may have already asked themselves, and one asked by Vincent Bugliosi (RH 1460; emphasis supplied):

> Let's assume, for example, that the CIA was behind the assassination. After the assassination, **how could the CIA have gotten the FBI, Secret Service, Dallas Police Department, the autopsy doctors, indeed, the Warren Commission itself, to go along with the horrendous crime the agency had committed** and do the great number of things the conspiracy theorists say these various groups and people did to cover up the CIA's complicity in Kennedy's murder? Wouldn't that be an impossible task?

Here Bugliosi asks a legitimate question. Yes, one or more plants/contract agents in the Dallas Police Department and FBI may actually have had knowing involvement with a conspiracy to assassinate the President from the beginning, but on the other hand, in a cover-up of that crime, many individuals would have needed to be unwittingly involved in a cooperative capacity. Can we really say that *all* these people were *knowing* co-conspirators?

Our intuition tells us "no!" A crime of this magnitude would have to have the *least* number of people involved as part of the "inner circle," if for no other reason to prevent discovery of the conspiracy and the ultimate identity of the perpetrators. Yet, numerous other people who would *not* have this knowledge would be called upon to cooperate after the fact as part of a cover-up operation. How could *these* people be drafted into the plot, however unwittingly?

Enter the World War III cover story.

To understand the methodology of surreptitious inclusion, one has to understand the psychology of the 1963 mindset. Just over a year earlier, the Cuban missile crisis occurred, and the United States seemed to be on the brink of nuclear war, as Americans woke up to headlines like these (*The New York Times*, October 23, 1962):

Following a steady dose of "duck and cover" civil defense training films that had earlier been seen by millions of kids in the 1950s, the Cuban Missile Crisis seemed to seal the deal and turn the most hardened scoffers of those training films into true believers.

The historical crisis was resolved when Kennedy and Kruschev together worked to bring America back from the precipice via mutual compromise, but this flirtation with the ultimate disaster — global annihilation — had to be fresh on people's minds, an omnipresent threat waiting in the wings.

An extremely useful tool for psychological leverage! This was not lost on President Johnson, who utilized this psychological tool to persuade his friend Richard Russell to serve on the Warren Commission. One version of the World War III cover story might have gone something like this: "This guy Oswald is a communist, and we have some pretty good evidence that this was a communist plot, instigated by either Cuba or Russia or both, but if we let the American people discover this, then we are going to have to take action, certainly a declaration of war, which could easily lead to a nuclear exchange. So to prevent the death of millions of innocent Americans, we are going to have to make sure that everyone thinks that Oswald is the lone assassin."

The author has been unable to locate any documentary evidence of this more detailed version, but there is on the record a transcript of the "lite" version of the cover story as transmitted to Russell on Novermber 29 by Johnson, with several of the details stated explicitly implied. Johnson meets Russell's reluctance to serve on the Commission with a good old-fashioned Texas power-play, the nuclear edition: [1]

DR	Well, now Mr. President, I know I don't have to tell you of my devotion to you..but I just can't serve on that Commission...I'm highly honored you'd think about me in connection with it..but I couldn't serve on it... with Chief Justice Warren...I don't like that man,.I don't have any confidence in him at all..I realise he is a much greater man in the United States..than anyone.. and so you get John Stennis.....
LBJ	Dick...it has already been announced and you can serve with anybody for the good of America and this is a question that has a good many more ramaifications than on the surface and we've got to take this out of the arena where thev're testifving that Krhuschev and Castro did this and did that and check us into a war that can kill 40 million Americans in an hour and you would put on your uniform in a minute and the reason I've asked Warren is because he is the Chief Justice of this country and we've got to have the highest Judicial people we can have. The reason I ask you is because you have that same kind of temperament..and you can do anything for your country and don't go giving me that kind of stuff about you can't serve with anybody..you'll do anything.

How many people besides Senator Russell were given this story, and in what form: in public places, or in smoke-filled rooms? If it is more than this one, we have an explanation for a methodology by which innocent, patriotic Americans could have been enlisted to cooperate in a conspiratorial effort without any knowledge on their part! Douglas Horne, Senior Analyst on the Military Records Team of the Assassination Records Review Board, citing author David Lifton, discussed this possibility in the context of medical personnel (an area of the case we have not yet investigated; *Inside The ARRB*, v. 4, pp. 1181-82; emphasis supplied):

---

[1] "Transcript of November 29, 1963 Phone Call at 855 P.M. Between Lyndon Baines Johnson and Richard Russell," http://www.historymatters.com/archive/jfk/lbjlib/phone_calls/Nov_1963/ html/LBJ-Nov-1963_0309a.htm (retrieved July 11, 2001: paragraphs on separate pages combined into one by author).

Lyndon B. Johnson . . . used the fear of a nuclear holocaust to persuade an extremely reluctant Chief Justice Earl Warren to chair the Presidential Commission whose primary goal was to quash rumors of conspiracy about Kennedy's assassination. Needless to say, this extreme form of arm-twisting — laying a guilt trip on Warren by telling him that unless he cooperated and chaired the Commission, 40 million people could be killed in a war between the United States and the U.S.S.R. because of rumors about an international Communist conspiracy — worked like a charm. **David Lifton has come to refer to the application of this psychology by LBJ as the 'World War III cover story,'** . . .

I say this because I do not for one minute believe that Robert Knudsen; Drs. Humes, Boswell, and Finck; Dr. Ebersole; Dr. Canada; nor Admirals Kenney, Galloway, or even Dr. Burkley, were knowing participants in the conspiracy to kill President Kennedy. They were, however, all clearly knowing participants in the medical coverup — but **if they were told that they had to suppress evidence of multiple shooters to prevent World War III, then they doubtless believed they were engaged in a coverup necessary for the survival of the nation and the prevention of a worldwide nuclear holocaust**.

If the distribution of this cover story was more widespread — and there is at least one key piece of evidence on the record that it is, the Katzenbach memo — then we have an explanation that could turn a possibility into a probability.

But could the cover story alone account for all the examples of unintentional cooperation that we may be coming across? No. The cover story was not the *only* method of surreptitious inclusion, and indeed, due to its sensitive nature, could only have been given to the most key parties, which then brings us to a second method.

Any key party given a cover story could then issue *orders* to their subordinates, and *their subordinates would follow orders without necessarily knowing the reason why*. The orders the subordinates were given could have been either to a) keep silent about something they had seen and/or b) provide testimony consistent with a "refreshed" memory (i.e. change their stories), and/or c) do an action and keep quiet about it, as the primary possibilities.

Regarding the first possibility, we know, for example, that medical personnel at President Kennedy's autopsy were ordered not to reveal what had transpired there, forced to sign "gag orders" which were in effect for approximately 15 years — so-called "rights" to free speech be damned. Here is what one of those gag orders looked like (ARRB MD 138):[1]

26 November 1963

From: Commanding Officer, U. S. Naval Medical School
To: RIEBE, Floyd Albert, 458-47-93, HM2, USN

1. You are reminded that you are under verbal orders of the Surgeon General, United States Navy, to discuss with no one events connected with your official duties on the evening of 22 November - 23 November 1963.

2. This letter constitutes official notification and reiteration of these verbal orders. You are warned that infraction of these orders makes you liable to Court Martial proceedings under appropriate articles of the Uniform Code of Military Justice.

J. H. STOVER, JR.
26 November 1963
(Date)

FIRST ENDORSEMENT

From: RIEBE, Floyd Albert, 458-47-93, HM2, USN
To: Commanding Officer, U. S. Naval Medical School

1. Above orders received this date.

2. I have read and fully understand them and am aware of the disciplinary action possible in the event that I disobey these orders.

FLOYD ALBERT RIEBE
27 Nov 63
(Date)

As far as the second and third possibilities go, the Johnson/Russell transcript indicates that President Johnson wanted to quash at the outset any investigatory threads that would lead to conspiracy. The mechanism for implementing this was the Warren Commission. With the Warren Commission in place, Johnson and Hoover would be able to control the flow of information, and nip in the bud any further investigations outside of White House and FBI control, as proven by this transcript of a conversation between Johnson and Hoover on November 29, 1:40 p.m:[2]

---

[1] http://www.history-matters.com/archive/jfk/arrb/master_med_set/md138/html/md138_0001a.htm (retrieved September 14, 2011).

[2] http://www.history-matters.com/archive/jfk/lbjlib/phone_calls/Nov_1963/audio/LBJ-Hoover_11-29-63.htm (retrieved September 21, 2011).

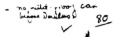

November 29, 1963
1:40 p. m.

TELEPHONE CONVERSATION BETWEEN THE PRESIDENT AND J. EDGAR HOOVER
(from Mr. Hoover)

LBJ   Are you familiar with this proposed group that they're trying to put together
         on this study of your report and other things..two from the House..two from
         the Senate.. somebody from the Court...a couple of outsiders?

JEH   I haven't heard of that. I've seen the reports on the Senate Investigating
         Committee that they've been talking about..

LBJ   Well, we think if we don't have...I want to get by just with your file and your
         report..

JEH   I think it would be very very bad to have a rash of investigations.. on this thing

LBJ   Well, the only way we can stop them is probably to appoint a high-level one
         to evaluate your report and put somebody that's pretty good on it ...that I
         can select, out of the Government...and tell the House and Senate not to go
         ahead with their investigations...because they'll get a lot of television going
         and I think it would be bad...

Once the mechanism for controlling the flow of information was in place, acting Attorney General Nicholas Katzenbach's November 25th memo (transmitting to the President's Press Secretary the directive that would create the necessary cognitive climate for what was about to proceed) would be given the teeth necessary to have legal and force and effect:

> 2. Speculation about Oswald's motivation ought to be cut off, and we should have some basis for rebutting thought that this was a Communist conspiracy or (as the Iron Curtain press is saying) a right-wing conspiracy to blame it on the Communists.

"Cutting off" speculation about Oswald's motivation: a pretty aggressive tactic, especially when at that stage a conspiracy of any sort was as probable as any other hypothesis! It's easy to see how what starts as a gag order can morph into an order to transmit false information. Since the vast majority of the individuals who were providing the most basic evidentiary testimony in the case to the Johnson-appointed Warren Commission were doctors under military control, FBI agents under Washington control, and Dallas police detectives under Dallas (and most likely Washington) control, all we really have to postulate is that innocent parties who were subordinates within the aforementioned hierarchies were given orders to do "X" and/or say or not say "Y" (and also ordered to remain silent about these directives if they wanted to keep their jobs, not to mention other possible consequences about which we have not been informed).

This technique would in effect create a vast functioning network of people in multiple domains "just doing their jobs" to achieve an objective about which they were *totally in the dark*. And since the media was broadcasting information fed to them by government operatives — operatives implementing orders to cut off speculation that Oswald was involved in a conspiracy, thanks to the Katzenbach memo — who could really blame these other individuals for following the party line? The "common" knowledge spraying from the firehoses of networks CBS, NBC et al. (piped by firemen Walter Cronkite and Huntley and Brinkley), and newspapers *The New York Times* and *The Washington Post* and magazines *Time* and *Life* (piped by firemen reporters), was now everywhere and in the minds of millions, defining the boundaries that separated the thoughts that were legitimate from the thoughts which were not.

And these were not the skeptical minds of a post-Vietnam, post-Watergate, post 911-world evaluating these boundaries, but naïve post-1950s minds shaped by a steady diet of *Andy Griffith* episodes and *Leave It To Beaver* reruns. It was a Norman Rockwell world indeed. Anyone who stepped out of the party line and alleged conspiracy on the part of a by-and-large trusted government would at the very least have been made a pariah, called "crazy," or confronted with other *ad hominem* attacks which persist to this vastly more well-informed day.

A profound psychological phenomenon, which can explain why otherwise upright individuals, like doctors with years of experience, became a part of the "silent majority." Dr. Charles Crenshaw gave a first-person account of this psychological phenomenon in his book *Conspiracy Of Silence* (pp. 153-6), and then explained that there was another psychological phenomenon contributing to his silence: the will to survive! (emphasis supplied)

> At a news conference in the hospital the previous day, Drs. Malcolm Perry and Kemp Clark suggested that the President must have been turning to his right when he was shot. They said this because they also believed that the bullet that ripped through President Kennedy's head had entered from the front. **When the films showed that the President was not turned when he was shot, nothing more was said, as I remember. I didn't blame Drs. Clark and Perry one bit. They, too, had observed the men in suits, and had heard about the scene**

with Dr. Earl Rose. [*BK: the Secret Service took possession of the President's body over the protestations of pathologist Rose who was supposed to conduct the autopsy*]. **Every doctor who was in Trauma Room 1 had his own reasons for not publicly refuting the "official line."**

I believe there was a common denominator in our silence — a fearful perception that to come forward with what we believed to be the medical truth would be asking for trouble. **Although we never admitted it to one another, we realized that the inertia of the established story was so powerful, so thoroughly presented, so adamantly accepted, that it would bury anyone who stood in its path. I had already witnessed that awesome, dictatorial force in the Earl Rose incident, the same fierceness that I would, for years to come, continue to recognize in the tragedies awaiting those people who sought the truth. I was as afraid of the men in suits as I was of the men who had assassinated the President. Whatever was happening was larger than any of us.** *I reasoned that anyone who would go so far as to eliminate the President of the United States would surely not hesitate to kill a doctor. . . .*

I've often wondered what would have been the consequences of looking directly into that camera and boldly stating, "President Kennedy was shot in the head and in the throat from the front." Now, after all these years, I realize that such courage would have been utterly ineffective and suicidal. **The truth, staring directly into the face of our government, stood about as much chance of coming to light as a june bug in a hailstorm, and I wouldn't have fared any better.**

Already, the eastern press had begun to discredit us as physicians and Parkland as a hospital. If you had any association with Dallas, you were suspect. To come forward and give an unwavering professional opinion that was contradictory to the official story would only have given them a personalized target. . . .

The hospital administration was paranoid about publicity, especially at a time like that. In view of all I had heard, seen, and sensed, I wasn't about to appear on the six-o'clock news, giving an interview about the death of the

President. **A nursing student had already fallen into disfavor, and was later thrown out of school, because she informed the press of the number of blood units Governor Connally had received. Although no official instructions had been issued by the hospital administration, there was a tacit implication, an unspoken warning in their general attitudes that said that anyone who was intelligent enough to pursue a medical career was also smart enough to keep his mouth shut.** Failure to do the latter would result in foreclosure on the former. **We were all young doctors who for years had struggled and sacrificed to achieve that level of success. And we had a fortune in money and time tied up in our professions. The thought of throwing all that away weighed heavily on my mind.**

That pretty much sums it up, doesn't it? Now just multiply that by 150 or so actors, and you'll have your answer to the question, "why would so many people consent to being unwilling participants in a conspiracy?"

There is one more follow-up question in this regard. It could be protested "who would launch a conspiracy *not knowing* precisely whether or not people would follow these orders or the party line?" This answer isn't too difficult: apparently this was not a concern for the professionals who had run dozens, if not hundreds, or thousands, of similar operations, and always managed to maintain the covert status of these schemes.

Remember the *Operation Northwoods* memo? As you will recall, under the *Northwoods* plan, announced to a very small and privileged part of the world by the Joint Chiefs of Staff on March 13, 1962, an airplane was to be loaded with college students, college students who would fly for a short while only to be later be disembarked at another location while an identical clone aircraft headed for Cuba that was supposedly carrying these college students was to transmit a "MAYDAY" message that it was under attack by Cuban MIG aircraft, said clone aircraft to then be destroyed by radio signal: [1]

---

[1] http://www.gwu.edu/~nsarchiv/news/20010430/doc1.pdf, p. 10 (retrieved September 22, 2011).

a. An aircraft at Eglin AFB would be painted and numbered as an exact duplicate for a civil registered aircraft belonging to a CIA proprietary organization in the Miami area. At a designated time the duplicate would be substituted for the actual civil aircraft and would be loaded with the selected passengers, all boarded under carefully prepared aliases. The actual registered aircraft would be converted to a drone.

b. Take off times of the drone aircraft and the actual aircraft will be scheduled to allow a rendezvous south of Florida. From the rendezvous point the passenger-carrying aircraft will descend to minimum altitude and go directly into an auxiliary field at Eglin AFB where arrangements will have been made to evacuate the passengers and return the aircraft to its original status. The drone aircraft meanwhile will continue to fly the filed flight plan. When over Cuba the drone will being transmitting on the international distress frequency a "MAY DAY" message stating he is under attack by Cuban MIG aircraft. The transmission will be interrupted by destruction of the aircraft which will be triggered by radio signal. This will allow ICAO radio

Now, every one of these college students would operate as a functional timebomb threatening to expose this little plot, but apparently the Joint Chiefs Of Staff did not find this to be a concern. The Chiefs probably realized from their years of experience creating plans organizing spooks, spies, and snipers that most people would be like the peers of Charles Crenshaw, who would simply keep their mouths shut, and if there were any outliers, like Crenshaw himself nearly 3 decades later, there was always the ever-reliable media with their well-placed, well-paid *Operation Mockingbird* "assets" ready, willing, and able to frame the outliers in the same way that Oswald was framed. It's the ever-familiar "wacko" spin: the people who go against the party line, like District Attorney Jim Garrison, don't get invited to join the party, as the ever-"objective" establishment pipeline *The New York Times* told us: [1]

---

[1] "Investigations: Some Say It's Garrison Who's In Wonderland," *The New York Times*, May 14, 1967.

Some Say It's Garrison Who's in Wonderland

If you know in advance that millions of people will be exposed to this frame, through newspapers, radio, and television, you are good to go.

Of course, on the outside chance that certain members of the media themselves would not cooperate, anyone who would order the murder of a President would most likely have a backup plan to take care of any contingencies like that — right?

So, as we close off this section, let's review what we've learned:

- That there were only *two*, and not *three*, shells on the sixth floor of the Texas School Book Depository Building is indicated not only by the early documentary evidence, including receipts and photographs, but also by a deductive proof related to the chain of custody based on the April 22 testimony of J.C. Day (as modified to the extent possible by Day's June 23 affidavit).
- The deductive proof results in a *checkmate* for *The Case Against Oswald*; if the aforementioned testimony is true, then there is no Case Against Oswald, and if it is *false*, then there is no Case Against Oswald.
- These two shells were turned over by a member of the Dallas Police Department to the FBI without explicit orders transferring jurisdiction, which would entail a level of coordination that is not formally explainable.
- Because there is a deductive proof that there were only *two* shells on the sixth floor, then all the testimony to the contrary indicates coordinated disinformation that by itself throws into doubt the credibility of all the evidence in the case, not just that related to the empty shells.
- Chain of custody issues related to the Brown and Williams possession (as well as the Day testimony) indicate that *at least two* of the shells that became Warren Commission exhibits were not those found on the floor of the Texas School Book Depository, a second deductive proof.
- Between 2 and 3 pm, there apparently were two sets of shells in play: the first set, a set of *three*, handed from

Day to Sims; the second set, a set of *two*, handed from Day to Brown. This provides a third deductive proof related to the following: if the Day/Sims testimony (and all corroborating testimony) is true, and if the Day/Brown documentation is true, then either *five* shells were found at the Depository (not *three*), or a fake set of shells was introduced early on. Alternatively, we can see the Day/Sims testimony as *falsified*, which would obliterate its value in establishing the chain of custody. If any of the above eventualities are true, the confidence level for Element One must remain zero, and deductive logic shows that at least *one* of them must be true.

- There is evidence on record that the Warren Commission misreported testimony, which if true would in and of itself obliterate faith in *any* evidence.
- Evidence against Oswald, when it can be demonstrated to be manufactured, is *automatically* converted into evidence for a conspiracy designed to hide the identity of the true assassins of the President, to allow these individuals to literally get away with murder — a crime for which there is no statute of limitations. And when the victim is the President of the United States, even more so than for any other person, *this simply cannot be allowed.*

To this last point, we now need to adopt a new attitude as we move through this book, and think in stereo. As we view the evidence, we need to see it from *two* perspectives:

Is this evidence *for* or *against* the elements of
The Case Against Oswald?

AND

Is this evidence *for* or *against* the notion that there was a conspiracy to cover up the identity of the true assassins of the President, with both witting and unwitting participants?

To answer this latter question, we ought to heed these words of wisdom from Vincent Bugliosi (RH 1439):

> **A conspiracy is nothing more than a criminal partnership. And although conspiracies obviously aren't proved by the transcript of a stenographer who typed up a conversation between the partners agreeing to commit the crime, there has to be some substantive evidence of the conspiracy or partnership's existence.** And in the conspiracy prosecutions I have conducted, I have always been able to present direct evidence of the co-conspirators acting in concert before, during, or after the crime, and/or **circumstantial evidence from which a reasonable inference of concert or meeting of the minds could be made.**

In this excerpt, we learn something important. The conspirators to murder the President (or to hide the true identity of his assassins) are not likely to be publishing their internal memos, such as existed. They didn't have court reporters present to record their conversations, nor tape recorders. So, how do we prove conspiracy? Through the existence of "circumstantial evidence from which a reasonable inference of concert or meeting of the minds could be made." Synchronized misstatements, planted evidence, forged documents, conclusions that violate the laws of physics: if we can see a pattern of improbable persuasion as we make our way through this book, we are able to rule out mere negligence as a hypothesis, and through sheer volume, are able to detect the presence of an "invisible hand" guiding otherwise innocent parties down a predetermined path.

So, both camps, the ones who maintain that Oswald is innocent, and the ones who maintain that Oswald is guilty, are in the same boat: forget claims, forget stipulations, and focus on *evidence*! And, when you analyze the evidence, look at it from the standpoint of *logic and intuition*: does this evidence *really* make sense?

To this point, we will let Mr. Bugliosi have the final word (RH 1437; emphasis supplied):

> **If . . . there is no evidence to support your allegation, from a legal standpoint you're out of court.** But even if you're out of court, if you can at least argue that "well, there's no evidence of this, but logic and common sense tell you it is so," you still have talking rights and you can still play the game,

as it were. **But when you not only have no evidence, but logic and common sense tell you it isn't so, it's time to fold your tent. No evidence plus no common sense equals go home, zipper your mouth up, take a walk, forget about it, get a life.**

My sentiments exactly, Mr. Bugliosi. Let's take a look at rest of the evidence, and see what it has to tell us.

THIS CONCLUDES VOLUME ONE.
THERE ARE TWO ADDITIONAL VOLUMES.

HIGHLIGHTS OF VOLUME TWO INCLUDE:

— The nine reasons why President Kennedy was shot in the back, not the neck;

— The methods for calculating the confidence level for *Proposition One, Element One,* and why one of them is certainly superior to the others;

— The most likely confidence level for *Proposition One, Element One,* based on the evidence;

— Six reasons we can be absolutely confident that not all the shots were fired from the Depository;

— And a whole series of "what is wrong with this photograph?" challenges.

HIGHLIGHTS OF VOLUME THREE INCLUDE:

— The Case of the Incredible Moving Boxes (*Proposition One, Element Three*);

— The 12 reasons why the single-bullet "theory" is a total fantasy;

— A final analysis of the confidence level for *Proposition One*;

— A Virtual Jury of 12, including two attorneys and an administrative law judge, provides their confidence level for the Case of the Incredible Moving Boxes;

— Overview of *The JFK Challenge* and *The JFK Mini-Challenge*, with a draft set of proposed rules, and a counter-rebuttal to a prototype JFK Challenge rebuttal written by an attorney;

— *Your Homework Assignment* (to get more background information on a bombshell document first released on the Internet in 2011).